ASIAN ECONOMIC INTEGRATION IN AN ERA OF GLOBAL UNCERTAINTY

ASIAN ECONOMIC INTEGRATION IN AN ERA OF GLOBAL UNCERTAINTY

EDITED BY SHIRO ARMSTRONG
AND TOM WESTLAND

Australian
National
University

PRESS

Pacific Trade and Development Conference Series
PAFTAD

ANU PRESS

Published by ANU Press
The Australian National University
Acton ACT 2601, Australia
Email: anupress@anu.edu.au
This title is also available online at press.anu.edu.au

A catalogue record for this
book is available from the
National Library of Australia

NATIONAL
LIBRARY
OF AUSTRALIA

ISBN(s): 9781760461751 (print)
9781760461768 (eBook)

Cover design and layout by ANU Press

Contents

List of figures

List of tables

List of contributors

Shiro Armstrong is a Fellow and Director of the East Asian Bureau of Economic Research at the Crawford School of Public Policy, The Australian National University.

Tom Westland is the WongCalthorpe Cambridge Australia PhD Scholar in Economic History at Sidney Sussex College, the University of Cambridge.

Mari Pangestu is Professor of International Economics at the University of Indonesia and is on the Board of Directors of the Centre for Strategic and International Studies, Indonesia.

Pascal Lamy is the former director-general and European commissioner for trade of the World Trade Organization.

Cyn-Young Park is the Director for Regional Cooperation and Integration in the Economic Research and Regional Cooperation Department of the Asian Development Bank.

Wendy Dobson is a Professor and Co-Director at the Rotman Institute of International Business, University of Toronto.

Hubert Escaith is the former chief statistician of the World Trade Organization; Visiting Scholar at SUIBE–WTO Research and Education, Shanghai University, China; and Associate Researcher at Aix-Marseille University, France.

Satoshi Inomata is Chief Senior Researcher at the Institute of Developing Economies, Japan External Trade Organization.

Sébastien Miroudot is Senior Trade Economist at the Trade and Agriculture Directorate, Organisation for Economic Co-operation and Development.

Somkiat Tangkitvanich is President of the Thailand Development Research Institute.

Saowaruj Rattanakhamfu is Senior Research Fellow at the Thailand Development Research Institute.

Dhiraj Nayyar is Officer on Special Duty and Head of Economics, Finance and Commerce at the National Institute for Transforming India, Government of India.

Ponciano Intal, Jr is Senior Economist at the Economic Research Institute for ASEAN and East Asia in Jakarta, Indonesia.

Shen Minghui is Professor at the National Institute for International Strategy, Chinese Academy of Social Sciences.

List of abbreviations

ACU	ASEAN Customs Union
ADB	Asian Development Bank
ADMM	ASEAN Defence Ministers Meeting
AEC	ASEAN Economic Community
AFAS	ASEAN Framework Agreement on Services
AFC	Asian financial crisis
AFTA	ASEAN Free Trade Area
AIIB	Asia Infrastructure Investment Bank
APEC	Asia–Pacific Economic Cooperation forum
APL	Average propagation length
ARCH	Autoregressive conditional heteroskedasticity model
ARF	ASEAN Regional Forum
ASEAN	Association of Southeast Asian Nations
ASEAN–ISIS	ASEAN – Institutes of Strategic and International Studies
ASW	ASEAN Single Window
AUSFTA	Australia–US FTA
AXC	Emerging East Asia excluding the People's Republic of China
BAC	APEC Business Advisory Council
BBIN	Bhutan, Bangladesh, India and Nepal
BEC	Broad economic categories
BIMSTEC	Bay of Bengal initiative for multisector technical and economic cooperation
BRI	Belt and Road Initiative

CCA	Coordinating Committee on ASEAN Trade in Goods Agreement
CEPEA	Comprehensive Economic Partnership for East Asia
CEPT	Common Effective Preferential Tariff
CER	Closer Economic Relations free trade agreement
CLMV	Cambodia, Laos, Myanmar and Vietnam
CLV	Cambodia, Laos and Vietnam
DCC	Dynamic conditional correlation model
EAFTA	East Asian FTA
EAS	East Asia Summit
EEA	Emerging East Asia
EGA	Environmental Goods Agreement
ERIA	Economic Research Institute for ASEAN and East Asia
ERIA RIN	Economic Research Institute of ASEAN Research Institute Network
EU	European Union
FDI	Foreign direct investment
FE	Fixed effects
FTA	Free trade agreement
FTAAP	Free Trade Area of the Asia–Pacific
G3	Group of Three
G8	Group of Eight
G20	Group of Twenty
GARCH	Generalised autoregressive conditional heteroskedasticity model
GATT	General Agreement on Tariffs and Trade
GDP	Gross domestic product
GFC	Global financial crisis
GRP	Good Regulatory Practice
GTAP	Global Trade Analysis Project
GVC	Global value chain
IMF	International Monetary Fund
ITA	Information Technology Agreement

LPG	Liquefied petroleum gas
MCIOTs	Multi-country input–output tables
MFN	Most-favoured nation
MPAC	Master Plan on ASEAN Connectivity
MRAs	mutual recognition arrangements
NAFTA	North American Free Trade Agreement
NGO	Non-government organisation
NIEs	Newly industrialised economies
NPLs	Non-performing loans
NTBs	Non-tariff barriers
ODA	Official Development Assistance program (Japan)
OECD	Organisation for Economic Co-operation and Development
PAFTAD	Pacific Trade and Development conference
PECC	Pacific Economic Cooperation Council
PRC	People's Republic of China
PTA	Preferential trade agreement
QFII	Qualified Foreigner Institutional Investors scheme
RCEP	Regional Comprehensive Economic Partnership
ROOs	Rules of origin
RTAs	Regional trade agreements
SAARC	South Asian Association for Regional Cooperation
SAFTA	South Asia Free Trade Agreement
SFA	Stochastic frontier approach
SOEs	State-owned enterprises
TiVA	Trade in value-added database
TPP	Trans-Pacific Partnership
TRIM	Trade-related investment measures
TTIP	Transatlantic Trade and Investment Partnership
US	United States
USITC	United States International Trade Commission
VAR	Vector auto-regression model

VAX	Ratio of value-added exports to gross exports
VIX	Volatility Index
VS	Vertical specialisation
WDI	World Development Indicators
WFDD	World Financial Development Database
WTO	World Trade Organization

We are indebted to Emily Hazlewood and ANU Press for working so patiently with us through the production process. We express our gratitude to Capstone Editing and Beth Battrick for their excellent copyediting work.

This is an important collection of essays at an important point in time for the global economy. Asia is the engine of growth in the global economy. Its economic success has been made possible by long-term commitment to open markets and economic integration, underpinned by a rules-based global trading system. Rising protectionism in the North Atlantic, but especially the United States, threatens that system. This volume helps to think of ways forward for Asia to protect and project its interests in the global system.

Shiro Armstrong and Tom Westland
Canberra, December 2017

1

Overview and issues

Shiro Armstrong and Tom Westland

Asia and the global system

The global economy is confronted by huge uncertainties and challenges to the global trading system and global growth. The slow recovery from the global financial crisis (GFC) of 2007 and 2008 has led to protectionist forces and a backlash against globalisation in Europe and the US that threatens the global openness on which many countries, especially those in Asia, rely for development, peace and stability. In 1950, Asian per capita income, averaged across the region, was about 7 per cent of US per capita income; 60 years later, it was 21 per cent of US per capita income (The Maddison Project, 2013). What is more, this conceals vast variation across the region. Whereas some countries have languished (especially in South Asia), several countries in East Asia now have higher per capita incomes than the US, and others—including, importantly, China and India—continue to enjoy growth rates well above those of developed countries, which will ensure continued convergence of incomes over time. The astonishing achievement of many of the Asian economies in this period fully merits the title of 'miracle' with which it has often been garlanded.

Nonetheless, it is worth recalling that this achievement took place in a specific economic and institutional context that is by no means permanently assured. A liberal trading order globally was enshrined in the General Agreement on Tariffs and Trade and there was strong growth in the advanced economies that ensured a market for exports from developing economies in Asia. After the GFC, there was no generalised repeat of the destructive beggar-thy-neighbour policies that followed the stock market crash of 1929; most countries understood that the maintenance of an open, rules-based order was a superior equilibrium outcome to one in which countries pursued economic policies at the expense of others, serving short-term interests but damaging longer-term ones.

The US's withdrawal from the Trans-Pacific Partnership (TPP) and Brexit in Europe, combined with unresolved economic and political difficulties in the Atlantic economies, signals a retreat of US and European leadership in global trade and investment liberalisation. The direction of US trade policy under the presidency of Donald Trump remains unclear, but the US could embrace a more aggressive bilateralism as it turns away from regional agreements with Europe and Asia. The cumbersome negotiating process used by the EU is opaque and deeply unpopular in the domestic politics of Europe. Given the pressures from political extremes, the weakness of economic growth and the underlying inward-looking nature of the single market, it is becoming more difficult for the nations of the EU to exercise joint leadership in pursuit of greater global economic integration. All the talk about a post-Brexit UK resuming its nineteenth-century role as a liberal vanguard notwithstanding, nor is it realistic to expect that Westminster (which will be obliged to spend most of its energy in the next decade or so extricating itself from the EU and, possibly, replicating trade agreements to which it was already a party) will supply much in the way of practical or intellectual leadership.

This is not an ideal time for such a vacuum to have opened. Trade growth has stalled since the GFC, falling from a rate close to double that of global gross domestic product (GDP) growth to one that barely keeps up with it. Asia was an engine of global trade and economic growth in the decade and a half after China's accession to the World Trade Organization (WTO), as Asian production networks proliferation and deepened. However, that rapid growth in trade from global value chains (GVCs) appears to have reached a plateau. The growth of trade in services has at least kept pace with global GDP growth. Stagnation of industrial country growth and the fall in investment appears to be responsible for three quarters of the slowdown in trade growth; the maturation of GVCs (in which finer and finer production fragmentation is reaching its limits) and rising protectionism have also played their part (International Monetary Fund [IMF], 2016, p. 65).

In this environment, economic reforms and liberalisation are politically more difficult to undertake. Countries are in search of a new strategy for development and opening up. The political economy of behind-the-border reforms and liberalisation is complicated and there are many new issues in cross-border commerce around the growth of information technologies. For the Asian nations, which have strong ambitions of development, there is a central interest in how to navigate these issues. There is much potential yet to be realised in South-East and South Asia and, of course, in China, where development remains dependent on engagement in the international system.

This volume reviews the current state of Asian economic integration but is primarily concerned with its future direction, given the new challenges thrown up by the adverse global context and the uncertainty that brings, and the new issues around international economic exchange in the twenty-first century.

The fourth industrial revolution in ecommerce, the internet, robotics and automation represent both a challenge and an opportunity for Asia and the world. Innovative policies regionally could contribute to positive and pre-emptive policies globally. Inspiration can be taken from the process that undergirded the Information Technology Agreement (ITA) and Environmental Goods Agreement (EGA) in the past. The ITA, which led to strong growth in the information communications technology sector in Asia at an early stage of its development and made GVCs possible, was an initiative first devised at the Asia–Pacific Economic Cooperation forum (APEC) and then subsequently implemented through the WTO. The EGA, a more recent example, is yet to progress as far. In this way, forums such as APEC can serve as intellectual proving grounds for ideas that are later taken to global institutions, including the WTO.

Both of the changes outlined here—the threat to globalisation led by the advanced economies of the North Atlantic and the new challenges to the way of conducting business—require creative and agile responses from Asia. A particular responsibility now devolves upon Asia to assume the mantle of leadership in open trade and economic policy strategy. **Mari Pangestu** and **Shiro Armstrong** begin to define what some of those responses might look like in **Chapter 2**. They describe the state of play in Asian economic integration and explain the 'new normal' for global and Asian economic integration. To do this, the situation up to now is reviewed, including the nature of the Asian economic cooperation and integration that has taken place. This provides an introduction to the new ways to think about the issues that are examined in greater depth throughout the volume.

The Asian economic integration agenda

Former Director-General of the WTO **Pascal Lamy** provides a perspective in **Chapter 3** on global trade that is not all bad news. Growth in trade volume may be slowing down globally, but more appropriate measures of international trade—such as growth in value added—indicate rising trade intensity. This is especially the case in the highly integrated Asia–Pacific region. At the top of the agenda in regional economic cooperation in Asia is the need to deepen trade intensity and economic integration.

East Asia's rise to become a centre of global trade growth is the result of a commitment to opening up to trade, investment and competition as the primary means of achieving economic development. Border barriers to trade in manufacturing goods, especially electronics, parts and components, are low in East Asia, and foreign investment in manufacturing is largely liberalised. This, combined with the ITA (which was agreed to through APEC and later the WTO), allowed information and communications technology to proliferate, and made the logistics of production fragmentation possible. GVCs, or vertical specialisation and fragmentation of production, proliferated in East Asia.

In **Chapter 6**, **Hubert Escaith**, **Satoshi Inomata** and **Sébastien Miroudot** examine the key features of GVCs in the Asia–Pacific and their evolution. The inter-industrial network moved from a simple hub-and-spokes cluster, centred on Japan in 1985, to a much more complex structure in 2005, with the emergence of China and the involvement of more countries. Production networks have only spread and deepened since 2005, but with the transition of China's growth model from an export and investment-led model to a services and consumption-led model, and the resulting shift in the structure of regional trade, growth in the Asia–Pacific value chains has slowed.

Trade in parts and components has slowed in production networks but these value chains have evolved to include services trade, and these trade networks now involve trade in tasks, including research and development and even the movement of people. This evolution in value chains is happening ahead of the policies that might secure, regulate and sustain it.

In **Chapter 5**, **Wendy Dobson** and **Tom Westland** examine the question of how Asian countries can move up regional value chains and boost growth by pursuing structural reforms that favour the development of high value-added export industries. They examine financial reforms underway in India and China. Noting that the reform process is much more advanced in China than India, they observe that policymakers in both economies need to ensure that domestic financial policy settings in China and the broader real economy in India are considered in conjunction with financial reform. They argue that, for economies trying to increase the sophistication of their export baskets, financial reform can be a complementary strategy.

However, much of South Asia, and even some of South-East Asia, is yet to really join the GVCs. Those nations have strong ambitions of development that will depend on engagement in the international system. India's 'Look East' and 'Make in India' strategies are aimed at joining the East Asian production networks as the easiest way to realise comparative advantage and integrate into the regional and global economies. Given India's size in the South Asian region—and globally—its success or failure in sustaining development will have significant implications for regional and global economies.

In **Chapter 8**, **Dhiraj Nayyar** reviews the progress, challenges and reform agenda for India to do just that. As wages in China rise rapidly and much low-cost or labour-intensive manufacturing shifts out of China, there is an opportunity for India to take up this role. With a young and growing population, many tens of millions of new entrants will have to be absorbed into the labour force each year. The agenda is relatively clear and well known to India's reformers but, as Nayyar explains, the political economy of the country's federal system is complex and there is a need to reform the arcane labour and land ownership laws, and restrictions on trade between states; undertake infrastructure reform and investment; and overcome other major impediments to trade and investment liberalisation. Institutional creativity is required.

The scale of the challenge is considerable. India's opening up and globalisation story is a deeply domestic one. The economic circumstances in which India hopes to industrialise are not necessarily as favourable as those enjoyed by China from the 1980s to the late 2000s, given slow growth in the advanced economies; technological change that may mean a large endowment of labour will be less valuable than in the past;

and strong competition at the 'low' end of value chains from countries including Cambodia, Bangladesh and Vietnam (as well as a few African economies with increasingly competitive unskilled labour costs and large endowments of labour, like Ethiopia). Given this, one question that faces Indian policymakers is how the reform process in India connects with broader regional integration. India is a member of the Regional Comprehensive Economic Partnership (RCEP), but has yet to play much of a constructive role in driving the process. However, it would be a mistake for India to think that required domestic reforms—especially those regarding the state-owned sector, agricultural subsidies and the still substantial barriers to internal and external trade—are best conceived of as bargaining chips to be given up in formal trade agreement negotiations. Such reforms will yield growth dividends whether they form part of RCEP or some other regional or bilateral agreement, and they cannot be delayed until the conclusion of a regional agreement.

Just as many in East Asia emulated Japan and its success, the hope is that India can lead South Asia by example. Beyond the domestic reforms that need to be sustained in India, infrastructure investment is needed in the rest of South Asia and in parts of East Asia. This includes major infrastructure investment *within* countries to realise growth potential, and also infrastructure *between* countries. In most cases, the finances are available internally or through external initiatives and donors, but there is a lack of bankable projects because of domestic impediments. Infrastructure investment can be used as a lever for domestic regulatory reform and structural reform.

Reforms that encourage infrastructure investment will be important, as large pools of capital seek higher returns internationally and Chinese initiatives, such as the Asian Infrastructure Investment Bank (AIIB) and the Belt and Road Initiative (BRI), present new opportunities to connect countries and regions. The infrastructure connectivity master plan of the Association of Southeast Asian Nations (ASEAN), China's BRI and increased financing through the multilateral development banks all set out strategies or present opportunities to which countries in Asia and beyond can respond.

One question that will weigh deeply on the minds of policymakers is the vexed issue of sovereignty. As the Brexit vote made clear, citizens are not always in favour of supranational institutions, and will sometimes resent, or seek to reverse, reforms that restrict the ability of national governments to make decisions in areas that have traditionally been considered their domain. This phenomenon poses deep challenges for reformers. How can deeper economic integration be designed in such a way that it does not provoke backlash? What kinds of social and political institutions—and forms of public engagement—are necessary to support this process? The kinds of reforms that are now being considered as part of the regional integration agenda are qualitatively different from those of previous eras, and careful thinking is required to tease out the political economy of integration in this new environment. In **Chapter 3**, **Lamy** explains that the increasingly multilocalised nature of production processes means that 'precaution' rather than 'protection' is becoming the frontier of multilateral trade governance. This refers to the harmonisation of value-based norms, and quality and safety-based standards, which reflect citizens' collective preferences. Multilocalisation also creates more opportunities for non-sovereign actors, such as corporations and non-government organisations, to engage in the international trade system, a trend that is becoming more apparent. The efficiencies created by this evolving international trade environment will affect welfare in ways that are dependent on domestic social systems. Policymakers must ensure that the economic gains from trade also translate into social gains across society, especially for developing countries where inequalities have been on the rise.

The future of Asian regionalism

What will the economic future of the region look like in the next decade or two, and what transnational public goods will the region need then? Leaders and policymakers require mechanisms to jointly develop policies at the country and regional levels, beyond the range of the normal political and business cycle. For example, how do Asian countries collaborate on the movement of people? Are the present forums adequate for the task, or is there a need to renovate or redesign the cooperative architecture to address the issues of the future, let alone the ones faced now? Answering these questions requires not only an understanding of the new issues that the region faces, but also an appreciation of the history of Asian integration.

Asia's integration with the global economy has always been different from the regionalism of Europe and North America. Many of the countries in the Asia–Pacific region formed part of imperial trading blocs in the colonial period, with trade preferences discriminating strongly in favour of imperial metropoles. However, in the post-war era, Asian integration has been outward looking. The countries in East Asia were much more diverse than those of Europe or the US—with different economic, political and social systems and institutions—and there was a lack of trust on a political level between many countries in the region. Without political closeness between the many countries in East Asia, for reasons including unresolved histories of conflict, territorial disputes and regional rivalry, the most congenial mode of cooperation was one of non-interference in the domestic affairs of other countries. In **Chapter 9**, **Ponciano Intal** explains that economic cooperation that did not impinge on sovereignty led to arrangements that had no supranational authority.

The intellectual principles of APEC were openness, equality and evolution of cooperation. It was difficult for many countries in East Asia to deepen economic ties with neighbours at the expense of relations with countries outside the region. The latter principle distinguishes the Asian style of cooperation from the inward-looking regionalisms of Europe and the US, while the former principle distinguishes it from traditional multilateralism of institutions such as the WTO. The Kuching consensus that ASEAN laid out in 1990, which formed the basis of its participation in the APEC process, emphasised that sovereignty remained with nation states, and that APEC would be a consultative, voluntary body—not coercive. It was difficult for many countries in East Asia to deepen economic ties with neighbours at the expense of relations with countries outside the region. Further, the process of forging consensus meant that larger countries could not dictate terms to smaller countries.

However, the question remains, are the current arrangements and their mode of cooperation suited to the current challenges that Asian economies face in deepening the integration of their economies with each other and the rest of the world? Border barriers are already relatively low and the real impediments to increasing trade, investment and commerce are behind the border. Regulatory barriers, non-tariff measures and port and infrastructure inefficiencies are much larger barriers to international trade and investment than the few remaining transparent border barriers. The reform challenge is domestic and it is typically more complex and involves a larger range of interests than reforms to external barriers. This suggests a form of cooperation that is domestically driven, not negotiated with other countries. For example, take China's state-owned enterprise (SOE) reform. Chinese SOEs have a significant effect on competition, for both domestic firms and foreign firms in China. The TPP includes a chapter on SOEs, largely aimed at Singaporean and Malaysian SOEs, but also with China in mind. However, China's SOE reform is a deeply domestic issue. While it is high on the Chinese reform agenda, there is an understandably strong desire for Chinese policymakers to define the timing, pace and nature of reform, as well as adapt to changing circumstances, instead of having those issues defined by external parties through negotiation. This is not a uniquely Chinese issue. Every country faces major structural reform challenges with similar sensitivities. Japan's labour market, corporate governance and other clearly identified issues on the structural reform agenda not only affect the domestic Japanese economy, but also its trade and investment. Given the backlash against globalisation, most acutely seen in the North Atlantic, economic cooperation that continues non-interference and avoids impinging on sovereignty would appear the most sustainable way forward.

What role, if any, is there for regional cooperation or regional arrangements in a world where the priority is domestic reform and countries are less inclined to negotiate away sovereignty?

ASEAN's economic cooperation and integration processes and achievements are often criticised for being 'talk shops' that do not deliver outcomes. **Somkiat Tangkitvanich** and **Saowaruji Rattanakhamfu** review progress towards the ASEAN Economic Community (AEC) in **Chapter 7** and conclude, as many already know, that the AEC falls short of many self-declared targets and is, indeed, a work in progress. However, economic cooperation the ASEAN way—that is, non-interference in other countries, no legally binding commitments (e.g. the North American Free Trade Agreement) and no supranational authority (e.g. the European Court of Justice)—has managed to sustain and slowly achieve high levels of integration on par with Europe and other integrated regions (Armstrong & Drysdale, 2011). With Europe and the US fighting to maintain open markets and to sustain their regional approaches to cooperation, Asia's track record looks better by comparison than it did even a few years ago.

Nonetheless, there is strong desire to strengthen cooperation in ASEAN and to elevate cooperation to include commitments to which member states adhere. With ASEAN cooperation acting as the hub for broader Asian cooperation, there is already progress towards binding commitments in RCEP, but with an economic cooperation agenda central to that agreement. **Shen Minghui** in **Chapter 10**, and **Tangkitvanich** and

Rattanakhamfu in **Chapter 7**, compare the TPP and RCEP and discuss some of the features that will be needed in Asia to further integration and reform. At best, such an arrangement would combine the capacity building and consensus forging that has characterised and sustained Asian cooperation through APEC and ASEAN. At worst, it may be a low-ambition RCEP agreement that does not have credibility and does not progress regional integration or provide the needed assistance for domestic reform programs. A poorly designed binding agreement in Asia could set the integration process back, as has occurred in other parts of the world.

Asian leadership

Asia has benefited from US and European leadership in the global economy in the past. However, such leadership is no longer assured. In his seminal work on the Great Depression, Kindleberger (1986, pp. 288–90) argued that the downturn of the 1930s was 'so widespread, so deep, so long' because it occurred at a time when Britain had more or less relinquished its role as a global economic leader but before the US had taken up the baton. Therefore, there was no country willing to lend counter-cyclically, no country willing to police an open trading order and a system of stable exchange rates (and, particularly, no country willing to accept 'distress goods' in a crisis, resulting in the Smoot–Hawley tariff war) and no country willing to provide emergency liquidity in the crunch. With the British tied up in squabbles with the French over the latter's sterling balances, and the US refusing to send 'good money after bad' by offering substantial discounting operations to the world economy, the global economy lacked a country that could take the lead in coordinating macro-economic policies and averting the worst of all outcomes. This is sobering history. It demonstrates the dangers inherent in a situation in which the leadership required to coordinate the supply of international public goods is lacking.

Although it is by no means clear yet that the US and European countries will step back fully from global leadership, in some ways this misses the point. Given the growth in the Asian economy, it is no longer possible, let alone appropriate, for the US to act alone in a leadership role. Indeed, the elevation of the Group of Twenty (G20) during the GFC as a critical leadership body and the sidelining of the G7/G8 demonstrated that the days in which the global order could conceivably be stewarded by a few, mainly Western, countries are over. Given the protectionist pressures in the US and Europe, where the focus is expected to be on internal challenges for the foreseeable future, and given the scale and influence of Asia on the global economy, a particular responsibility now devolves upon Asia to assume the mantle of leadership of an open trade and economic policy strategy. The dimensions of that leadership include articulating a diplomacy that pushes back on anti-globalisation, forging ahead with regional liberalisation and reform initiatives and shaping policies that reach out in an inclusive way beyond the region. It needs to ensure that regional integration strategies—and, with the probable stagnation or collapse of the TPP, this means RCEP in particular—are structured in such a way that they buttress, rather than undermine, the global system. Such leadership should focus on areas of international economic interest in which cooperation has been lacking. For example, collective Asian leadership could examine connecting and providing coherence to the provision of infrastructure funding, ensuring that new (and welcome) regional initiatives, such as the AIIB and older bodies, such as the Asian Development Bank, are complementary and adhere to principles that ensure investment in regional connectivity yields the maximum benefit. Even more ambitiously, such leadership could begin to tackle the almost complete absence of global rule making on investment that has led to a confused and confusing web of bilateral and plurilateral treaties.

What is clear from these efforts is that the idea of Asian leadership is easier to state as a concept than to actually deliver. It is too much to ask of China—still a developing country that is properly cautious and not ready to step forward—nor can ASEAN provide leadership on its own. Collective Asian leadership is called for, in the tradition of other successful regional initiatives, such as APEC in the past. China, Japan, South Korea, Australia, Indonesia and India all need to be engaged. What then are the methods by which such leadership could be mobilised? Cooperation and coordination among Asian members within international forums such as the G20 has merit. Informal bilateral agreements on areas of positive-sum cooperation—such as the China–US agreement on climate change—may play some part. Since the supply of international public goods will always require some disproportionate contribution from leaders (without supranational enforcement mechanisms, of which very few successful examples can be found, as there will always be some degree of free-riding), it is natural that China be central to any regional or global provision of international public goods.

The BRI, China's major strategic initiative, could be a significant international public good. As **Shen** explains in **Chapter 10**, the BRI attempts to build closer economic, physical and institutional links between different countries, as well as between those countries and China. While there are domestic imperatives for the BRI, such as excess capacity that could be exported and the need to develop China's western regions, it is an international initiative that aims to link both land and maritime regions, with comprehensive agendas ranging from infrastructure and industrial parks to port networks and cultural exchanges. Whether the BRI succeeds or fails will depend on the extent to which other countries welcome it, and that will depend on whether it is open, transparent and in the interests of participating countries. Shen explains that China's economic success has relied on the open multilateral trading system and that China has a deep interest in the preservation and strengthening of that system for continued growth.

The best and most effective leadership that any country can provide is to undertake reforms and grow; leadership must start at home. Economic growth can provide neighbours, trading partners, the region and—in the case of Asia's largest economies—the rest of the world with some buoyancy. Sustaining Chinese or Indian growth or reviving the Japanese market would provide large positive spillovers to other Asian countries as well as to the US and Europe.

However, to be effective, Asian economic leadership in the provision of global public goods needs to engage with the rest of the world. This point is brought out by **Cyn-Young Park** in **Chapter 4**. She revisits the decoupling issue—that is, whether Asian growth has decoupled from that of the North Atlantic economies of the US and Europe. The GFC proved that debate to be wrong in the mid-2000s, and Park demonstrates that it is not true now. Asian economies have opened up to the global economy, not just to their neighbours, and the integration that has resulted means that there is great interdependence with other major markets internationally. The implications of Park's chapter are clear. Future Asian regional cooperation aimed at deepening regional integration and building Asian institutions for managing that integration cannot become inward looking and must remain open to US and other global interests. Deeper integration in Asia cannot come at the expense of those outside the region, especially at a time when many are looking for excuses to raise protectionist barriers.

Shen makes it clear in **Chapter 10** that to achieve the next phase of development in Asia—that is, for poorer countries to achieve middle-income levels, and for middle-income countries to become fully prosperous—an open global economic system is needed. As **Park** demonstrates in **Chapter 4**, Asian economies remain reliant upon global demand. Difficult domestic reforms are made easier with a more open and dynamic external economy that can absorb export expansion. Such reforms are also much easier, politically, when effective systems of income distribution and regional policy exist to cushion those who lose out from the opening process. The experiences—positive and negative— of advanced countries in the Americas and Europe can be instructive, although domestic policies must, of course, be sensitive to the local context.

Asia now has the economic weight, interest and responsibility to lead in the preservation and strengthening of the global trading system. Asia has an opportunity to contribute to the global economic system through regional initiatives like RCEP, APEC and the AEC, and through groupings that lead to broader membership, such as the idea of the free trade area of the Asia–Pacific. Importantly, economic diplomacy initiatives will not carry the day. What matters is what key countries in Asia do at home in terms of economic reform, further opening up and in learning the lesson that it is not trade protection or protection against competition and globalisation but social protections that will bring sustainable development.

References

Armstrong, S. & Drysdale, P. (2011). The influence of economics and politics on the structure of world trade and investment flows. In S. Armstrong (Ed.), *The politics and the economics of integration in Asia and the Pacific* (pp. 65–92). London, England: Routledge.

International Monetary Fund (IMF). (2016). Subdued demand: Symptoms and remedies, *World Economic Outlook October 2016*. Retrieved from www.imf.org/external/pubs/ft/weo/2016/02/

Kindleberger, C. P. (1986). *The world in depression 1929–1939*. Berkeley, CA: University of California Press.

The Maddison Project. (2013). Retrieved from www.ggdc.net/maddison/ maddison-project/home.htm

2

Asian economic integration: The state of play

Mari Pangestu and Shiro Armstrong[1]

Introduction

Economic integration in Asia has progressed over the last 30 years through the formation of greater trade and investment linkages, which have been driven by market-led integration, underpinned by international commitments. A strategy of economic development based on export orientation and integration into regional and global value chains (GVCs) has served the countries in the region well. For most of the period during which the Asian economies experienced rapid growth, they faced a global economy that was growing and open to trade and was, therefore, conducive to their growth. East Asia experienced higher economic growth and growth in trade and investment than did other regions, even when China's growth is not taken into account. Poverty rates also declined as a result of this growth, with more people in Asia moving out of poverty than anywhere else in the world. Trade has been the engine of growth for the region, with regional economic integration acting as a key driver. Expanding global trade outpaced and buoyed global economic growth, which Asia both benefited from and contributed to—until the global financial crisis (GFC) in 2007–08.

1   We are grateful to Matthew Jacob and Son Chu for their excellent research assistance. Any and all errors remaining are our own.

The slow recovery of the advanced industrial economies of Europe and the US since the GFC has created a challenging global situation, characterised by continued slow economic and trade growth. In addition, anti-globalisation, anti-immigration and strong nationalistic sentiments are on the rise, as seen in Brexit and the populist, anti-trade and anti-immigration outcomes of the US elections. Such dissatisfaction has arisen from the perception that globalisation and trade agreements have led to the loss of jobs, stagnating incomes and increased inequality.

East Asia's supply chains and production fragmentation deepened trade and economic integration in Asia and were an engine of global trade and economic growth, particularly prior to the GFC (see Constantinescu, Aaditya & Ruta, 2015). The global slowdown in trade growth has been attributed, in part, to a slowing in this mode of Asian economic integration since the GFC, compared with the three decades preceding it. For instance, after joining the World Trade Organization (WTO) in 2001, China became the largest goods trader in the world, and the largest trading partner for almost all countries in Asia and beyond. However, its trade grew only grew 3 per cent in 2014 and, in 2015, it fell 7.6 per cent.[2] It appears that China's rapid growth in goods trade could not be sustained because it is shifting away from an export-led growth model to a consumption and services-led model.

A further cause of the slowdown in global trade growth is that, even before the GFC, there was little progress and, seemingly, little international leadership and commitment on any major trade agreements. Multilateral trade negotiations under the WTO have stalled and there has not been any movement on the Doha Round since 2008, with the exception of the Trade Facilitation Agreement in 2013. The main game for trade liberalisation has since shifted to regional and bilateral agreements. The US-led plurilateral agreement in the Asia–Pacific, the Trans-Pacific Partnership (TPP), has been on hold since President Donald Trump withdrew the US from the agreement,[3] and the US–EU Transatlantic Trade and Investment Partnership (TTIP) appears to be stalled. However, in East Asia, a number of regional agreements have progressed and continue

---

2   Not all countries had reported trade statistics for 2015 at the time of writing and the fall in Chinese trade may reflect this fact.
3   President Trump withdrew the US from the TPP on 23 January 2017. Since then, the remaining 11 countries have made efforts to continue their processes of ratification and to decide on the next steps. The remaining members are proceeding with an agreement that freezes some chapters until the US rejoins the agreement.

to be negotiated. Implementation of the Association of Southeast Asian Nations (ASEAN) Economic Community (AEC) and the five ASEAN+1 free trade agreements (FTAs) with China, Korea, Japan, Australia–New Zealand and India, are occurring. There is also the ongoing negotiation of the East Asian Regional Comprehensive Economic Partnership (RCEP) agreement, which is intended to consolidate the five ASEAN+1 FTAs. Bilateral agreements have proliferated since the turn of the twenty-first century and have become the major focus of trade liberalisation and international commerce.

Asia continues to grow faster than the rest of the world; therefore, it has a peculiar responsibility to protect the global system. Maintaining a robust global trading system is important to keep markets open. Much of South-East and South Asia are yet to enjoy the middle or high incomes achieved by some of their Asian neighbours. A great deal is at stake for North-East Asia as well, as the framework of national reforms in East Asia have been driven by international commitments. Deepening reforms is a much harder task in the face of a global trading system in retreat. Asia's major economies face difficult structural reform programs, including Japan's third arrow of Abenomics, China's supply-side reforms and India's 'Make in India' reforms. Having an external environment that facilitates these and other reforms in Asia and globally is important.

Given the current challenging global context for trade liberalisation, trade agreements and external economic expansion that the world faces, the important question to ask is: how will economic integration in Asia proceed and what form is it likely to take in the near future? To begin providing an answer to this question, this chapter examines the characteristics and current state of play of regional economic integration in Asia.

In the next section, we provide a summary of the trends in economic integration in the region in the last 30 years. The two following sections examine explanations for the pattern of regional economic integration observed in Asia. The first explanation relates to what is often termed market-driven integration (or the trade–investment nexus), which occurs without regional trade agreements (RTAs), as border barriers come down in response to unilateral reforms, and as production networks and GVCs evolve. The second explanation examines the effect of the RTAs in Asia on regional economic integration and explores the nature and scope of intra-regional and extra-regional trade patterns. In the fourth section, we provide a summary of the state of play regarding the mega-RTAs. In the final section, we confront the issue of the day; given the 'new normal' context, in which trade (and investment) have stalled as an engine of growth, what is the future of regional economic integration?

Trends in regional economic integration in Asia

Economic integration is simply about the liberalisation and facilitation of the flow of trade in goods, services, investment and movement of people across borders. Borders involve a discontinuity in relative prices as a result of trade barriers, regulatory differences, natural and institutional impediments to trade, and differences in relative endowments. Therefore, trade within and across borders differ; however, both allow for further division of labour and specialisation in production. Economic integration is the process of removing border barriers and behind-the-border impediments to trade—whether they are regulatory or involve information asymmetries. This helps to allocate resources to their most productive uses, given the set of technologies available.

Regional economic integration means the free flow of trade in goods and services, investment, capital and financial flows, as well as the movement of people, within a region. The EU is probably close to achieving this state of integration. In Asia, regional economic integration has mainly focused on trade in goods and services and, to some extent, investment. Regarding trade in goods, most intra-ASEAN trade, or trade between ASEAN and its six FTA partners (China, Korea, Japan, Australia, New Zealand and India) already involves tariffs that are very close to zero. However, non-tariff measures (NTMs) and restrictions on services and the movement of professional people remain. Freedom of movement of people for tourism purposes already exists for the ASEAN countries, but does not yet exist between ASEAN countries and the ASEAN+1 partners.

As Figure 2.1 indicates, although the level of intra-regional trade is highest in Europe, intra-Asian trade is higher than trade within the North American Free Trade Agreement (NAFTA). Moreover, the growth rate of intra-Asian trade is much higher than for any other RTA, having grown from 45 to 55 per cent from 1990 to 2014. Intra-regional trade in North America through NAFTA peaked in 2002 at 45 per cent, declined to 35 per cent, and has remained flat since then. The highest level of intra-regional trade within Asia is in East Asia (the 10 ASEAN countries plus South Korea, Japan and China) and also in South-East Asia (i.e. the ASEAN countries). In addition, there has been a high share of intra-regional investment in Asia, with the five largest investors being Japan, China, South Korea, Singapore and Hong Kong.

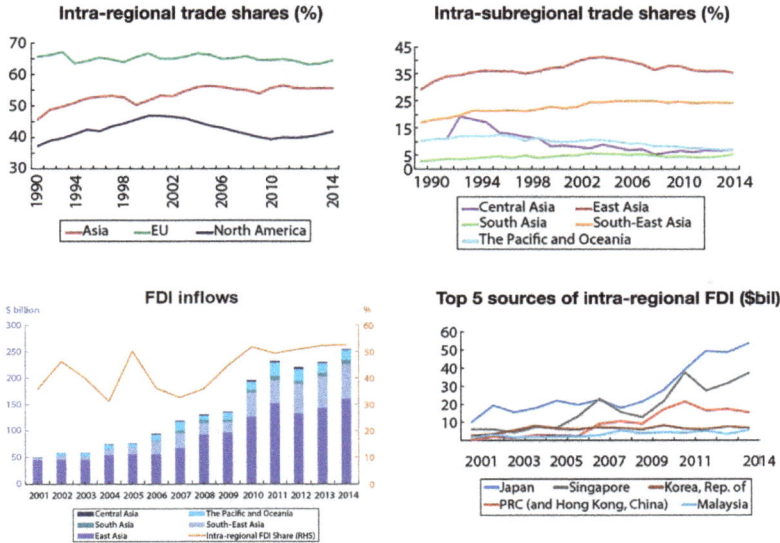

Figure 2.1: High growth in intra-regional trade and investment in Asia, especially East Asia
Source: Asian Development Bank (ADB, 2015).

In this chapter, we mainly focus on regional economic integration in the context of trade and investment. Other chapters in this volume examine financial integration issues. For the last three decades, there have been various catalysts and modes for the reduction of barriers to trade and investment in Asia that have led to greater intra- and extra-regional trade and investment. We examine the two main drivers of regional economic integration in East Asia. First, we consider the regional trade and investment integration that occurred without any RTAs—including through unilateral liberalisation, reforms and the evolution of production networks and GVCs. Second, we review and evaluate the effects of the regional integration agreements that are in place.

Market-driven integration: Reforms and production networks

In Asia, the largest episode of opening up to trade and investment occurred unilaterally from the 1980s through to the 2000s. The story is a familiar one in East Asia. In the 1980s and 1990s, there was a growing consensus among policymakers involved in integrating Asia that trade and openness were the key drivers of development. Consequently, the removal of border barriers and deeper integration were achieved without formal or binding external agreements. This process is often termed market-driven integration, as it did not involve RTAs. Competitive unilateral liberalisation in the 1980s and 1990s was followed by reforms and further liberalisation, influenced by economic crises, regional institutions such as the Asia–Pacific Economic Cooperation forum (APEC) and ASEAN, and global commitments through the General Agreement on Tariffs and Trade (GATT) and WTO processes.

South Korea had already industrialised by the mid-1980s, having followed its successful 'Korea Inc.' export orientation and *chaebol*-led[4] economic development model. Outward Japanese investments had departed in waves to North-East and then South-East Asia. The trade and investment nexus led to intra-regional trade in parts and components, mainly in electronics and automotive sectors. North-East Asian companies began to move offshore to South-East Asia in search of lower labour and land costs. This pattern of development—in which the more advanced Asian countries, starting with Japan, moved production to lower cost locations—is often referred to as development in response to 'push factors' or 'flying geese' development. Japan's outward investment started in the 1970s when Japanese labour became more expensive; it accelerated in the mid-1980s, following the Plaza Accord, when the yen rapidly appreciated. South Korea and Taiwan were next to follow this export-led development pattern. Japanese production was initially relocated to South-East Asia following the Plaza Accord. Non-Asian companies also established production in Asia as part of this trend. In the mid-1990s, the rise of China attracted significant investment; it became the hub of the production network after its accession to the WTO in 2001.

---

4   *Chaebol* are large industrial conglomerates in South Korea that are run and controlled by an owner or family.

In addition to these push factors, a pull factor—that is, the process of liberalisation and the reforms undertaken in South-East Asia—contributed to development from the mid-1980s. The impetus for liberalisation and reform in the 1980s varied between countries. In the case of Indonesia, the decline of oil prices in the mid-1980s led to a period of devaluation, bold reforms and deregulation to diversify exports away from oil. The changes involved customs reforms, reductions in tariffs, establishment of bonded zones and free trade zones, and duty drawback schemes, to allow exporters to access internationally priced inputs. To attract investment and foster increased trade, all Asian countries undertook deregulation and reforms based on the competitive liberalisation model. The Asian countries grew on the basis of trade, investment and a conducive global economy. Indonesia, in particular, succeeded in diversifying its exports away from oil and gas to labour and resource-intensive exports in line with its comparative advantage. As a result, the share of oil and gas exports declined from 80 per cent in 1983 to 40 per cent in 1989–90. The main non-oil and gas exports were in manufacturing, such as textiles, garments, footwear and electronics.

As Indonesia grew more confident in its export-oriented strategy, support grew for the proposed ASEAN Free Trade Area (AFTA), which envisaged the reduction of intra-ASEAN tariffs to zero in 15 years. AFTA was agreed to in 1991 and implemented on 1 January 1992. In line with the program to reduce tariffs under their AFTA commitments, many ASEAN countries aligned their most-favoured nation (MFN) tariff rates at the same time. For instance, Indonesia announced major trade reforms in 1993 to rationalise its tariffs.

In the 1990s, the impetus for reforms and trade liberalisation came from APEC and the establishment of the WTO in 1995. In the early years of APEC, countries typically pushed for concerted unilateral liberalisation when it was their turn to host APEC meetings. When Indonesia hosted APEC in 1994, and launched the APEC Bogor Goals of free trade and investment, it also announced a major deregulation of foreign investment. Other APEC host economies followed suit, including the Philippines in 1995 and China in 2001.

The creation of the WTO in 1995 led to a program of tariff reduction in accordance with the commitments made by member countries, as well as the elimination of local content regulations under the Agreement on Trade-Related Investment Measures and discipline in the use of export subsidies. The WTO led to number of national regulations and laws being passed on customs and intellectual property under the Agreement on Trade-Related Aspects of Intellectual Property Rights, and trade remedies. A number of the East Asian countries that were not initially part of the GATT—including China, Vietnam and Cambodia—went through a process of comprehensive trade and tariff reform as a result of their accession to the WTO.

China's unilateral liberalisation on the path to accession to the GATT/ WTO is a clear example of this comprehensive opening up process. Figure 2.2 shows that China's average tariff rate fell from 55 per cent in 1982 to around 15 per cent in 2001. China announced a major liberalisation package at the 1995 APEC summit in Osaka. Its 15-year march to WTO accession involved major unilateral reforms and a substantial opening up of its economy.

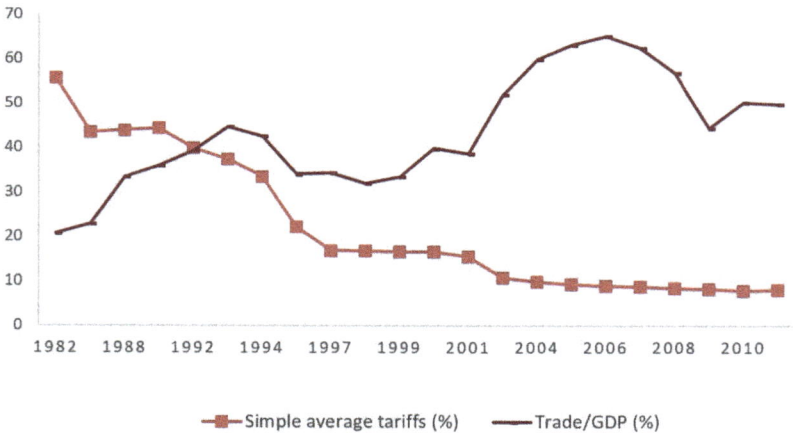

Figure 2.2: China's total trade-to-GDP ratio and average tariff rate, 1982–2011

Sources: UN Comtrade (comtrade.un.org/); World Development Indicators (data.worldbank. org/data-catalog/world-development-indicators); Ministry of Commerce, People's Republic of China (english.mofcom.gov.cn/article/statistic/).

The APEC Bogor Goals, which aimed for free, open trade and investment for developed economies by 2015 and for developing economies by 2020, provided a framework for countries to undertake unilateral liberalisation in concert, thus making it easier to sell domestically and compounding the benefits of openness.

In addition to the Bogor Goals, APEC members initiated the Information Technology Agreement (ITA) in 1997, which limited tariffs on information communications technologies—then a burgeoning, but yet to be established, industry—before they became a major factor in trade and before protectionist interests could be marshalled. Alongside reductions in transportation costs arising from technological advancements, the ITA provided a significant boost to trade in information and communication technology and the proliferation of Asian supply chains.

The Asian financial crisis of 1997–98 led to three Asian countries[5] requiring International Monetary Fund (IMF) rescue packages, with accompanying measures of liberalisation and reforms. This provided the impetus for these countries, and others competing with them, to undertake serious reforms on trade, investment and other institutional and governance issues.

By the early 2000s, tariff rates for manufacturing in East Asia were low and production networks in manufacturing had proliferated. However, tariffs and other barriers to services and agricultural trade, which are more politically sensitive, largely remained in place. Reform of services and investment barriers, which reach deeper behind the border, is complex.

Production networks and the evolution of GVCs explain a large part of the growth in intra–East Asia trade during the 1990s to mid-2000s. As noted above, the earlier development phase, during the 1980s to mid-1990s, was characterised by the more traditional production network model, involving the flying geese development pattern, under which investments were relocated from North-East to South-East Asia as costs increased. The regional production centre developed to export to third markets, notably the markets of the advanced countries. However, in the 1990s, the rise of China and technological changes were accompanied by greater fragmentation of production; intra-regional trade became dominated by intermediate goods and components with China as the hub.

---

5   The three countries were Thailand, Indonesia and South Korea.

Different catalysts and modes of achieving deeper integration

There has been a proliferation of bilateral and regional FTAs in the Asian region in the last three decades. This section examines empirical analyses of these agreements in Asia, with a focus on whether they have led to trade creation or diversion, their utilisation and to what degree they have influenced intra- and extra-regional trade. Although ecommerce, trade in services and other cross-border flows are important, the focus here is on trade in goods because goods trade is the easiest to measure; it can assist in gaining an understanding of the nature of Asian economic integration more broadly, and how it might differ from patterns in the rest of the world.

Trade creation and trade diversion

Bilateral preferential trade agreements, otherwise known as free trade agreements or regional trade agreements, remove tariffs and other trade barriers between members to the agreement, but keep the trade and economic exchange barriers in place for non-members. If preferential tariff rates are utilised, they can create trade among members and divert trade away from non-members, which means that some of the trade expansion that occurs can be at the expense of non-members. For partner countries, preferential tariff rates may make the products of less efficient, member country producers cheaper compared with those of more efficient producers that are outside the arrangement and not granted preferred tariff treatment. If utilisation of preferential tariffs is low in a trade agreement—and trade occurs under the MFN rate available to all trading partners—then the trade agreement has little effect on the merchandise trade between partner countries. However, if the utilisation rate of the FTA preferences is high, there is scope for trade to be created among the members, as well as for trade to be diverted away from non-members.

Today, with trade liberalisation through the WTO stalled, and the global trading system seriously weakened and under threat by the policies of the US and Europe, bilateral agreements constitute much of the policy action in trade liberalisation. Such agreements bear the responsibility for securing current levels of openness. The net effects of FTAs on trade, investment and economic integration are not obvious. Continuing to negotiate and sign FTAs without a broader strategy that is consistent with the international trading system will complicate trade and may introduce new distortions and trade diversion.

On balance, whether an FTA is trade creating or trade diverting is an empirical question. It is often said that agreements that are net trade creating are stepping stones to broader multilateral trade liberalisation, as they contribute more trade to the global system than they divert. FTAs that divert trade are welfare reducing and represent stumbling blocks towards multilateral trade liberalisation.

The empirical literature on the effects of RTAs has rapidly expanded as trade agreements have proliferated since the 2000s. Given the preferential and reciprocal treatment for members underlying the formation of the FTAs, a common expectation is that there will be trade creation within the trading blocs for member economies and the potential for trade diversion between FTA members and non-members. Most ex-post empirical studies are based on the gravity model—the workhorse of bilateral trade flow analysis. Empirical findings on the effects of FTAs on trade have been diverse, with the magnitude depending on a range of factors such as the types of FTAs, what countries are under study, the time periods, estimation methods and model specifications.

Although there are many bilateral FTAs, the most widely assessed FTAs are regional agreements involving more than two trade partners, including the AFTA in Asia; NAFTA in North America; the European Economic Area and the EU in Europe; and, in Latin America, the Latin American Integration Association, Mercosur and the Andean Community (see Cipollina & Salvatici, 2010).

Large and significant trade creation effects from FTAs have been found by a majority of empirical studies. By contrast, trade-diversion effects, which are not always estimated in such models, have been found to be small in magnitude and, in some cases, insignificant. This tendency was identified by Freund and Ornelas (2010) and validated by Cipollina and Salvatici (2010) in their large data analysis of empirical works on the effects of FTAs on trade flows. Cipollina and Salvatici (2010) estimated a robust and positive effect of FTAs that is associated with increasing trade by around 40 per cent. The dominance of trade creation effects can be observed from reviewing selected studies, as shown in Table A2.1 (see Appendix A). These studies show that most intra-bloc trade effects of FTAs and RTAs are significant and large in magnitude, whereas extra-bloc trade effects are small or insignificant, despite some evidence of trade diversion.

Studies have found that ASEAN has extra-bloc creation effects, as indicated by the estimates shown in Table A2.1 (see Appendix A). Urata and Okabe (2007) concluded that the EU, NAFTA and Mercosur have created trade-diversion effects at product levels, but that ASEAN, which appears to be a more open FTA, has not.

There are two factors that could explain the substantial and significant trade creation effects of FTAs. The first is the natural trading partner hypothesis, as elaborated by Freund and Ornelas (2010), that suggests positive welfare effects result from FTAs due to highly complementary trade structures. Baier and Bergstrand's (2004) findings on the likelihood of an RTA being formed lend support to this view, with proximity and relative remoteness of the trading country pair being important determinants. The second factor is the endogeneity of FTAs. Baier and Bergstrand (2007) suggested that the positive effect of RTAs could be quintupled after controlling for the endogeneity of RTAs, which are caused by country-pair and country-specific effects that can be time varying or time invariant. Controlling for all of these effects may result in statistically insignificant effects of RTAs or a reduction in the magnitude of the estimates of trade creation effects, as shown in Magee (2008). Magee (2008) also demonstrated the importance of devising an appropriate dynamic specification for FTA dummies.

There are two different views on the small and insignificant results found for the trade-diversion effects of FTAs. One explanation, suggested by Freund and Ornelas (2010), is that strategic cost–benefit calculations by governments signing FTAs lead to lower external tariffs for extra-bloc trading partners. That explanation does not appear to fit in the case of the Australia–US FTA (AUSFTA), for which Armstrong (2015) found large trade-diversion effects and a lack of trade creation. This suggests that poorly designed and implemented FTAs, completed under time pressure and primarily for political reasons, do not further broader trade liberalisation. Another explanation is methodological in nature. Cheong, Kwak and Tang (2015) suggested that the small trade-diversion effects estimated by many empirical studies could result from a failure to utilise the appropriate model specification or variables to capture the effects of FTAs.

Urata and Okabe (2007) and Okabe (2015) did not find significant trade creation effects for the ASEAN+1 FTAs (ASEAN plus China, Japan or Korea), perhaps because the FTAs had not been in force for long enough to have generated sufficient relevant data, given that the results of gravity model studies usually estimate the cumulative effects of FTAs.

Utilisation rates of FTAs

Previous research based on survey data has found low utilisation rates, below 30 per cent, for FTAs in Asia (see Table 2.1). By way of comparison, 90 per cent of preference-eligible imports into Canada, the EU and the US take advantage of these preferences (Keck & Lendle, 2012). This suggests that the 'noodle bowl' of Asian FTAs has not been effective in driving trade growth.

Table 2.1: Summary of previous survey results on FTA utilisation rates in Asia

Paper	Utilisation rate	Main reason for underutilisation
Baldwin (2008)	Percentage of intra-ASEAN trade that benefited from AFTA—3%	• Low MFN tariffs (less than 2%) on high-volume goods, including computers and electrical goods
Kawai & Wignaraja (2010)	Asian Development Bank survey of 841 firms in 6 East Asian economies—28%	• Lack of information (35%) • Low margins of preference (17%) • Costs associated with rules of origin laws (15%)
Takahashi & Urata (2010)	Based on a survey of 1,688 Japanese firms by the Research Institute of Economy, Trade and Industry—22.9%	• Limited trade volumes with FTA partners • Small margins of preference
Ing, Urata & Fukunaga (2016)	Based on a survey of 630 manufacturing firms across 9 ASEAN economies for utilisation of AFTA by the Economic Research Institute for ASEAN and East Asia (ERIA)—15%	• Low margins of preference • Limited information
Hayakawa, Hiratsuka, Shiino & Sukegawa (2009)	Based on the 22nd survey by the Japan External Trade and Research Organization of 1,852 Japanese affiliates operating in 13 Asian countries—20%	• Incentive schemes have already eliminated tariffs (48.9%) • Importers are exempted from tariffs (37.6%) • No FTAs with main export destinations (22.9%)

Paper	Utilisation rate	Main reason for underutilisation
Wignaraja, Olfindo, Pupphavesa, Panpiemras & Ongkittikul (2010)	Survey of 221 Thai exporters in textiles, electronics and automotive sectors—24.9%	• Rules of origin laws add to business costs (26%)
Chirathivat (2007)	Thailand Department of International Trade, Ministry of Commerce certificates of origin data—26.7%	• Complex rules of origin laws

Source: Author's work.

In the surveys reviewed in Table 2.1, the main reason cited for the poor uptake of FTAs was low or no significant margins of preference. This can arise when the MFN tariff rate is zero, or not much higher than the FTA rate. In 2013, the average intra-ASEAN tariff rate was slightly above 1 per cent (ASEAN, 2014). To demonstrate this effect, Jongwanich and Kohpaiboon (2008) examined the utilisation of AFTA using Thai export data in 2005. They found that, for the 10 commodity lines (identified by two-digit Harmonized Commodity Description and Coding Systems, or HS) with margins of preference greater than 10 per cent, the average utilisation rate was 52.4 per cent. Other survey results have found higher rates of utilisation in the machinery and automotive industries than in electronics and textiles. This accords with the lower margins of preference in the latter sectors (ASEAN, 2015).

Surveys have also been used to identify the main costs and benefits of FTAs for businesses. Based on the Asian Development Bank (ADB) survey of 841 East Asian firms (Kawai & Wignaraja, 2010), the most cited benefits to firms were wider export markets and preferential tariffs, which encouraged imports of intermediate goods. The most frequently cited costs were increased competition from imported products and the documentation required to take advantage of existing FTAs.

Intra- and extra-regional trade patterns: Open regionalism

The EU has had intra-regional trade at 60 per cent and more, accounting for up to two thirds of total trade within the region since the 2000s (see Figure 2.3). In comparison, the intra-regional trade share of ASEAN has been at around 25 per cent over the previous decade, slowly rising since the 1990s. Intra-regional trade for North America and the RCEP grouping is roughly the same, both at 40 per cent. This indicates that

Europe's extra-regional trade share is 40 per cent and that three quarters of ASEAN's trade is with the rest of the world. South Asia is one of the least integrated regions globally, with 5 per cent intra-regional trade.

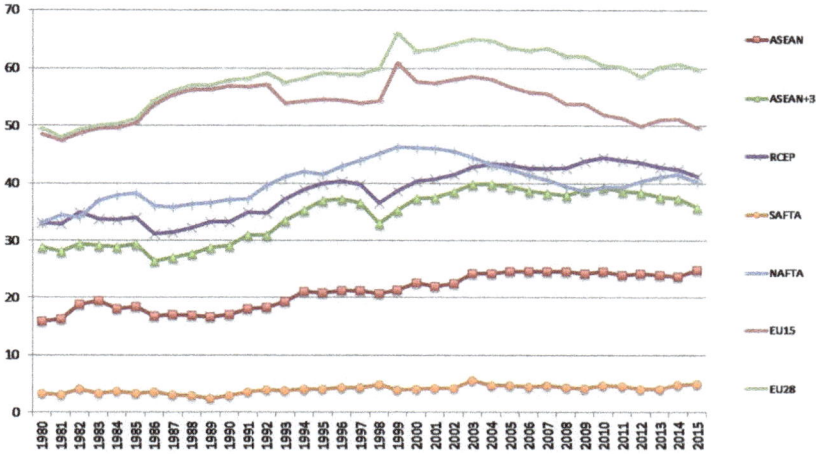

Figure 2.3: Intra-regional merchandise trade shares for regional groupings, 1980–2015
Source: UN Comtrade (comtrade.un.org/) and authors' calculations.

Is Europe's high intra-regional trade occurring at the expense of trade with the rest of the world? In other words, is Europe inward looking? Are European countries trading more with each other than we would expect, given the determinants of their trade, or the proximity and size of European economies? How much do we expect Asian economies to be trading among Asian partners and the rest of the world, given their location, proximity and scale?

A gravity model can estimate the amount of trade expected between any two countries given the key underlying determinants of trade, which are scale and distance. Comparisons of actual and predicted trade, provided in Tables 2.2 and 2.3, indicate whether trade flows more easily than 'average', controlling for the determinants. The model specification and results are explained in detail in Appendix C.

As Tables 2.2 and 2.3 indicate, intra-regional trade outperformed extra-regional trade for all country groups. ASEAN appears to have had the highest level of intra-regional trade relative to the level predicted by the model (Table 2.2), whereas NAFTA and the RCEP grouping achieved slightly more than ASEAN in potential trade (Table 2.3). Intra-EU trade (whether calculated with 15 or 28 members) did not perform as well as North America or East Asia, once trade determinants were controlled for. This result contrasts with the pattern observed when using the simple measure of intra-regional trade shares, for which Europe had the highest level. Interestingly, ASEAN and RCEP achieved better extra-regional trade performance, which is in line with their high achievement in intra-regional trade performance. This trend is consistent with the ratio of actual to predicted trade for ASEAN. The ratio for ASEAN's intra-regional trade declined significantly between 2005 and 2015, whereas its extra-regional trade shrank much more slowly.

Table 2.2: The extent of regional trade integration: Ratios of actual trade/ predicted trade values

Country group	Trade direction	1980s	1990s	2000s	2010s
ASEAN	Intra-regional	154.5	184.3	189.2	125.7
	Extra-regional	19.7	21.0	21.5	18.0
RCEP	Intra-regional	26.6	25.4	31.5	29.3
	Extra-regional	11.3	10.0	11.6	11.9
NAFTA	Intra-regional	52.2	68.1	58.3	55.3
	Extra-regional	7.1	6.3	4.8	5.1
EU28	Intra-regional	36.6	32.1	33.2	36.3
	Extra-regional	9.2	7.3	7.3	8.1
World	All	0	0	0	0

Note: This measure of trade integration is based on the conventional estimation approach using the fixed-effects (FE) estimator. The FE estimator controls for fixed effects that are specific to trading pairs, which include natural determinants such as the distance between the countries, whether they speak a common language, have a shared border or are land locked. Predicted trade values are derived using $y = xb$. With this formula, fixed effects are included in the residuals, so it is likely that trade gaps (the residuals between actual and predicted trade) are large. We use this measure of the trade gap to make the results more easily comparable with measures of the trade gap based on the stochastic frontier approach (SFA).

Source: Authors' estimation.

Table 2.3: The extent of trade integration: Achievement of actual trade compared with trade potential (simple average performance level)

Country group	Trade direction	1980s	1990s	2000s	2010s
ASEAN	Intra-regional	0.434	0.499	0.517	0.495
	Extra-regional	0.389	0.426	0.436	0.431
RCEP	Intra-regional	0.431	0.476	0.504	0.505
	Extra-regional	0.366	0.389	0.414	0.417

Country group	Trade direction	1980s	1990s	2000s	2010s
NAFTA	Intra-regional	0.455	0.496	0.516	0.533
	Extra-regional	0.303	0.301	0.293	0.313
EU	Intra-regional	0.340	0.346	0.376	0.400
	Extra-regional	0.343	0.331	0.327	0.342
World	All	0.347	0.343	0.336	0.332

Note: This measure of trade integration is based on the SFA, following Battese and Coelli (1995). The SFA is applied to the gravity model to identify the maximum trade volume (potential trade) of trading pairs and derive a measure of trade performance in terms of a ratio between actual and potential trade values.

Source: Author's estimation.

The European, North American and East Asian RTAs have promoted trade and economic integration within their respective regions. Figure 2.3 shows that European intra-regional trade shares are higher than those of Asia or North America, but Europe does not perform as well when distance, scale and other determinants are taken into account (see Tables 2.2 and 2.3). Relative to Europe and the rest of the world, and given geography and other characteristics, Asia and North America trade more within their regions. Importantly, Asia trades more with the rest of the world—that is, extra-regionally—given its characteristics, than Europe or North America. This is the case both in terms of what is expected (Table 2.2) and achievement of potential (Table 2.3). To date, Asian FTAs and arrangements regarding trade liberalisation among members have been more open to trading partners outside Asia. This is to be expected, given the open regionalism mode of integration in Asia and the inability of regional countries to conclude binding formal arrangements that favour regional partners. Asia's reform and opening up was largely undertaken in a global context and underpinned by the global trading system.

The regional architecture of mega-RTAs

There are a number of mega-regional agreements in the Asian region: the AEC, RCEP and the TPP, as well as the planned Free Trade Area of the Asia–Pacific (FTAAP). RCEP and the TPP are comparable in terms of their member countries' share of world gross domestic product (GDP) at 30 per cent and 37 per cent, respectively. They are also comparable in terms of shares of world trade at 29 per cent and 24 per cent, respectively. However, the RCEP exceeds the TPP in terms of purchasing power (see Figure 2.4) and it comprises 48 per cent of the world's population, compared with 11 per cent for the TPP. Further, the nature of these trade agreements are very different in terms of comprehensiveness and the approach taken in negotiations.

Table 2.4: Key economic trends of regional agreements and cooperation in the Asia–Pacific

		GDP current price (US$bn)	Population (millions)	Export of goods (US$bn)	Export of services (US$bn)	Trade value (US$bn)
		2015 (%)	2015 (%)	2015 (%)	2015 (%)	2015 (%)
1	Malaysia	269.3	31.2	199.9	34.8	234.7
2	Singapore	292.7	5.5	350.5	139.6	490.1
3	Brunei Darussalam	12.9	0.4	6.4	0.6	6.9
4	Vietnam	191.5	91.7	162.1	11.2	173.3
5	Philippines	292.5	102.2	58.6	28.2	86.8
6	Thailand	395.3	68.8	214.4	60.6	275.0
7	Indonesia	859.0	255.5	150.3	21.9	172.2
8	Cambodia	17.8	15.5	12.3	3.9	16.3
9	Lao PDR	12.6	7.0	2.8	0.8	3.6
10	Myanmar	62.9	51.8	11.1	-	11.1
	ASEAN (rows 1–10)	2433.3 (3.3)	629.7 (8.6)	1,168.3 (7.1)	301.7 (6.3)	1,470.0 (6.9)
11	China	11,181.6	1,373.5	2,274.9	286.5	2,561.5
12	South Korea	1,377.9	50.6	526.8	97.9	624.6
13	Japan	4,124.2	127.0	624.9	162.2	787.1
14	Australia	1,225.3	23.9	188.4	49.1	237.6
15	New Zealand	172.3	4.6	34.4	14.3	48.7
16	India	2,073.0	1,292.7	267.1	155.8	423.0
	RCEP (ASEAN+ rows 11–16)	22,587.5 (30.2)	3,502.1 (47.7)	5,084.9 (30.7)	1,067.5 (22.1)	6,152.5 (28.8)
17	US	18,036.7	321.6	1,504.9	710.2	2,215.1
18	Canada	1,550.5	35.8	408.5	77.5	486.0
19	Mexico	1,143.8	121.0	380.8	22.6	403.4
20	Chile	240.2	18.0	63.4	9.7	73.1
21	Peru	192.1	31.1	34.2	6.2	40.4
	TPP (rows 1–4, 13–15 and 17–21)	27,478.5 (36.8)	812.0 (11.0)	3,958.3 (23.9)	1,238.1 (25.7)	5,196.4 (24.3)

		GDP current price (US$bn)	Population (millions)	Export of goods (US$bn)	Export of services (US$bn)	Trade value (US$bn)
		2015 (%)	2015 (%)	2015 (%)	2015 (%)	2015 (%)
22	Hong Kong SAR	309.2	7.3	510.6	104.2	614.8
23	Taiwan Province of China	523.0	23.5	285.4	56.8	342.2
24	Russia	1,326.0	143.5	340.3	51.8	392.1
25	Papua New Guinea	21.2	7.7	8.7	0.1	8.8
	FTAAP (rows 1–7, 11–15, 17–21 and 21–25)	43,764.1 (58.5)	2844.5 (38.7)	8,328.3 (50.3)	1,946.1 (40.3)	10,274.4 (48.1)
	WORLD	74,753.1	7,349.5	16,551.6	4,826.0	21,377.6

Source: Author's calculations, using data from IMF's International Financial Statistics and UNCTAD (unctadstat.unctad.org/EN/).

It is notable that the FTAAP grouping, which comprises the 21 APEC economies, includes close to 60 per cent of world GDP, 48 per cent of world trade and 39 per cent of the world population. The FTAAP has not been concluded, but remains in the study stage.

With global trade liberalisation stalled and unable to tackle behind-the-border barriers until the WTO is reformed—and with bilateral agreements proliferating, often with large sectoral exceptions and a lack of cohesion— regional agreements such as the AEC, RCEP and the TPP are potentially the most effective way forward in deepening integration. At a time when global trade growth is slowing and advanced economies seem to be more inward looking, it is important for regional agreements to be catalysts for broader reform and liberalisation, and—as has been the case with ASEAN (see Tables 2.2 and 2.3)—to support trade beyond the regional grouping over time.

The mega-regional agreements in Asia, the TPP and RCEP, and also the TTIP agreement between the US and Europe, present new opportunities to make progress with larger groups of countries. They have the potential to increase, and change the patterns of, trade and investment. They also raise the issue of how they might best relate to the global trading system.

The aim of the TPP was to be a high-quality, twenty–first century economic agreement that defined new rules for commerce relevant to modern business. The TPP negotiations concluded in 2015; its 12 members are Australia, Brunei, Canada, Chile, Japan, Malaysia, Mexico, New Zealand,

Peru, Singapore, the US and Vietnam. All TPP members are APEC members, including all of the North and Latin American members of APEC. Indonesia, China, South Korea and some other ASEAN states are not members of the TPP.

However, it unlikely that the US-led TPP will be implemented any time soon, either with its current membership or in its current form. Without the US ratifying the TPP, it cannot come into force. A version of the TPP without the US is unlikely to eventuate, given the centrality of the US to the cost–benefit calculations and commitments of many of the members. A US withdrawal from the TPP has major adverse consequences beyond US economic engagement in Asia, as it signals a retreat from US leadership in global trade. Even worse, were the Trump administration to impose massive tariffs on China and Mexico, and across the board tariffs on the rest of the world, the world would face a potential trade war.

RCEP comprises the 10 ASEAN member states plus Australia, China, India, Japan, South Korea and New Zealand. It was initiated by Indonesia in 2011, based on the five existing ASEAN+1 FTAs, and inspired by the formation of the TPP with ASEAN at its core. At best, RCEP will expand and reinforce the AEC. It aims to bring binding targets to Asian economic cooperation, but will also build an ongoing cooperation and reform agenda. The scope of RCEP includes trade in goods, services, investment, ecommerce and other issues, including environmental, labour and competition policies. As RCEP is a consolidation of the five existing ASEAN+1 FTAs, these are the sectors that were in the different FTAs. The main problem with current RCEP negotiations is that there are no FTAs between the major '+6' non-ASEAN countries; in particular, there are no FTAs between China and India or between Japan and China.

RCEP does not include any TPP or APEC members from the other side of the Pacific. The TPP also has membership gaps in Asia (see Figure 2.4). Open accession to both mega-regional FTAs, and the fate of the TPP, will be important for the expansion of membership but also for increasing the benefits of both agreements. The proposed FTAAP could encompass the best features of RCEP and the TPP and assist in keeping markets in Asia open to each other and the rest of the world.

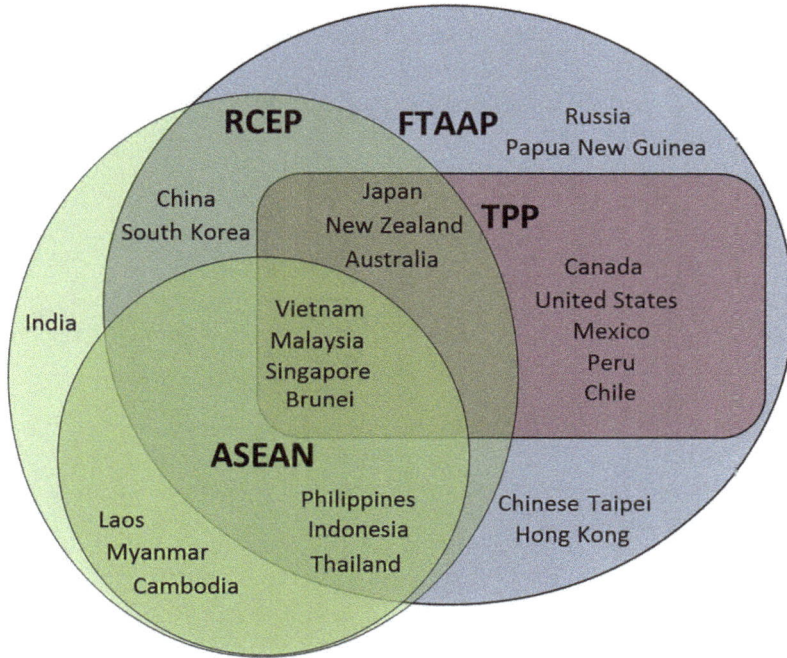

Figure 2.4: ASEAN, RCEP, TPP and possible FTAAP membership

Source: East Asian Bureau of Economic Research and China Center for International Economic Exchange (2016).

The RCEP countries already constitute a larger part of the global economy than do the TPP countries. In addition, RCEP includes some of the fastest growing countries, led by India and China, but also some of the least-developed countries in the region, including Cambodia, Laos and Myanmar, which are not members of APEC or the TPP. The GDP of the RCEP group—based on conservative projections—could be close to double that of the TPP in 15 years (Figure 2.5).

Many RCEP members are in the midst of economic transitions that will be made easier by a more open and dynamic external environment. The presence of large neighbours that are committed to serious reforms and to opening up their economies will not only benefit these individual countries but also make it easier for others in the region to implement domestic reforms. Many RCEP members, including India, are coming from behind on economic and trade reform and have economies that are relatively more protected from international competition. As a result, the gains from opening up will be large. Given RCEP's openness to less-developed countries, and the special, differential treatment afforded to them, there are significant potential gains from assisting those countries to make and, over time, achieve ambitious commitments on trade openness and growth.

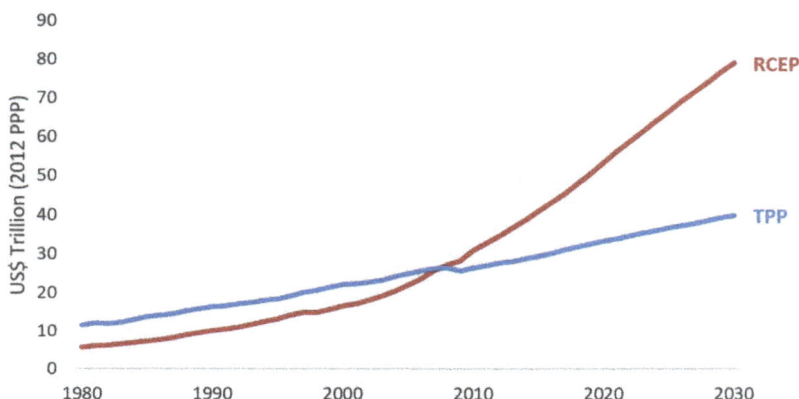

Figure 2.5: GDP projections of RCEP and TPP groups, 1980–2030 at purchasing power parity

Note: Based on IMF projections to 2020; subsequent projections based on an estimate of potential labour productivity for countries currently in transition, given institutional quality, as measured by the World Economic Forum's Global Competitiveness Index.

Source: Hubbard and Sharma (2016).

The future of Asian regional economic integration in the 'new normal'

Although it recovered from the sharp decline in trade during the GFC, growth in world trade has been slower than in the pre-crisis period. World trade grew by less than 3 per cent in both 2012 and 2013, compared with the pre-crisis average of 7.1 per cent for 1987–2007. In 2014 and 2015, it grew at less than 3 per cent and growth for 2016 was only 2.3 per cent.

Most Asian and Asia–Pacific countries experienced contractions in trade from 2015, and some experienced them earlier; contractions began in 2012 for Japan and Indonesia. Chinese merchandise trade growth has slowed dramatically. During the 1990s and 2000s, it grew, on average, 13.7 per cent per year and 20.8 per cent per year, respectively, even accounting for the 13.9 per cent contraction during the GFC. In the decade after accession to the WTO, Chinese merchandise trade grew even faster, at 22.6 per cent per year. However, average trade growth has since slowed to 5.7 per cent up to the end of 2014 and it experienced a contraction in 2015. With the exceptions of Cambodia, Laos, Myanmar and Vietnam, all Asian countries experienced a contraction in trade in 2015 (see Appendix B, Table B2.1).

Figure 2.6 shows the decline in Asian trade growth. As trade growth is linked to GDP growth, it has more than halved since the GFC. In the heydays of the 1990s, with bold reforms providing a boost to trade and investment, the prominence of export-oriented development strategies, production networks and a world economy generally conducive to growth, growth in trade was three times the growth in GDP (or the income elasticity of trade was around three). In the late 1990s and into the 2000s, prior to the crisis, the relationship was closer to 2 to 1. Post-GFC, it is now roughly 1 to 1, though it has been estimated to be less than 1 (0.9) in 2016 (WTO, 2016).

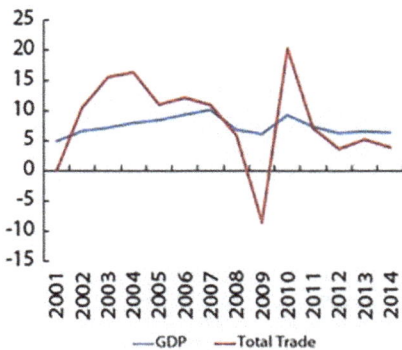

Figure 2.6: Asian trade trends
Source: ADB (2015).

The fall in trade growth is even sharper in Asia because of the China factor. The interdependence between China and Asian regional trade means that China's sharp growth slowdown—growth fell from 9–10 per cent a year prior to the crisis and, in the stimulus years after the crisis, to 6.5–7 per cent a year—has had a large effect on the other Asian trading partners (see Figure 2.7). The Asian neighbours are part of the GVC that has China at its centre; they provide the essential inputs to China's growth, including natural resources (oil, coal and rubber products) and food (palm oil). The rebalancing of China away from exports and investment towards services and domestic consumption has influenced its trading partners. The income–trade elasticity before and after the GFC fell from 2.69 to 1.31 (ADB, 2015).

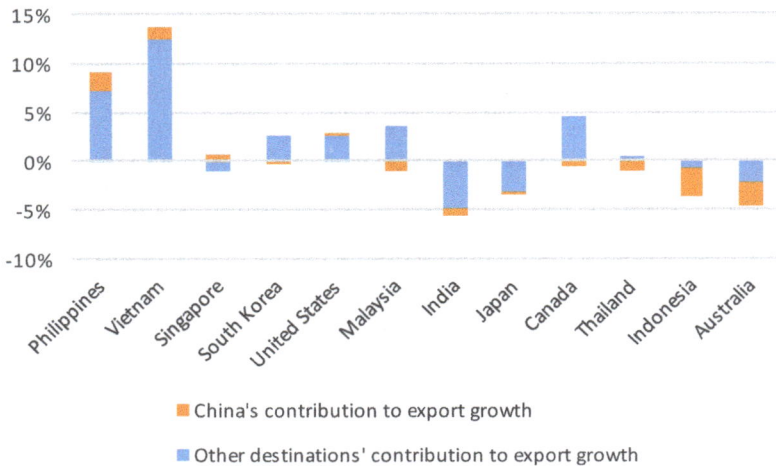

Figure 2.7: China's slowdown: Contribution of China versus other export markets to total 2014 export growth
Source: UN Comtrade (comtrade.un.org) and authors' calculations.

Of course, this places the basic premise of Asian growth during the last three decades (prior to the GFC)—that trade and investment serve as an engine of growth and development, which leads to a reduction in poverty—under question. Therefore, we ask: what are the causes for this structural slowdown?

The recent levelling off in global trade growth may be a particular trend that is reaching its limits (Krugman, 2014). Trade dependence, or trade as a share of GDP and its contribution to growth, may have reached its limits in some countries. After all, some advanced countries have had relatively steady trade-to-GDP ratios for long periods, indicating that a steady state may exist (see Figure 2.8). Perhaps the contribution of merchandise trade to growth has reached a limit in China and the drivers are now services and consumption. It is notable that the global trade in services has not slowed as much as the trade in merchandise.

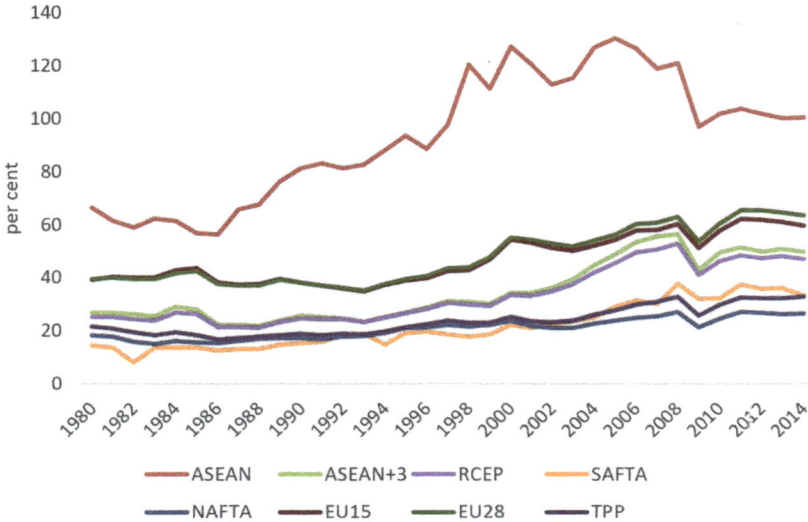

Figure 2.8: Merchandise trade as a percentage of GDP for economic groupings, 1980–2014

Source: UN Comtrade (comtrade.un.org/) and authors' calculations.

According to the most recent analysis by the IMF (2016, p. 65), about three quarters of the structural slowdown in trade is the result of slower growth, especially slower investment. The stagnation of global economic growth and low investment levels have caused a decline in the import of capital and intermediate goods; low growth also means low consumption needs. As already mentioned, the rebalancing of China away from exports and investment towards consumption and services has also had an effect on the Asian region, given China's size and role as the centre of GVCs. Prior to the GFC, growth in trade was twice the growth in GDP; after the crisis, the link between GDP growth and trade growth is closer to one.

The other factors explaining the structural slowdown in trade are shown in Figure 2.9. The first reason is the maturation of the GVC and increased import substitution in China. China is sourcing more goods domestically than before, as more and more intermediate goods and components are being produced within the country.

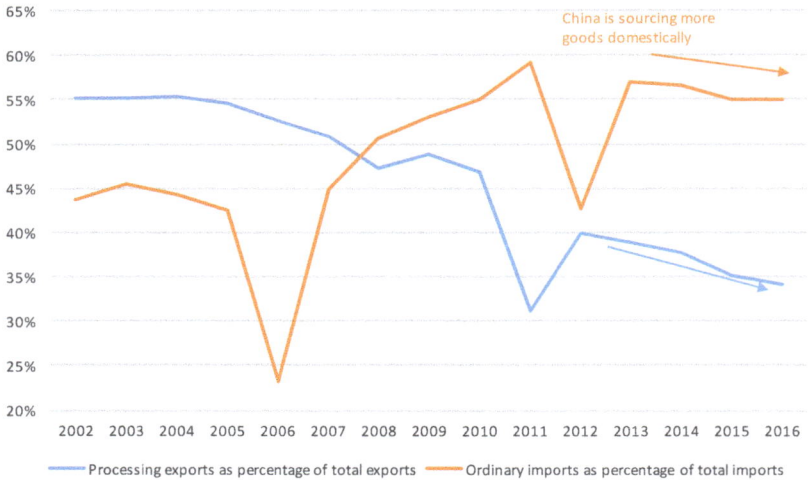

Figure 2.9: China's move to innovation and services

Source: Compiled from data from China Statistical Yearbook and China Customs Information Center.

The second reason for the structural slowdown in trade is the increased protectionism experienced by Asian exporters (see Figure 2.10). Even though there has not been an increase in tariffs, there has been an escalation of trade 'remedy actions' imposed on Asian exports, mainly those from China, and an increase in the use of NTMs. In regard to trade remedy actions, these are being imposed by non-Asian and Asian countries, against each other. The main categories of products affected are basic chemicals and metals, and fabricated metal products, which reflects excess capacity and the falling prices of metal. The main exporting countries that have faced these trade remedy actions are China, South Korea and Taiwan, with actions taken by non-Asian countries including the EU, Brazil, South Africa and Turkey. Intra-regional actions have been taken by India, Thailand, Indonesia and Australia against these exporters, especially for basic metals and fabricated metal products. Affected countries' exports of those products have fallen as a result.

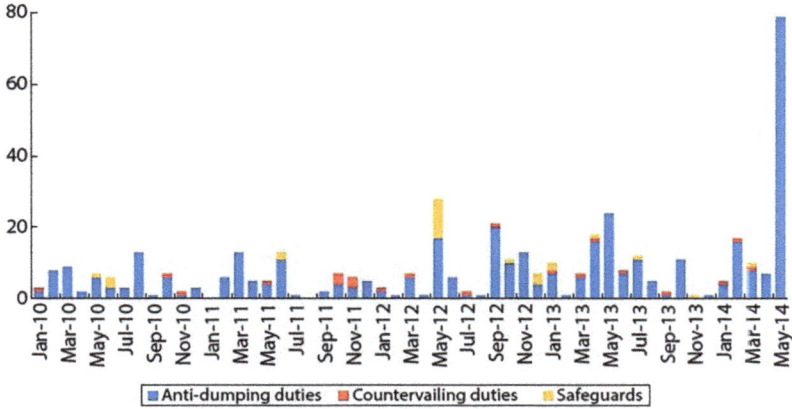

Figure 2.10: Increased protection: Number of trade remedy actions affecting Asia (by type)

Source: ADB calculations using data from the Global Trade Alert (www.globaltradealert.org/).

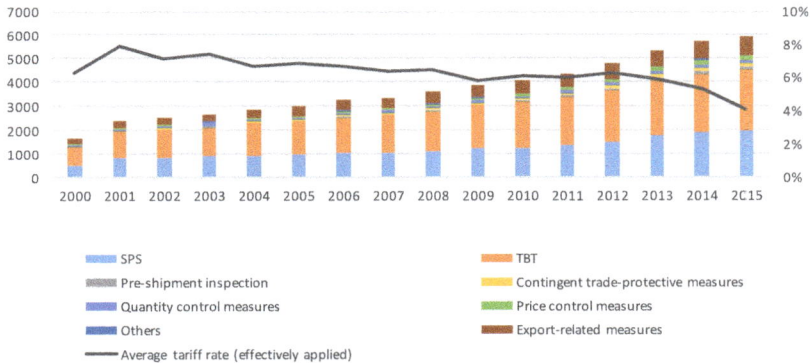

Figure 2.11: Trends in the number of NTMs versus tariffs

Note: SPS = sanity and phytosanity; TBT = technical barriers to trade.

Source: Compiled from data from the New Database of ASEAN Non-Tariff Measures (asean.i-tip.org) and UNCTAD Stat (unctadstat.unctad.org).

Table 2.5: NTMs by type

Code	NTMs by type	Number of NTMs	%
A	Sanitary and phytosanitary (SPS) measures	125	19.7
B	Technical barriers to trade (TBT)	321	50.6
C	Pre-shipment inspection and other formalities	53	8.4
D	Contingent trade protective measures	44	6.9
E	Non-automatic licensing, quotas, prohibitions and quantity control measures, other than SPS or TBT	8	1.3
F	Price control measures, including additional taxes and charges	5	0.8
P	Export-related measures	74	11.7
G–O	Other measures	4	0.6
	Total coded NTMs	634	100

Note: The NTM classification is based on that used by UNCTAD.
Source: UNCTAD-ERIA (2015).

Although the average applied tariff rates of the ASEAN countries declined from 8.92 per cent in 2000 to 4.52 per cent in 2015, the number of NTMs increased from 1,634 to 5,975 measures over the same period (Ing, Urata & Fukunaga, 2016).

The third reason explaining the structural slowdown in trade is the lack of any bold trade reforms, such as have occurred in the past. Changes in transportation, logistics and telecommunication technology, which have substantially boosted trade growth in the past, have had more limited effects on trade in recent years.

Despite the need for structural reforms to boost trade, investment and growth, in the absence of fiscal stimulus and given the limits of monetary policy, very few countries—not just Asia but also the advanced countries—have been able to enact bold structural reform programs. China's implementation of its structural reform program has been slow, especially with regard to the state-owned sector. The situation is worsened by the strong, worldwide anti-globalisation sentiment that has led to the election of politicians running anti-globalisation, inward-looking platforms. The Brexit vote and result of the US election are evidence of this trend.

In the North Atlantic advanced countries, the source of dissatisfaction (and politics of anger and fear) lies in the stagnating incomes of the lower middle class, the loss of jobs in the rust belt, where some industries have been declining, as well as in the older, more rural and less educated segments of the population (Autor, Dorn & Hanson, 2015). In the Asian context, there is dissatisfaction regarding the distribution of the benefits of globalisation and the rising inequality between and within countries. This issue has not affected Asia uniformly as some parts of Asia lack geographical connectivity, with areas that are not connected to the main centres of economic activity missing out on the benefits of the economic boom. Other issues are the lack of participation by micro-, small- and medium-sized enterprises in the modern economy, the lack of capacity and skills in human resources and the lack of quality soft infrastructure such as institutions and other domestic settings. These issues will need to be addressed to progress the national reform agenda and push for RTAs.

Other than the slowdown in world trade, the 'new normal' includes the advent of the 'fourth industrial revolution', which has disrupted conventional trade and investment business models, and will continue to do so. One dimension of this revolution is the digital technology and ecommerce platforms that bypass normal trade channels and are growing in importance and reach. Access to the internet allows for further outsourcing of many services without labour movement, as has already occurred with call centres, software development and back-office support in India, the Philippines and China. This trend is now increasingly moving into the area of higher value-added services including animation, research and design, and development. The growth in, and declining costs of, automation, robotics, artificial intelligence, and digital and 3D printing embedded in machinery used to produce and process have meant an increase in reshoring. The replacement of unskilled labour with machines and more skilled labour is part of this trend, which presents challenges in terms of retraining and skill development.

What next for regional economic integration in Asia?

Regional economic integration in Asia in the last three decades, up to the GFC, flourished under a conducive global economy, leadership from developed countries on the openness agenda and progress being made on various international commitments. This provided a conducive climate for Asian countries to pursue unilateral reform agendas as well as regional agreements.

The new normal is quite different now. There is structural slowdown in world trade, an absence of leadership from the US or Europe in the push for openness and international commitments are stalling. Further, the reforms that need to be undertaken now are the more difficult 'second generation' and behind-the-border reforms, as well as institutional reforms.

The difficulty of undertaking further bold unilateral reforms in developed and developing countries is clear. This is true for Asia, which faces several difficulties and challenges. The reforms that need to be implemented are more difficult than the first generation of reforms, which were largely related to tariffs and border issues. Now, the barriers that must be addressed are NTMs, services and investment dispute settlement, behind-the-border measures, such as domestic regulation and intellectual property rights, and ensuring a level playing field vis-à-vis government, through procurement and state-owned enterprises.

There are large, poor and young populations in Asia, concentrated in India and Indonesia, but also elsewhere in South-East and South Asia, which means the growth potential will be high for decades to come. In addition, China faces the challenge of becoming a high-income country. Much is at stake; whether or not Asia is ready, it can no longer rely on developed countries to show leadership in furthering international trade, investment and commerce. Integrating South and South-East Asia into GVCs would provide a large stimulus to regional and global trade. Infrastructure investment, trade and investment liberalisation, and economic cooperation are all important.

Despite the slowdown in the world economy, Asia is still growing at a higher rate than any other region. There is an opportunity and responsibility for Asia to take the leadership role in continuing necessary reforms and progressing RTAs that contribute to, and strengthen, the global economic system.

Asia needs to rise to the current challenges by championing unilateral reforms and supporting processes in the multilateral arena, such as through the WTO and the implementation of the Trade Facilitation Agreement. If the era of major, single-undertaking, multilateral rounds is past, then plurilaterals and other initiatives that promote international commerce and the global system must be promoted from the bottom up. Asia needs to be a proactive and positive force in that arena. Most importantly, Asia can conclude ambitious regional agreements within Asia.[6] For RCEP, the issue is leadership and whether there can be breakthroughs with bilateral issues between the '+6' partners. Getting bogged down in bilateral differences risks missing the larger opportunities and failing to recognise what is at stake.

There is the risk of RCEP appearing to be too China-led. The experience in East Asia has been one of shared leadership, ASEAN centrality and benign leadership by major powers. China and Japan can play an important role in capacity building, whether in physical or soft infrastructure, to ensure connectivity, education and skills development, or to ensure that the inclusive agenda is addressed—for example, by empowering small and medium-sized enterprises. China's Belt and Road Initiative (BRI), the Asian Infrastructure Investment Bank (AIIB), the Japanese Official Development Assistance (ODA) program and other such programs and initiatives can be positive forces in this process. Particular attention must be paid to equitable growth, so that concerns with the benefits of globalisation do not derail the process of integration in Asia. The design of the AEC, as well as of RCEP, provides potential for this balance to be achieved in the way that the agreement is conceptualised, but there needs to be a serious effort to realise it because there is still a lack of thought and political leadership in ASEAN.

The analysis in this chapter has shown that Asia's integration has been qualitatively different from that in North America or Europe. Agreements and arrangements in Asia need to continue to be open to those outside the region. If Asia, the largest and most dynamic part of the global economy, becomes inward looking at this point in time when the US and Europe are retreating from leadership in keeping the global system open, it could be more damaging to both Asian and broader global interests than at any time in recent history. Asia needs to practise open regionalism in RCEP and other initiatives to buttress the global economic system.

---

6   The smaller Pacific Alliance in Latin America is another option to promote international commerce.

The combination of stagnating investments in advanced economies and development needs in Asia means that there is an urgency in mobilising infrastructure investment. The AIIB, China's BRI and Japan's ODA should be welcomed, and they should also be extended. Countries looking to boost investment in infrastructure need to undertake investment reform and work towards a more conducive investment environment. There is a major role for policy cooperation between countries and regionally, as well as for capacity building to improve policies, better coordinate cross-border investments and enhance regional connectivity.

In addition to facilitating regional investment, regional economic cooperation—whether capacity building or experience sharing—will be central to meeting the major challenges brought about by technological disruption, dealing with distributional issues, the movement of people and tackling new cross-border issues, such as energy transformation and climate change. The disruptions or shocks from these and other sources, including policies, will have both negative and positive effects across borders. Regional solutions will assist in managing cross-border or regional challenges, and economic cooperation will assist countries at different levels of development to better manage these challenges domestically.

With the main game of economic integration now in services and investment behind the border, consistent standards between countries, regulatory reform and regulatory coherence matter much more than in the past. These issues need to be dealt with collectively, not negotiated bilaterally.

The lessons of the advanced economies need to be learned and economic integration in Asia needs to proceed in combination with measures to address inequities and the sense of imbalance. National policies need to be complemented with development policies that are separate from trade and investment policies, and targeted at those who will not benefit or lose from the reforms. In the RTAs, it will be important to integrate capacity building, participation of small- and medium-sized enterprises and development programs that include the building of infrastructure. These issues must be seen as prerequisites to proceed with the regional trade agreement agenda. This is not an easy task, given constraints on government budgets and the difficulty of devising well-targeted and effective programs. However, it is the number one issue that needs to be considered and addressed for further progress on reforms at the national or regional levels, which will ensure continued and sustained opening up for intra-regional trade and investment and enable deeper forms of integration to take place.

For sustainable economic integration, the lessons of success and failure globally need to be learned. International agreements that affect sovereignty cannot be imposed from the outside; the domestic reform battle has to be won. Coalitions for reform have to be built and the argument articulated and communicated to the public.

In the absence of leadership on global trade from the US and EU, must leadership be sought somewhere else—in Asia, perhaps? All the Asian economies have to undertake further structural reforms to address issues of productivity and innovation and to grow. Without the previous anchor in the global trading system and economy, can the impetus and leadership come from Asia? The logical platforms right now are the AEC and RCEP, particularly given that the TPP has stalled. RCEP is already relatively comprehensive, excluding the difficult behind-the-border issues that the TPP aimed to address. However, as indicated by the recent experiences in the US and Europe with externally imposed, behind-the-border reforms, or attempts at reform without the necessary domestic constituencies being established, it would have been difficult for many countries to comply because these reforms strike at sovereignty issues. Asia's regional cooperation, which is less intrusive and based instead on building consensus, appears to have avoided the difficulties of Europe since the GFC. Nevertheless, the lessons from the US and Europe should not be ignored by the rest of the world.

The stakes are too high for a lack of support for continued openness. A reversal towards protectionism or looking inward in Asia is unthinkable—it would lead to continued stagnation of the global economy and economic hardship, and the issues of balanced growth and inclusiveness would remain unaddressed.

Entering this period of uncertainty in the global economy, the region needs to consider carefully how to develop champions and leadership in Asia. Asia cannot just rely on China—leadership is too heavy a burden for a developing country to carry alone. Instead, Asia should embrace a shared leadership, with ASEAN prepared to push ahead on unilateral reforms, as well as on the RTAs that are already under negotiation. This is the challenge for the next phase of economic integration in East Asia.

References

Armstrong, S. (2015). The economic impact of the Australia–US free trade agreement. *Australian Journal of International Affairs, 69*(5), 513–37. dx.doi.org/10.1080/10357718.2015.1048777

Asian Development Bank (ADB). (2015). *Asian economic integration report 2015: How can special economic zones catalyze economic development.* Manila, Philippines: Asian Development Bank.

Association of Southeast Asian Nations (ASEAN). (2014). *ASEAN community in figures: Special edition 2014.* Singapore: ASEAN Secretariat. Retrieved from: www.asean.org/storage/images/ASEAN_RTK_2014/ ACIF_Special_Edition_2014.pdf

Association of Southeast Asian Nations (ASEAN). (2015). *ASEAN integration report 2015.* Singapore: ASEAN Secretariat. Retrieved from: asean.org/asean-integration-report-2015-4/

Autor, D. H., Dorn, D. & Hanson, G. H. (2015, May). Untangling trade and technology: Evidence from local labor markets. *The Economic Journal, 125*, 621–46. dx.doi.org/10.1111/ecoj.12245

Baier, S. L. & Bergstrand, J. H. (2004). Economic determinants of free trade agreements. *Journal of International Economics, 64*(1), 29–63. doi.org/10.1016/S0022-1996(03)00079-5

Baier, S. L. & Bergstrand, J. H. (2007). Do free trade agreements actually increase members' international trade? *Journal of International Economics, 71*(1), 72–95. doi.org/10.1016/j.jinteco.2006.02.005

Baldwin, R. (2008). Managing the noodle bowl: The fragility of East Asian regionalism. *The Singapore Economic Review, 53*(3), 449–78. dx.doi.org/10.1142/S0217590808003063

Battese, G. E. & Coelli, T. J. (1995). A model for technical inefficiency effects in a stochastic frontier production function for panel data. *Empirical Economics, 20*, 325–32. doi.org/10.1007/BF01205442

Carrère, C. (2006). Revisiting the effects of regional trade agreements on trade flows with proper specification of the gravity model. *European Economic Review, 50*(2), 223–47. doi.org/10.1016/j.euro ecorev.2004.06.001

Cheong, J., Kwak, D. W. & Tang, K. K. (2015). It is much bigger than what we thought: New estimate of trade diversion. *The World Economy, 38*(11), 1795–808. dx.doi.org/10.1111/twec.12297

Chirathivat, S. (2007). Thailand's strategy toward FTAs in the new context of East Asian economic integration. *Chulalongkorn Journal of Economics, 19*(2), 185–214. Retrieved from: www.econ.chula.ac.th/public/publication/journal/2007/cje190204.pdf

Cipollina, M. & Salvatici, L. (2010). Reciprocal trade agreements in gravity models: A meta-analysis. *Review of International Economics, 18*(1), 63–80. dx.doi.org/10.1111/j.1467-9396.2009.00877.x

Constantinescu, C., Aaditya, M. & Ruta, M. (2015). The global trade slowdown: Cyclical or structural? *IMF Working Paper No. 15/6.* Washington, DC: International Monetary Fund. Retrieved from: www.imf.org/external/pubs/ft/wp/2015/wp1506.pdf

Dai, M., Yotov, Y. V. & Zylkin, T. (2014). On the trade-diversion effects of free trade agreements. *Economics Letters, 122*(2), 321–25. doi.org/10.1016/j.econlet.2013.12.024

East Asian Bureau of Economic Research and China Center for International Economic Exchanges. (2016). *Partnership for Change: Australia–China Joint Economic Report.* dx.doi.org/10.22459/PC.08.2016

Egger, P., Larch, M., Staub, K. E. & Winkelmann, R. (2011). The trade effects of endogenous preferential trade agreements, *American Economic Journal: Economic Policy,* 3(3), 113–43. dx.doi.org/10.1257/pol.3.3.113

ERIA-UNCTAD. (2016). *Non-Tariff Measures in ASEAN*. Retrieved from: unctad.org/en/PublicationsLibrary/ERIA-UNCTAD_Non-Tariff _Measures_in_ASEAN_en.pdf

Freund, C. L. & Ornelas, E. (2010). Regional trade agreements. *World Bank Policy Research Working Paper Series No. WPS5314.* Retrieved from: documents.worldbank.org/curated/en/367221468337914543/pdf/WPS5314.pdf

Hayakawa, K., Hiratsuka, D., Shiino, K. & Sukegawa, S. (2009). Who uses free trade agreements? *ERIA Discussion Paper Series no. ERIA-DP-2009-22*. Retrieved from: www.eria.org/ERIA-DP-2009-22.pdf

Hubbard, P. & Sharma, D. (2016). Understanding and applying long-term GDP projections. *EABER Working Paper, 119*. Retrieved from: www.eaber.org/node/25601

Ing, L., Urata, S. & Fukunaga, Y. (2016). How do exports and imports affect the use of free trade agreements? Firm-level survey evidence from Southeast Asia. *ERIA Discussion Paper, ERIA-DP-2016-01*. Retrieved from: www.eria.org/ERIA-DP-2016-01.pdf

International Monetary Fund (IMF). (2016, October). Subdued demand: Symptoms and remedies. In International Monetary Fund, W*orld economic outlook 2016*. Washington, DC: International Monetary Fund. Retrieved from: www.imf.org/external/pubs/ft/weo/2016/02/

Jongwanich, J. & Kohpaiboon, A. (2008). Export performance, foreign ownership, and trade policy regime: Evidence from Thai manufacturing. *ADB Economics Working Paper Series No. 140*. Retrieved from: www.adb.org/sites/default/files/publication/28379/economics-wp140.pdf

Kawai M. & Wignaraja, G. (2010). Asian FTAs: Trends, prospects, and challenges. *ADB Economics Working Paper Series No. 226*. Retrieved from: www.un.org/esa/ffd/wp-content/uploads/2010/11/20101115_ADB_WPs.pdf

Keck, A. & Lendle, A. (2012). New evidence on preference utilization. *World Trade Organization Staff Working Paper, ESRD-2012-12*. Retrieved from: www.wto.org/english/res_e/reser_e/ersd201212_e.pdf

Krugman, P. (2014, 3 November). Flattening flattens. *New York Times*. Retrieved from: krugman.blogs.nytimes.com/2014/11/03/flattening-flattens/

Magee, C. S. P. (2008). New measures of trade creation and trade diversion. *Journal of International Economics, 75*(2), 349–62. doi.org/10.1016/j.jinteco.2008.03.006

Okabe, M. (2015). Impact of free trade agreements on trade in East Asia. *ERIA Discussion Paper Series, ERIA-DP-2015-01*. Retrieved from: www.eria.org/ERIA-DP-2015-01.pdf

Productivity Commission. (2010). *An econometric analysis of the links between the formation of trade agreements and merchandise trade, supplement to bilateral and regional trade agreements* (Productivity Commission research report). Canberra, ACT: Productivity Commission.

Takahashi, K. & Urata, S. (2010). On the use of FTAs by Japanese firms: Further evidence. *RIETI Discussion Paper Series, 09-E-028.* dx.doi.org/10.2202/1469-3569.1310

UN Comtrade (United Nations Commodities Trade database), various years. comtrade.un.org/

UNCTAD-ERIA. (2015). *TRAINS: Non-Tariff Measures (NTMs) based on official regulations.* Retrieved from: asean.i-tip.org

Urata, S. & Okabe, M. (2007). The impacts of free trade agreements on trade flows: An application of the gravity model approach. *RIETI Discussion Paper Series No. 07-E-052.* Retrieved from: www.rieti.go.jp/en/

Wignaraja, G., Olfindo, R., Pupphavesa, W., Panpiemras, J. & Ongkittikul, S. (2010). How do FTAs affect exporting firms in Thailand? *ADBI Working Paper Series No. 190.* Retrieved from: www.adb.org/sites/default/files/publication/156045/adbi-wp190.pdf

World Trade Organization (WTO). (2016). *Trade in 2016 to grow at slowest pace since the financial crisis.* Press release 779. Retrieved from: www.wto.org/english/news_e/pres16_e/pr779_e.htm

Appendices

Appendix A

Table A2.1: Selected studies on trade creation and trade diversion of free trade agreements

Year	Author	Dataset and time period	Dependent variable	Explanatory variables	Estimation method	FTA/RTA	Findings			
							Intra-bloc effect	Extra-bloc effect: Exports	Extra-bloc effect: Imports	Extra-bloc effect: Both sides
2006	Carrère	Panel data, 130 countries, 1962–96	Imports	GDP, multilateral resistance terms, distance, border, landlocked, infrastructure	Hausman–Taylor	ASEAN	0.88	−0.48	0.76	
						NAFTA	0.65[+]	0.06[+]	−0.5	
						CACM	0.7	−0.21	0.8	
						Mercosur	−0.9[+]	−0.18	−1.09	
						Andean	0.6	−0.92	−0.097	
						EU	0.71	0.29	0.2	
2014	Dai, Yotov & Zylkin	Panel data at two-digit ISIC manufacturing industry, 41 trading partners, 1990–2002	Trade	Bilateral fixed effects, time-varying importer and exporter fixed effects and FTAs (structural gravity model)	Poisson pseudo-maximum likelihood (PPML) estimator	FTA (Dummy for all FTAs signed)	0.343	−0.196	−0.852	

Year	Author	Dataset and time period	Dependent variable	Explanatory variables	Estimation method	FTA/RTA	Findings			
							Intra-bloc effect	Extra-bloc effect: Exports	Extra-bloc effect: Imports	Extra-bloc effect: Both sides
2007	Baier & Bergstrand	Panel data, every five years, 1960–2000; 47,081 observations	Trade	GDPi, GDPj, distance, common border, common language, FTAs (Bilateral and multilateral)	FE with pair fixed effects and year dummies	FTAs	0.68			
					FE with pair fixed effects and year dummies and MTP	FTAs	0.46			
					FE with pair fixed effects and year dummies, MTP and lagged effects	FTAs	0.76			
2011	Egger, Larch, Staub & Winkelmann	Panel data of 126 economies in period, 121 PTAs/FTAs; 15,750 country pairs	Exports	Sum of real GDPs (log), similarity of real GDP, difference in factor endowments, distance, border, language, colony, and PTAs	Two-way FE model, controlling for endogeneity of PTAs–PPML estimator	PTA (exogenous)	0.642			
						PTA (endogenous)	1.27			

Year	Author	Dataset and time period	Dependent variable	Explanatory variables	Estimation method	FTA/RTA	Findings			
							Intra-bloc effect	Extra-bloc effect: Exports	Extra-bloc effect: Imports	Extra-bloc effect: Both sides
2008	Magee	Panel data, 133 countries in period 1980–1998; 285,180 observations	Imports	GDPi, GDPj, distance, FTA dummies	PPML estimator with country-pair fixed effects	CU	0.829			−0.01[+]
						FTA	0.508			−0.004[+]
						PTA	0.169			0.039[+]
						RTAs (All)	0.638			−0.002[+]
					PPML estimator with country-pair fixed effects	ASEAN AFTA	1.165			0.624
						Andean	1.021			−0.002
						NAFTA	0.829			0.189
						Mercosur	0.441			0.022[+]
						EU13	0.81			0.037[+]
2015	Okabe	Panel data at BEC sector level for 182 countries in 2000–12 with ASEAN focus	Imports	GDPi, GDPj, Distance, ASEAN+1 FTA dummies and other bilateral FTAs dummies	Fixed effects PPML with year fixed effects	ASEAN–China	Positive (intermediate and capital goods)			
						ASEAN–Korea	Positive (intermediate and capital goods)			
						ASEAN-Japan	Small and insignificant effect			

Year	Author	Dataset and time period	Dependent variable	Explanatory variables	Estimation method	FTA/RTA	Findings			
							Intra-bloc effect	Extra-bloc effect: Exports	Extra-bloc effect: Imports	Extra-bloc effect: Both sides
2007	Urata and Okabe	Panel data of 178 countries for 1950–2005	Trade	GDPi, GDPj, GDP per capita, distance, adjacent, common language, dummies for FTAs of different types	Generalised method of moment estimator for general FTA dummies and FE estimation method for specific FTA dummies	General FTAs (1950–1983)	0.207			
						General FTAs (1984–2005)	0.106			
						ASEAN–AFTA	0.534			0.336
						NAFTA	0.805			0.043+
						Mercosur	0.71			-0.028+
						EU	0.544			0.063+
						ASEAN–China	0.301+			0.152
2010	Productivity Commission	Panel data of about 140 countries during 1970–2008; 1,139,283 observations	Exports and imports	GDPi+GDPj; GDP similarity, Difference in GDP per capita	PPML with pair fixed effects	ASEAN AFTA	0.32	0.12	0.24	
						Andean	0.65	0.05	0.13	
						NAFTA	0.32	0.06	-0.20	
						Mercosur	0.86	0.18	-0.07	
						EU27	0.37	0.07	0.05	

Year	Author	Dataset and time period	Dependent variable	Explanatory variables	Estimation method	FTA/RTA	Findings			
							Intra-bloc effect	Extra-bloc effect: Exports	Extra-bloc effect: Imports	Extra-bloc effect: Both sides
2014	Armstrong	Panel data of about 140 countries during 1970–2012; 1,361,549 observations	Exports & imports	GDPi+GDPj; GDP similarity, difference in GDP per capita	PPML with pair fixed effects	AFTA	0.264	0.085	0.198	
						Andean	0.729	0.293	0.423	
						NAFTA	0.271	0.009	-0.156	
						Mercosur	0.87	0.161	-0.054	
						EU27	0.644	0.21	0.247	
						AUSFTA	-0.394	-0.12	-0.18	

Notes: Estimated coefficients with [+] are not statistically significant. PTAs = preferential trade agreements; FTAs = free trade agreements; CU = currency union; CACM = Central American Common Market; BEC = broad economic categories; MTP = multilateral price effect; FE = fixed effects; PPML = Possion pseudo-maximum likelihood.

Source: Authors' compilation.

Appendix B

Table B2.1: Merchandise exports by country and region, 2009–15

		Merchandise exports (US$ billions)							Growth rate	
		2009	2010	2011	2012	2013	2014	2015	2009–11	2012–15
1	Malaysia	157	199	228	228	228	234	200	20.6	−3.9
2	Singapore	270	352	410	408	410	410	351	23.4	−4.7
3	Brunei Darussalam	7	9	12	13	11	11	6	31.8	−1.9
4	Vietnam	57	72	97	115	132	150	162	30.3	12.3
5	Philippines	38	51	48	52	57	62	59	13.9	4.3
6	Thailand	152	193	223	229	229	228	214	21.0	−2.2
7	Indonesia	120	158	203	190	183	176	150	30.4	−7.4
8	Cambodia	4	5	7	8	9	11	12	26.5	16.3
9	Lao PDR	1	2	2	2	2	3	3	45.6	7.1
10	Myanmar	7	9	9	9	11	11	11	18.3	8.5
	ASEAN (rows 1–10)	814	1050	1239	1254	1273	1295	1168	23.5	−2.2
11	China	1202	1578	1898	2049	2209	2342	2275	25.8	3.7
12	South Korea	364	466	555	548	560	573	527	23.7	−1.2
13	Japan	581	770	823	799	715	690	625	19.7	−7.8
14	Australia	164	213	272	257	253	241	188	32.8	−9.3
15	New Zealand	25	31	38	37	39	42	34	23.0	−2.1

		Merchandise exports (US$ billions)							Growth rate	
		2009	2010	2011	2012	2013	2014	2015	2009–11	2012–15
16	India	165	226	303	297	315	323	267	35.5	-2.9
	RCEP (ASEAN+ rows 11–16)	3304	4334	5129	5240	5364	5506	5085	24.8	-0.9
17	US	1056	1278	1483	1546	1580	1621	1505	18.5	-0.8
18	Canada	316	387	451	456	458	475	408	19.5	-3.3
19	Mexico	230	298	350	371	380	397	381	23.5	1.0
20	Chile	55	71	81	78	76	76	63	21.4	-6.3
21	Peru	27	36	46	47	43	40	34	31.2	-10.3
	TPP (rows 1–4, 13–15 and 17–21)	2936	3717	4291	4353	4327	4385	3958	21.0	-3.0
22	Hong Kong SAR	329	401	456	493	535	524	511	17.7	1.3
23	Taiwan Province of China	204	275	308	306	311	320	285	23.5	-2.1
24	Russia	303	401	522	529	523	498	340	31.2	-12.5
25	Papua New Guinea	4	6	7	6	6	9	9	25.5	13.3
	FTAAP (rows 1–7, 11–15, 17–21 and 21–25)	5652	7245	8511	8756	8939	9117	8328	22.8	-1.5
	WORLD	12,556	15,302	18,339	18,497	18,939	18,996	16,552	20.9	-3.4

Source: Authors' calculations using data from UNCTAD (unctadstat.unctad.org/EN/).

Appendix C: Regression results

Fixed effects and stochastic frontier gravity models (see Appendix D, Table D2.1) are estimated to calculate the predicted and potential trade values, respectively, discussed in the chapter. The gravity model that is applied to a panel data structure is specified as follows:

$$\ln X_{ijt} = \beta_0 + \beta_1 \ln Y_{it} + \beta_2 \ln Y_{jt} + \delta_t \ln Dist_{ij} * Year + \gamma_t + u_{ij} + \varepsilon_{ijt},$$

in which X_{ijt} is the volume of exports between country i (reporter) and its trading partner (country j), Y_{it} and Y_{jt} are, respectively, the current GDPs of countries i and j, as proxies of economic mass. $Dist_{ij}$ represents geographical distance between two trading partners as the main variable of trade costs identified in the gravity model literature. The fixed-effects estimator means that other variables commonly used to explain trade between two countries, such as a common language, shared border and distance (without interacting with year) are controlled for, but cannot estimate coefficients. In this conventional gravity model, year fixed effects that are common to all trading country pairs are taken into account with γ_t. Unobservable country-pair fixed effects are accounted for by u_{ij}. In addition, an interaction variable between $\ln Dist_{ij}$ and $Year$ is included to account for changes in the effect of geographical distance over time. ε_{ijt} is the random error term.

With the same set of explanatory variables, a stochastic frontier gravity model is constructed, based on Battese and Coelli's (1995) model, with two identifying equations. The trade frontier equation is defined by the key determinants of the gravity model, including GDP_i, GDP_j and $Dist_{ij}$, and year effects are included to account for changes over time in the trade potential of a trading country pair, as follows:

$$\ln X_{ijt} = \beta_0 + \beta_1 \ln Y_{it} + \beta_2 \ln Y_{jt} + \beta_3 \ln Dist_{ij} + \gamma_t * Year + v_{ijt} + u_{ijt}$$

In this specification, v_{ijt} is the random error term and is the one-sided non-negative random variable. By construction, the term u_{ijt} is defined as trade inefficiency effects, which cause actual bilateral trade between two trading partners to deviate from the potential trade level. In the setting of an augmented gravity model, trade inefficiency is assumed to be a function of natural and socio-economic factors and policy variables, which are presented by a trade inefficiency model as follows:

$$\mu_{ijt} = \delta_0 + \delta_1 Landlocked_i + \delta_2 Landlocked_j + \delta_3 Lang_{ij} + \delta_4 Border_{ij} + \omega_{ijt}$$

Landlocked$_i$ and *Landlocked$_j$* are two dummy variables accounting for a fixed country characteristic indicating whether country i and country j are landlocked. The other two dummy variables, *Lang$_{ij}$* and *Border$_{ij}$*, take a value of one if a trading pair shares a common official language and common border.

A big panel dataset that includes information on the model variables for about 205 countries in the period 1980–2014 is constructed for empirical estimation of these two models, using different data sources. Exports data are taken from the United Nations Comtrade database, using the World Bank's World Integrated Trade Solution platform. Data on the GDP of trading pairs are obtained from the World Bank's World Development Indicators Database. Data on distance and other country or country-pair characteristics, such as being landlocked, possessing a common language and a common border, are obtained from the Centre d'Études Prospectives et d'Informations Internationales (CEPII) database.

Appendix D

Table D2.1: Fixed effects and stochastic frontier gravity models

Dependent variable ln(exports)	Fixed effects gravity model	Stochastic frontier gravity model
lnGDP_i	0.82*** (−0.009)	1.089*** (0.0017)
lnGDP_j	0.72*** (−0.007)	0.822*** (0.00133)
ln$Dist_{ij}$		−1.274*** (0.00374)
Year dummies	Yes	Yes
Year*ln$Dist_{ij}$	Yes	
Constant	−7.91*** (−0.1)	1.631*** (−0.04)
Non-negative residual estimation		
Landlocked$_i$		2.782*** (−0.11)
Landlocked$_j$		4.711*** (−0.16)
Common language		−5.734*** (−0.22)
Shared border		−18.944*** (−0.91)

Dependent variable ln(exports)	Fixed effects gravity model	Stochastic frontier gravity model
Constant		−10.082*** (−0.51)
Observations	486,955	486,955
Country pairs	27,876	27,876

*** denotes significance at the 1 per cent level.

Source: Authors' estimation.

3

The global setting for Asian economic integration

Pascal Lamy

Introduction

East Asia has been part of the globalisation trend that has brought development to the Asian region as a whole, and reduced the vast numbers of people who were living below the poverty line. Globalisation has occurred as firms around the world have continually reallocated labour and capital to new and different uses in response to changing regulations, trade barriers and business opportunities. Increasingly, the tasks that these firms perform can be moved with relative ease to a different country or a different firm with a totally dissimilar process of production. Naturally, the efficiency created through this transformation is the direct consequence of industrial relocation and transfer.

A Ricardo–Schumpeterian model of trade illustrates how this process creates efficiency. Ricardo (1817) argued that manufacturing efficiency stems from greater international division of labour. Schumpeter (1942) described the ongoing process of remaking manufacturing systems as a 'gale of creative destruction', whereby less efficient structures give way to more efficient ones. These more productive systems take on the labour and capital 'freed up' by the transformation.

This path of increased openness, with the reduction of cross-border barriers to trade leading to increased investment and trade flows and efficiency gains, has defined the globalisation of the past few decades. Much of East Asia's economic integration has occurred within this context.

The efficiencies created by the evolving international trade environment affect welfare in ways that are dependent on domestic social systems. As ever, policymakers must make it a priority that the economic gains from trade translate into social gains at all levels of society. Without such a focus, anti-globalisation sentiments will arise. We return to this imperative in this chapter's final section.

In the last few decades, most countries have reduced cross-border barriers, motivated by a combination of multilateral and regional commitments, as well as unilateral reform programs. As cross-border barriers have come down, and as production processes have become increasingly multilocalised, the frontier of multilateral trade governance has shifted to 'precaution' behind the border rather than 'protection' at the border. This refers to the harmonisation of value-based norms, and quality and safety-based standards that reflect citizens' collective preferences. It creates more opportunities for non-sovereign actors, such as corporations and non-government organisations (NGOs), to engage in the international trade system, a trend that is becoming more apparent. Multilateral and regional efforts need to ensure that they address the issue of standards.

Trade globalisation will keep changing. Growth in international trade volumes is projected to converge to a lower average rate globally by 2050. Part of this slowdown is the result of lower expected gross domestic product (GDP) growth and investment, but it is also the result of a slower average rate of expansion of global value chains (GVCs) in recent years. Despite this reduced pace, international trade is not moving backwards— the momentum remains towards further integration and multilocalisation of production.

Trade will continue with the changing nature of GVCs and the increased tradability of services. This is evident when trade is measured not by volume, but in terms of value added. This provides a more complex picture of the global trade environment, one in which service trades assume much greater importance and participation in GVCs that are linked closely to economic growth. These trends have affected, and are likely to continue to affect, the nature of East Asian economic integration.

The remainder of this chapter is divided into four sections to discuss globalisation, which has been and will continue to be the setting for economic integration in East Asia. In the first section, the past pattern of globalisation is reviewed in the context of the Ricardo–Schumpeterian framework. The second section discusses the longer-term trends of multilocalisation and consumer protection, while the third section discuss the short-term trends, with a focus on whether there is a deglobalisation trend. Finally, the chapter presents concluding remarks regarding globalisation and the political context of trade.

The Ricardo–Schumpeterian framework: Globalisation

Historically, globalisation has been driven by technological progress; one early example is the invention of the steam engine and the drastic reduction in the cost and speed of transportation that followed. In recent decades, major technological revolutions, especially in information and communications technology, have resulted in vast reductions in the cost of trade. These technological revolutions increased economic growth by improving productivity.

Ricardo (1817) theorised that a system is at its optimum when each component is specialising in its area of comparative advantage. Schumpeter (1942), expanding on this process, argued that efficiency is created through confrontations that redefine each component's competitive position. Whether domestic or international, these confrontations between systems of production inherently lead to the reallocation of resources or 'creative destruction'.

International trade keeps moving forward, regardless of whether it is measured by volume or value added. As the Ricardo–Schumpeterian model illustrates, more efficient systems of production up-end and replace less productive ones—in other words, openness to trade works because it is painful and it is painful because it works. Individuals, firms and countries trade with the objective of becoming more efficient. Technological developments in transportation, logistics and information and communications technology have facilitated efficient multilocal value chains, which are cross-border in nature.

The distribution of 'winners' and 'losers' from trade has changed over time. In part, this occurs because of the shifting positions of developing countries on GVCs (a subject that will be discussed further below); however, domestic social policies also play a role. For example, considering the example of the US, openness to trade can be considered only very minimally responsible for the continued stagnation of US manufacturing wages. Lawrence (2007) argued that the greater causes of stagnating pay cheques in the US are the increasing shares of wealth going to the population's top 1 per cent of earners, the amount of income going to corporate profits and the staggering increases in healthcare costs.

Bradford, Grieco and Hufbauer (2005, p. 73) estimated that an increase in US trade exposure by 10 per cent would increase the country's incomes by roughly 2 per cent. Therefore, it would be deeply counterproductive to attempt to mitigate wage stagnation by introducing trade barriers. Policymakers need to shift their focus to other areas to deal with the economic problems facing workers. Supranational institutions can do little to address wage inequality within individual countries or to repair their ailing health and welfare systems. These and related issues can only be addressed through domestic taxation and spending. Ultimately, if confidence in trade is to be rebuilt among a country's citizens, the right domestic policies must be in place.

Longer-term trends: Multilocalisation and consumer protection

Recently, discussions regarding world trade regulation have been dominated by inter- and intra-regional initiatives for integration, including the mega–free trade agreements, represented by the East Asia Regional Comprehensive Economic Partnership (RCEP), the Trans-Pacific Partnership (TPP) and the Transatlantic Trade and Investment Partnership (TTIP). With the demise of the TPP almost certain, there has been a shift in focus towards bilateral agreements.

Trade agreements will continue to focus, in part, on required actions in relation to 'old-world' trade barriers, including tariffs, trade facilitation and distortions in agricultural policy. The Doha Round, which addresses many of these issues, is yet to be completed, notwithstanding the good progress made on trade facilitation in 2014 in Bali. Many developing countries and emerging markets continue to maintain high tariff rates. In most developing countries and, to an increasing extent, in some emerging countries, trade-distorting agricultural subsidies stand in the way of further integration.

Lowering trade barriers through such initiatives does indeed level the playing field of world trade and should continue to be prioritised. Yet, the nature of these barriers is changing with the transition to the 'new world' of trade. In the past, trade was characterised by domestic production processes and the focus of barriers was to protect producers. Hence, opening trade primarily involved lowering tariffs, subsidies and quotas; although this was far from easy, it was conceptually straightforward for negotiators.

However, a long-term trend, which is connected to multilocalisation, is the growing importance of consumer protection barriers. These new-world trade barriers are increasingly oriented towards precautionary, behind-the-border measures, rather than protectionary cross-border measures. This means a greater focus on the tastes and preferences of consumers rather than industries. Reducing these new-world barriers is more difficult because it necessitates the harmonisation of value-based standards across economies.

The progressive or graduated method of implementing trade openness,[1] which is based on the level of development—and which has been successfully applied to old-world, producer-oriented trade barriers—does not always apply to new-world barriers. Although tariff reductions may vary in terms of the speed and the level of reductions depending on the level of development, this graduated approach is much harder to justify when attempting to reduce precautionary regulations across borders. For example, consider trade regulations regarding maximum pesticide levels on flowers grown for export. It makes little sense to have different maximum pesticide levels for flower-exporting countries based on income levels (see Lamy, 2015a).

---

1   That is, to use the terminology of the multilateral trading rules in the World Trade Organization (WTO), 'special and differential treatment'.

The implementation of new-world trade regulation transforms the analysis of the implications of bilateral and multilateral initiatives because the central critique of bilateralism—that it is preferential and discriminatory—is invalid for precautionary regulation. Bilateral equalisation of safety regulations in the US and the EU would not be discriminatory. Indeed, exporters in both markets would benefit.

At the same time, the success of developing countries' exports still hinges on the efficacy of international regulatory institutions. This remains the case in East Asia, as well as in Eastern Africa and Central America, despite the relative success and growing influence of intra-regional integration projects.

The multilocalisation of production processes increases the opportunities for non-sovereign actors to engage in the process of lowering barriers to trade. Consider again the example of standards for maximum pesticide residue levels in flowers. A Rwandan exporter of flowers would benefit substantially if countries such as the US or Japan adopted the same regulatory standards as in Rwanda. Different levels of regulation force exporters to segregate their production based on market destinations, which prevents them from achieving economies of scale and reaching their potential comparative advantage. Moreover, it is unlikely that trade negotiators will be responsible for determining the maximum levels of pesticide residues permitted in flowers, as this task would be allocated to phytosanitary experts, informed by research on the health effects of pesticides. This illustrates one way in which the scope for private actors and NGOs to act in harmonising trade regulations will increase with the pace of multilocalisation.

This shift in agency reflects the discrepancy between the potential efficiency of the Westphalian system, which is treaty- and convention-based, and the bottom-up, GVC-based introduction of social standards to international trade. In future decades, the environmental and social standards of supply chains could become even more significant for workers' conditions than the classical international trade regime. This should be borne in mind in the forthcoming regional and bilateral trade arrangements that are part of the East Asian process of economic integration.

In addition, multilocalisation and the expansion of GVCs means that governments must rethink how best to pursue trade-led growth in ways that are both effective and fair. Government guidance can help instil a 'virtuous circle' of competitiveness and trade growth, with implications for continued development. For developing economies, public–private cooperation attracts foreign direction investment (FDI) and, with it, new technology. Foreign investment in infrastructure, along with the support services required to successfully pursue such investment, can bolster ties between countries. Ultimately, this may result in greater GVC participation. For these mechanisms to be effective, active policies regarding labour, innovation and education are indispensable.

Short-term trends: Is there a deglobalisation trend?

Despite the recent deceleration, growth and trade are now increasing globally, and it is likely that they will continue to do so, especially in developing economies and emerging markets. The growth of the global economy is expected to pick up slightly, to 3.5 per cent in 2017, and it is expected to stabilise at around 3 per cent per year over the next 50 years. Emerging markets and developing economies should grow at a rate of close to 4.5 per cent in 2017 and reach 5 per cent in 2022, compared with growth rates of 1.7 per cent in Europe and 2.3 per cent in the US in 2017, which are expected to reach 1.5 and 1.7 per cent, respectively, in 2022. Emerging and developing economies in East Asia are expected to continue to achieve the highest growth rate, remaining at 6.4 per cent growth in 2017, despite the slowdown in China. India and a number of the Association of Southeast Asian Nations (ASEAN) countries are experiencing high growth of 7–8 per cent and it is projected that this region will grow at 6.3 per cent in 2022. Thus, East Asia will remain the emerging world's engine of growth in coming decades (International Monetary Fund [IMF], 2017).

International trade growth, as measured by volume, could rebound briefly to 3.8 per cent in 2017. A healthy level of trade volume growth of around 3 per cent can be expected over the next 15 years. It seems unlikely, however, that the global economy will return to the steep trade growth path experienced prior to the global financial crisis (GFC) in the next decade (IMF, 2017) (see Table 3.1).

East Asian economies are some of the world's most integrated economies, along with those of the EU. In East Asia, almost 50 per cent of the region's trade is intra-regional. Five of the world's six fastest-growing export economies are Asian; they are expected to experience export growth of 8–11 per cent annually from 2014–30. In addition, the rising global trade share of the emerging economies will bolster the expanding trade between developing countries. South–south trade proved uniquely resilient to the GFC. Real growth in south–south trade is predicted to be close to 6 per cent each year in the period up to 2030—nearly double the global average (Lamy, 2015b). This has resulted in an increase in the developing countries' share of world trade. The share of today's advanced countries (the EU, US, UK, Japan and Canada) is expected to decline from 48 per cent in 2012 to 37 per cent in 2030 and to 33 per cent in 2060 (Figure 3.1). Shares of global trade are changing to account for greater shares of south–south and north–south trade (Figures 3.1 and 3.2).

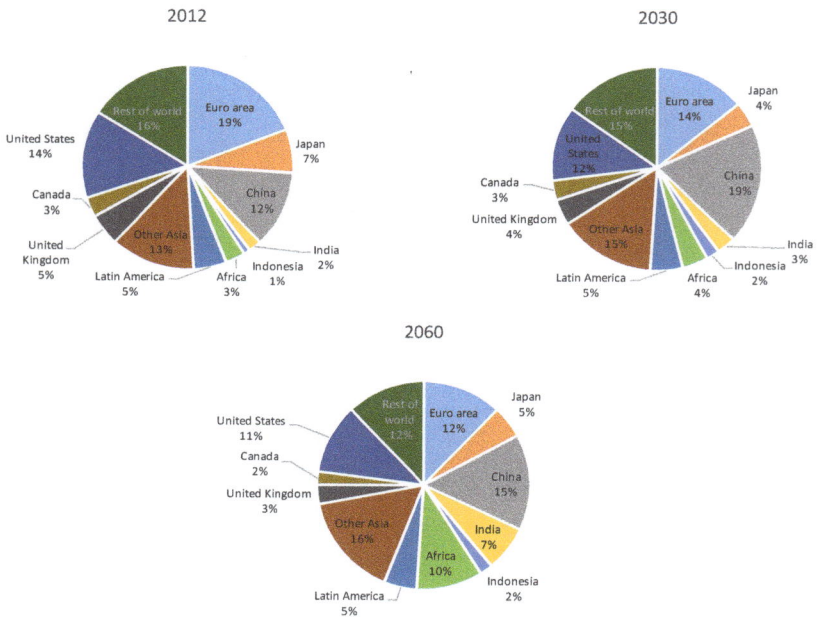

Figure 3.1: The changing distribution of global trade (exports as a share of global exports)

Source: Projections from Château et al. (2014).

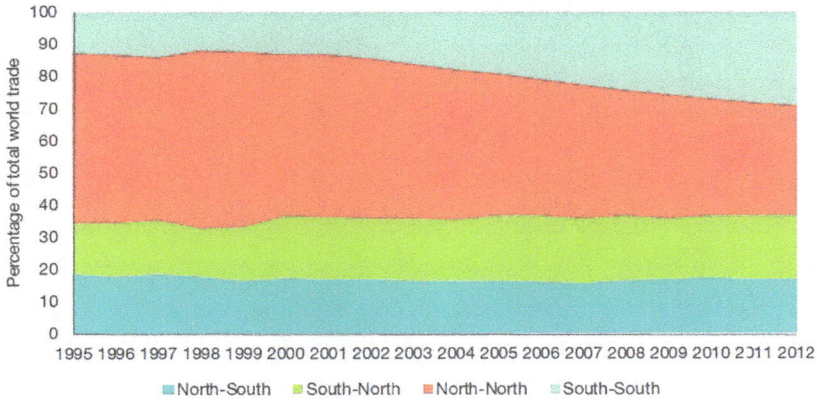

Figure 3.2: The south–south trade corridor, 1995–2012

Note: For each pair of regions, the figures represent exports from the first region
to the second.

Source: United Nations Conference on Trade and Development (UNCTAD, 2014, p. 34).

Emerging economies are attracting an ever greater share of global FDI
flows. Although it can be difficult to develop long-term predictions of
FDI flows, the strong correlation between FDI and trade indicates that
it is likely that FDI flows will continue to follow trade flows in being
reoriented towards developing economies (Lamy, 2015b, p. 134).
However, trade volumes alone cannot tell the whole story when it comes
to changes in the global trade environment. International trade is growing
slowly not only because of slow GDP growth following the GFC, but
also because of structural change that has occurred in the trade–GDP
relationship in recent years.

The recent relative decline in trade growth by volume has resulted from
a slowdown in the expansion of GVCs and the faltering performance in
reducing obstacles to trade. However, this slowdown indicates very little
about the effect of trade on growth. It is not necessarily the case that the
slowing of global trade—or, to be precise, the slowing of the increase
of international trade *volume*—will lead to weaker global growth once
the effect of value added on the trade numbers is taken into account
(Lamy, 2015b, p. 139). Measuring trade by volume estimates the end
point effect of GVCs, whereas measuring trade in value added provides
estimates of trade as a driver of growth. The latter is what ultimately
matters most.

Research based on measuring trade in value added has established that private-sector competitiveness and export performance increasingly depends on openness and participation in GVCs (i.e. Organisation for Economic Co-operation and Development [OECD] 2016). Services, in particular, add substantial value to manufacturing exports through their role in value chains. Indeed, the facilitation of services imports is one of the most effective ways for economies to boost the value of their manufacturing exports.

Intermediate goods often cross borders several times during the production stage. This can lead to miscounting and statistical errors in estimating trade volumes, whereas measuring with value added avoids these problems. It also helps to track commercial value at each country's point of entry, helping to distinguish when countries are simply re-exporting foreign components. Moreover, value addition can be decomposed into assets that are particular to the exporting industry, as opposed to the value-added contributions made by domestic suppliers.

The value-added measurement of trade enables more precise bilateral trade balance figures for analytical purposes. Conventional measurement by trade volume assigns all value to the final link in the production chain, even if the value added at this final stage was relatively minor. Take the well-known example of the iPhone—if measured conventionally, 100 per cent of the phone's value is counted at its assembly in China, deepening the US trade deficit by that amount when the phone is imported into the US. The phone's actual effect on China's GDP, in contrast, is around 5 per cent of that value (Lamy, 2013b).

Table 3.1: Average trade growth by volume, value and unit value (per cent)

Period	Volume	Unit Value	Value
1981–1985	2.9	–3.5	–0.7
1986–1990	5.8	6.2	12.3
1991–1995	6.2	1.9	8.4
1995–2000	7.0	–2.1	4.8
2001–2005	5.0	5.1	10.5
2006–2010	3.7	4.6	9.0
2011–2015	3.1	–1.3	1.8
2013–2015	2.6	–6.0	–3.6

Source: World Trade Organization Secretariat (2016).

What can one learn from measuring trade by value added? First, it provides a sectoral picture of trade that differs substantially from the conventional approach. This can be seen most clearly in the share of services in global trade. Services have been referred to as the 'poor relation of globalisation'—agriculture, which accounts for just 7 per cent of trade, often attracts greater attention than services (Lamy, 2013b).

However, services play an indispensable role in value chains, whether domestic or international. This is because the services that drive value chains—whether information technology, logistics, marketing or distribution—are most likely to be subcontracted to an external firm.

If measured by value added, the proportion of services in global trade is nearly twice that measured by volume. For 2008, immediately before the GFC, services accounted for 23 per cent of total trade when measured in the traditional way; however, this increases to 45 per cent if the direct and indirect value added ascribed to services is incorporated. For 2013, services were the chief contributors to global trade, whereas the manufacturing industry's share of international trade declined proportionally (Lamy, 2013b).

Examining value-added trade reveals that there are more actors in the supply chain, particularly smaller suppliers and subcontractors, than are often imagined. In contrast, the volume-based statistics appear to reduce the production process to a few massive players, such as the aeronautical, pharmaceutical and automotive industries.

The contribution of services to export value is most significant in advanced economies. Further, the services sector is where an increasing share of jobs is being created. This is a significant development because it pertains to developed countries' comparative advantages. The competitiveness and sophistication of advanced economies' services, including management, logistics and research and development, is crucial to their comparative advantage in trade.

Another perspective offered by the value-added account of global trade is that effective importers can often make the best exporters. If an industry's competitiveness hinges substantially on the suppliers and subcontractors that are integral to its production process, it is in that industry's interest to continually improve its access to high-quality services.

The emerging economies' trade growth in recent years has been highly dependent on their rapid integration into GVCs, including through services provision. Between 1990 and 2010, the share of developing countries in global value-added trade rose from 20 to over 40 per cent. More than half of all the exports of the emerging economies are related to participation in GVCs. In particular, south–south global linkages are growing rapidly and, over the last 25 years, the proportion of trade between developing countries that is related to GVCs has quadrupled (Lamy, 2015b).

Most developing regions are increasing their participation in GVCs at a much faster rate than advanced economies. Consequently, many of the 25 highest-ranked economies in terms of GVC participation are developing countries. East Asia, in particular, is the world's leading region in terms of GVC participation because of its dominance in the processing of export-oriented manufactured goods (Lamy, 2015b).

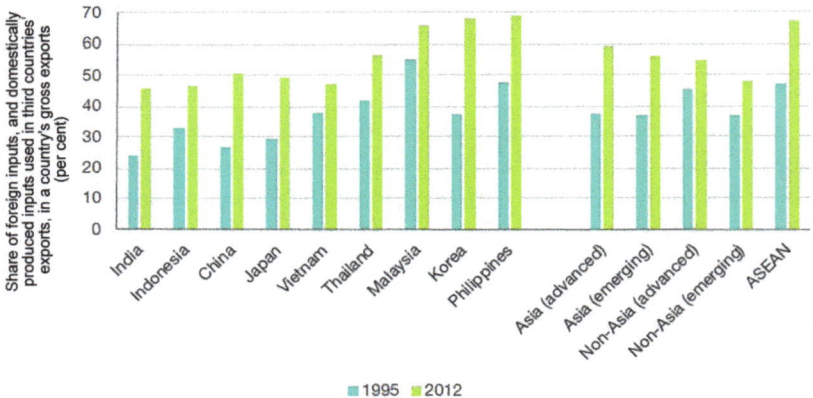

Figure 3.3: Emerging economies' participation in global value chains, 1995 and 2012

Note: Non-Asia includes comparable advanced and emerging economies.

Source: Cheng, Rehman, Seneviratne and Zhang (2015, p. 6).

South Asia remains the region with the lowest participation in GVCs. A major share of South Asian service exports serve domestic demands. Nonetheless, South Asia also has the world's highest *growth* in GVC participation, although this is from a low base (Lamy, 2015b).

Countries can be defined as either upstream or downstream in GVCs, with upstream countries furthest from final demand and downstream countries closest. Upstream countries are more likely to produce components and inputs, whereas downstream countries focus more on product assembly. A number of East Asian economies have succeeded in moving upstream through specialisation, particularly China, the Philippines, Malaysia and Singapore. These Asian economies have seen exceptional growth in the values of their initial inputs, with increases of over 8 per cent during 1995–2008 (Lamy, 2015b, p. 141).

Today, partly as a result of the expansion of GVCs, countries tend to specialise in particular business functions—that is, roles in the supply chain—rather than in individual industries.

These trends in GVC development are expected to continue, with East Asia remaining a key part of their evolution. In the next stages of the East Asian economic integration, these trends in GVC development, including the important role of services, should be kept in mind.

Recent contractions in trade have sometimes occurred because of a lack of access to trade finance, or heightened perceptions of risk brought on by the GFC, which has caused producers to swap from international to domestic suppliers. This process of domestic-focused consolidation suggests that there is an 'optimal level of fragmentation' (De Backer & Miroudot, 2013). At the same time, there is not yet sufficient evidence to determine whether cyclical or structural factors are behind recent GVC contractions. The flexibility of GVCs during the financial crisis is a positive sign for medium-term trade growth. This is especially the case for regions such as Africa, where trade intensity is set to increase.

Although the expansion of GVCs is slowing—particularly in advanced economies—international trade is still tending towards longer and more specialised value chains.

The growth of a country's exports is highly correlated with its participation in value chains through the import of inputs and intermediate goods. This relationship is particularly strong for emerging economies, but it is also important for industrial powers, such as Germany. The ability to import relatively inexpensive intermediates frees up domestic firms at the margin to invest in their areas of greater comparative advantage. This enables advanced economies, including the US, Europe and Japan, to specialise further in providing value chain-based services, such as research and development, and industrial engineering, creating jobs in these countries rather than destroying them. Indeed, investment in these kinds of services generates particularly high-paying jobs (Lamy, 2013b).

Globalisation and the political context of trade

The Ricardo–Schumpeterian model of international trade has been pushed to extremes by three things: the sheer scale and disruption of economic shocks, the high and growing number of actors, and the political limits confronting certain trade concessions (e.g. agricultural subsidies in the US and Japan). This is political economy in its fullest sense: the negotiators are negotiating with themselves.

These political limits are even harder to navigate in times of crisis when economies are more fragile. The agency of negotiators declines as a result (Lamy, 2012). It is natural that the process of trade liberalisation and growth raises concerns of fairness, sustainability and social justice. Trade integration leads to growth by up-ending and reshaping the global web of production, creating new efficiencies; however, the way that these efficiencies translate into welfare depends, as ever, on responsible social policies, usually at the domestic level. It is crucial that governments play a leading role in ensuring that trade liberalisation works in the interest of all income levels, especially in developing countries. I have previously referred to this imperative of 'free trade for all' as the 'Geneva consensus' (see Lamy, 2013a).

A discrepancy exists between the benefits of globalisation and the legitimate values shared by diverse communities. The gains of globalisation tend to accrue in favour of large firms and economies, simply because of the economies of scale that are linked to competitiveness in trade. In contrast, the utility that stems from identity and cultural and political legitimacy comes from closeness, rather than openness, and from uniqueness, rather than from scaling up to large volumes of production for export.

The recent wave of Western populism has resulted partly from socio-economic disruptions, the costs of which are relatively widely known and studied, and partly from cultural disruptions. These disruptions are largely unexplored in the literature on international trade, even though international trade is often blamed for the disruptions. Therefore, it is imperative that policymakers' agendas should turn to the broader question of how best to mitigate social and cultural insecurity. In formulating trade and social policy, these insecurities must be given careful consideration if the legitimacy of policymaking in these areas is to be preserved.

Even if the pace of globalisation slows, 'deglobalisation' is not likely to occur. Technological progress, the key driver of globalisation, has never regressed. The clock cannot be turned back, nor would this even be desirable. Turning our backs on globalisation would do nothing to address the biggest issues facing the world, which range from climate change to nuclear proliferation to economic inequality. Severing economic and cultural linkages cannot meaningfully improve employment.

The central problem with globalisation is one of insufficient governance. In the nineteenth century, the first age of globalisation disintegrated because of the lack of coherent political and policy responses in the face of unprecedented social and economic changes. Similarly, the threats confronting today's global economic order are political in nature.

The need to reinvent international institutions is one challenge in addressing these problems. The birth of the Group of Twenty (G20) in place of the Group of Eight (G8) was a great innovation and signified that the international system could adapt to change. More broadly, the scope and capacity for international cooperation has never been so significant— whether stopping pandemics or rewriting technical standards, tackling drug trafficking or combating deforestation. Yet, it has not been sufficient to date. Transforming our institutions will not just be about building new ones, but about 'networking' the existing organisations in a more effective way. Increasingly, the United Nations, the WTO and the IMF must operate as a coherent whole (see Lamy, 2011).

Policymaking has become more complex as international integration has advanced. For example, negotiations on climate change concern international economics as well as the environment. How are the technologies, costs and benefits of environmental policy to be distributed? Similarly, the push to further integrate developing countries into the global economy requires a focus on building the capacity of those countries, far beyond the passive imposition of a set of financial rules. These issues are not just international—more coherent policy must also be a domestic aim.

There is much to be done to strengthen the legitimacy of the global system—to build trust and better align these institutions with societies' interests. This will mean designing and implementing policies for a globalised world, in which education, training and income distribution are prioritised. Deliberation over the most significant causes of wage stagnation (e.g. trade or technology) obscures the more important fact that people in advanced and developing countries need more assistance in coping with profound economic transformations. People will only continue to support globalisation and openness if they share in its benefits. These are all lessons that East Asia should bear in mind as its process of economic integration continues.

References

Bradford, S. C., Grieco, P. L. E. & Hufbauer, G. C. (2005). The payoff to America from global integration. In C. F. Bergsten (Ed.), *The United States and the world economy: Foreign economic policy for the next decade.* pp. 65–109 Washington, DC: Peterson Institute for International Economics. Retrieved from: www.piie.com/publications/chapters_preview/3802/2iie3802.pdf

Château, L. F., Fouré, J., Johansson, Å. & Olaberría, E. (2014). Trade patterns in the 2060 world economy. *OECD Economics Department Working Paper No. 1142*. Paris, France: OECD Publishing. dx.doi.org/10.1787/5jxrmdk5f86j-en

Cheng, K., Rehman, S., Seneviratne, D. & Zhang, S. (2015). Reaping the benefits from global value chains. *IMF Working Paper No. 15/204*. Washington, DC: IMF. Retrieved from: www.imf.org/en/Publications/WP/Issues/2016/12/31/Reaping-the-Benefits-from-Global-Value-Chains-43311

De Backer, K. & Miroudot S. M. (2013). Mapping global value chains. *OECD Trade Policy Paper No. 159*. Paris, France: OECD Publishing. dx.doi.org/10.1787/5k3v1trgnbr4-en

International Monetary Fund (IMF). (2017). *World economic outlook April 2017*. Washington, DC: IMF. Retrieved from: www.imf.org/en/Publications/WEO/Issues/2017/04/04/world-economic-outlook-april-2017

Lamy, P. (2011). *Lamy underlines need for 'unity in our global diversity'.* Speech presented at the Centre for Strategic and International Studies, Jakarta. Retrieved from: www.wto.org/english/news_e/ sppl_e/sppl194_e.htm

Lamy, P. (2012). *Has international trade reached a deadlock?* Interview, *Knowledge@Wharton*, Wharton School of the University of Pennsylvania. Retrieved from: knowledge.wharton.upenn.edu/article/ has-international-trade-reached-a-deadlock-an-interview-with-pascal-lamy-director-general-of-the-wto/

Lamy, P. (2013a). *The Geneva consensus: Making trade work for all.* Cambridge, England: Cambridge University Press.

Lamy, P. (2013b). *The new mapping of international trade.* Speech presented at École Polytechnique Fédérale de Lausanne. Retrieved from: www.wto.org/english/news_e/sppl_e/sppl267_e.htm

Lamy, P. (2015a). The role of aid for trade and technical trade assistance in regional economic integration. *International Trade Forum Magazine*, *2*(12), 28–29.

Lamy, P. (2015b). Where will emerging markets stand in global trade? In H. S. Kohli (Ed.), *The world in 2050*, pp. 133–167, Oxford, England: Oxford University Press.

Lawrence, R. Z. (2007, 15 June). *Slow wage growth and US income inequality: Is trade to blame?* Paper presented at the 'Is free trade still optimal in the 21st century?' conference, Brandeis University. Retrieved from: sites.hks.harvard.edu/fs/rlawrence/Lawrence%20for %20Brandeis.pdf

Organisation for Economic Co-operation and Development (OECD). (2016). Re-thinking upgrading: Benefitting from participation in global value chains. *OECD Trade Policy Notes*, October. Paris: OECD. Retrieved from: www.oecd.org/tad/policynotes/benefitting-participation-gvcs.pdf

Ricardo, D. (1817). *On the principles of political economy and taxation.* London, England: John Murray.

Schumpeter, J. (1942). *Capitalism, socialism and democracy.* New York, NY: Harper & Brothers.

United Nations Conference on Trade and Development (UNCTAD). (2014). *World economic situation and prospects* (WESP/2014). Geneva: UN Publications. Retrieved from: www.unctad.org/en/pages/ PublicationWebflyer.aspx?publicationid=771

World Trade Organization Secretariat. (2016). *World trade statistical review*. Retrieved from: www.wto.org/english/res_e/statis_e/wts2016_e/ wts2016_e.pdf

4

Decoupling Asia revisited

Cyn-Young Park

Introduction

Asia's integration and rise as a main driver of global production and trade has been reshaping the global economic landscape. East and South-East Asia, grouped together as emerging East Asia (EEA),[1] now account for about 25 per cent of total global trade and 21 per cent of global gross domestic product (GDP), whereas the comparable figures in 1985 were about 10 per cent and 5.8 per cent respectively. The region has made remarkable economic progress, with an annual growth rate averaging 7.6 per cent between 1985 and 2015. This performance has been underpinned by dynamic growth in the People's Republic of China (PRC), which contributed around 4.5 percentage points to this growth during the 30-year period.

The PRC has emerged as a major player in the world economy, as a producer, exporter of manufacturing goods and consumer of primary commodities. The PRC also plays a central role in the Asian production network, with the tightening of intra-regional trade and investment links fundamentally changing the nature of macro-economic interdependence and growth spillovers between the region and major advanced economies.

---

1   Throughout this study, Asia refers to nine selected countries in East and South-East Asia. The nine Asian economies that are selected for the study include the PRC; Hong Kong, China; Indonesia; the Republic of Korea; Malaysia; the Philippines; Singapore; Taipei, China; and Thailand.

The issue of decoupling is controversial.[2] The decoupling hypothesis was based on the observation that EEA's sustained high growth in the 2000s, prior to the global financial crisis (GFC) of 2008, was seemingly unaffected by the ups and downs experienced by the major advanced economies. In a narrow sense, the decoupling hypothesis involves the question of whether the regional economy will maintain its strong growth, regardless of a slowdown elsewhere, particularly in the US. In a broader sense, decoupling concerns the emergence of regional economic dynamics in EEA that are independent of economic swings in major industrial countries.

This chapter reinvestigates the decoupling hypothesis using the most recent data and focusing on the potential transmission of economic shocks between the EEA and Group of Three (G3) economies—the US, Japan and the EU. It is likely that the progress of regional economic development and integration has influenced the direction and magnitude of macro-economic interdependence and growth spillovers through regional and global trade and investment links. The ongoing reforms and economic restructuring in the PRC also indicate potential changes in its role in the regional production network.

Following strong policy efforts to rebalance, EEA's economic performance has been solid, despite the visible slowing in the US, Japanese and EU economies in the aftermath of the GFC. Given the weaker than expected economic recovery in the US, and subdued growth prospects in Europe in the post-GFC period, EEA's potential to lead the global economic recovery as an independent source of growth is of particular policy interest.

The three broad purposes of the chapter are as follows. First, the chapter evaluates the progress of regional trade and financial integration, which has implications for the direction and magnitude of macro-economic interdependence and growth spillovers, both intra-regionally and inter-regionally. Global macro-economic interdependence should be time varying and subject to structural changes in economies that are interrelated

---

2　The decoupling hypothesis gained considerable attention from market participants and commentators (see e.g. The decoupling debate, 2008; Are Asian economies decoupling from the US?, 2008). EEA's sustained high growth since the Asian financial crisis nonetheless faltered in the wake of the GFC and the economic downturn that followed. A sharp increase in the business cycle co-movement between Asia and major advanced economies after the crisis seemed to discredit the decoupling hypothesis and reconfirm that Asia remains highly dependent on the global economy.

through trade, investment and financial links. Therefore, it is important to understand the changing dynamics in each of these transmission channels for economic shocks.

Second, the chapter reviews the special role of the PRC in the closely knit regional trade and investment relationship. Intra-Asian trade has been driven, in part, by strong expansion of regional supply networks established by multinational companies. The PRC has become a regional hub of manufactured production by hosting the production process of many multinationals and attracting most inward foreign direct investment (FDI) to the region. The effect of ongoing structural changes in the PRC's production and trade patterns is of particular interest to the region's business cycle analysis and the issue of whether a regional component has strengthened in the region's business cycles.

Finally, the chapter will examine the evolution of business cycle synchronisation in Asia and investigate macro-economic interdependence and growth spillovers between EEA and developed economies. We employ a vector auto-regression (VAR) model to assess the effect of the US output, world trade, financial volatility and the PRC output shocks on EEA. Evidence presented in this chapter indicates how global and regional shocks transmit to the regional economy and which channel works prominently in the transmission of economic shocks.

The chapter is organised as follows. The first section presents a concise literature survey on the issues of economic integration and business cycle synchronisation, focusing on both intra-regional and inter-regional integration for EEA. The second section examines the recent trends in the region's trade and financial linkages, both within and beyond the region, and investigates the changing role of the PRC in these linkages. The third section reviews the evolution of Asia's business cycles and evaluates the growth spillover effects and the degree of macro-economic interdependence between EEA and G3 economies, using a VAR model. The fourth section concludes the chapter.

Literature review: Economic integration and business cycle synchronisation

In economic theory, the effect of economic integration on business cycle co-movement is ambiguous. A substantial literature has investigated the effect of trade linkages on business cycle synchronisation. Frankel and Rose (1998) empirically showed that increased trade integration leads to greater convergence in business cycles by allowing aggregate demand shocks to spread more easily across borders. Such spillover effects can also occur through changes in the relative prices of factors and products. For example, a change in the relative price of labour-intensive goods, resulting from a positive shock in an economy, can spill over to higher wages and employment in other countries through free trade (Kraay & Ventura, 2007). Following the seminal paper by Frankel and Rose (1998), many empirical studies have confirmed that trade intensity increases business cycle synchronisation, albeit at varying degrees, depending on country-specific economic structures (e.g. Baxter & Kouparitsas, 2005; Imbs, 2004; Inklaar, Jong-A-Pin & de Haan, 2008).

However, free trade may not necessarily lead to convergence in cross-country business cycles if stronger trade linkages induce the specialisation of production. Kose and Yi (2002) argued that increased trade linkages would encourage countries to specialise in certain types of production and that increased inter-industry specialisation across countries would decrease the co-movement of international business cycles. In this context, it is not just the size of trade, but also the similarities in industrial structures, that would be important in explaining output co-fluctuations.

A few related studies have focused specifically on the similarity of production structures as an important determinant of output co-movements. They showed the effect of industrial structure in cross-border spillovers through the trade channel. Industry-specific shocks can cause more business cycle synchronisation among countries with similar production structures. Clark and van Wincoop (2001), Imbs (2004) and Shin and Wang (2004) provided evidence that greater similarity in industry structure is associated with more synchronicity in output and employment. Imbs (2004) emphasised that when bilateral trade is driven more by intra-industry trade than by inter-industry trade, output co-movement tends to strengthen.

The effect of financial integration on output co-movement is even more controversial. Financial integration can help increase the efficiency of financial resource allocation across countries, for example, by moving capital from a country with a negative shock to one with a positive shock, implying a negative output correlation. Kalemli-Ozcan, Sørensen and Yosha (2003) demonstrated that better risk sharing through greater financial integration can lead to higher specialisation of production and, hence, less symmetric output fluctuations. Heathcote and Perri (2004) presented evidence that higher financial integration can lead to a decline in the correlation of output in a two-country, two-good model.

However, Imbs (2006) empirically showed that a higher degree of financial integration leads to greater business cycle synchronisation between two economies. The empirical literature on financial crises and financial contagion has also tended to highlight the direct and positive effects of financial integration on business cycle synchronisation (Calvo & Reinhart, 1996; Claessens, Dornbusch & Park, 2001; Kose, Prasad & Terrones, 2003, 2007). Especially in a crisis context, with imperfect information or liquidity constraints, a flight to safety can cause investors to withdraw capital from many countries simultaneously, contributing to positive output correlation. Kim, Kim and Wang (2003) illustrated how shocks to capital flows generate positive business cycle correlation for countries in Asia and the Pacific. Kim and Kim (2013) also examined the role of capital market liberalisation in business cycle synchronisation among Asian economies by providing empirical evidence of the positive effect of international capital flows on output co-movement.

The effect of trade and financial linkages on business cycle co-movement hinges more broadly on socio-economic and policy factors, including cross-country differences in industrial structure, factor intensity, macro-economic policies and foreign exchange regimes. With increasingly globalised trade and financial settings, policymaking (particularly in regard to monetary policy) shows a tendency towards cross-country convergence. In general, greater integration may call for greater macro-economic policy cooperation across borders to more effectively manage spillovers and macro-economic interdependence.

The nature and extent of business cycle co-movement is ultimately an empirical question. Several studies have adopted dynamic factor models that decompose an economy's output fluctuations into contributions by different factors, such as global, regional and country-specific factors. Using various specifications of a dynamic factor model, Moneta and Ruffer (2006) found a significant common factor in outputs of 10 East Asian economies, not including the PRC and Japan. Their findings showed that the common factor was mainly the result of co-movements in exports, as well as some exogenous factors, such as the oil price and the JPY–USD exchange rate. However, cross-country spillover effects do not explain a large share of the co-movement in Asia.

Other empirical studies suggest that the business cycles of Asian economies have increasingly synchronised, partly as a result of deepened trade integration. Shin and Wang (2004) employed a panel regression to show that intra-industry trade is the major channel for business cycle convergence between the Republic of Korea and other Asian economies. Abeysinghe and Forbes (2005) developed a structural VAR model to examine how a shock to a country would transmit to 11 Asian economies, as well as to the US and the rest of the Organisation for Economic Co-operation and Development (OECD). They estimated the multiplier effects of a shock using trading linkages, which are large and significant, although they differ from the predicted patterns using a bilateral trade matrix. Kim and Lee (2008) examined the extent of output interdependence among Asian economies, and between Asia and the world, using a VAR approach, and found that regional influence increased as much as global influence in Asian outputs after the Asian financial crisis (AFC) of 1997–98.

Overall, the empirical studies suggest varying degrees of macro-economic interdependence in Asia, depending on the choice of empirical methodology and measures of integration. Although recent studies have found evidence of increasing output interdependence among Asian economies, especially after the AFC, the results remain inconclusive as to whether the outputs of Asian economies have become more independent and decoupled from those of the industrialised economies. Helbling et al. (2007) and Kose, Otrok and Prasad (2008) found that global and regional common shocks have accounted for a sizeable fraction of business cycle fluctuations in both industrial countries and emerging market economies, but that the relative importance of global factors has decreased while that of regional factors has increased. This result provides support for the decoupling, or divergence, of business cycles between industrialised countries and Asian economies. However, Kim, Lee and Park (2009) provided empirical evidence to support the 'recoupling', rather than decoupling, of Asian economies with major advanced countries, as their findings indicated that economic interdependence between Asian and major advanced economies increased significantly after the AFC.

Trade and financial linkages

Intra-Asian trade: The PRC's role and vertical supply networks

Trade is often considered an important channel through which economic shocks are transmitted from one country to another. Export-driven growth may expose countries to the economic conditions of their trading partners and external market environments. EEA has achieved rapid economic expansion over the past few decades, underpinned by strong export performance. Its export-to-GDP ratio rose rapidly from 25 per cent in 1985 to a peak of 46 per cent in 2006, before declining steadily to 29 per cent in 2015. The region's average ratio over 1985–2015 was 35 per cent, much higher than the world average of 19 per cent, attesting to the export-oriented growth strategy in the region.

EEA's high reliance on exports has been accompanied by significant progress in diversifying its export base. Figure 4.1 shows the composition of EEA's exports by destination. The geographical composition of Asia's export market has become much more diversified, with the share of the single largest market, the US, at only 14 per cent in 2015, down from 23 per cent in 1990. The G3 economies collectively accounted for 29 per cent of EEA's total exports in 2015, down from almost 50 per cent from 1990. In contrast, EEA's exports to other developing economies (Africa, Latin America and the Middle East) rose from only 5 per cent to 12 per cent.

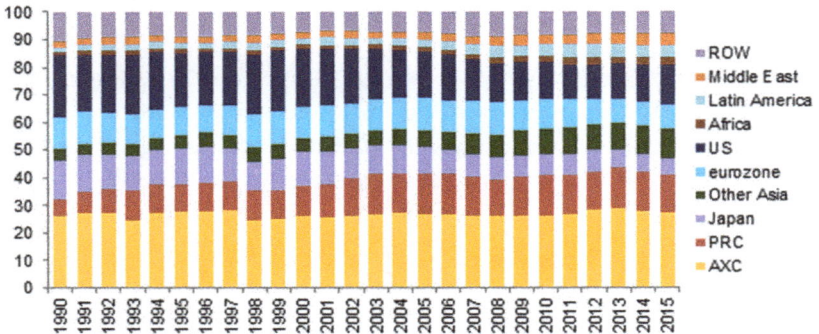

Figure 4.1: Destination of EEA exports (percentage of total exports)

EEA = emerging East Asia; AXC = EEA excluding PRC; ROW = rest of the world; PRC = People's Republic of China; US = United States.

Note: EEA includes ASEAN–4 (Indonesia, Malaysia, the Philippines and Thailand), NIE (Hong Kong, China; the Republic of Korea; Singapore; and Taipei, China) and the PRC.

Source: Park (2017).

Greater diversification in the destination of Asian exports suggests that an idiosyncratic demand shock from a single market may be mitigated, to some extent, by stronger growth in other export markets. At the same time, the share of intra-regional trade of EEA economies in total exports rose from 32 per cent in 1990 to around 41 per cent in 2015. The PRC now accounts for around 30 per cent of EEA's intra-regional exports, up from 20 per cent in 1990. Strong growth in intra-regional trade, including with the PRC, has been regarded as evidence of EEA's greater resilience to cyclical fluctuations in the major trading partners outside the region.

However, changing demand conditions in the world's major economies— particularly the US—appear to remain a dominant factor in EEA's export growth. Figure 4.2 demonstrates the close relationship between US non-oil import growth and Asian export growth. The US non-oil imports account for about 60 per cent of total G3 non-oil imports, and are highly synchronised with the movements of G3 non-oil imports. Consequently, the correlation between EEA exports and G3 non-oil import growth should be quite significant. Although the share of G3 markets in Asia's total export market is declining, Figure 4.2 indicates that the relationship has strengthened; the decadal correlations between the growth rates of US non-oil imports and Asian exports confirm that this linkage is significant and tighter in the 2000s.

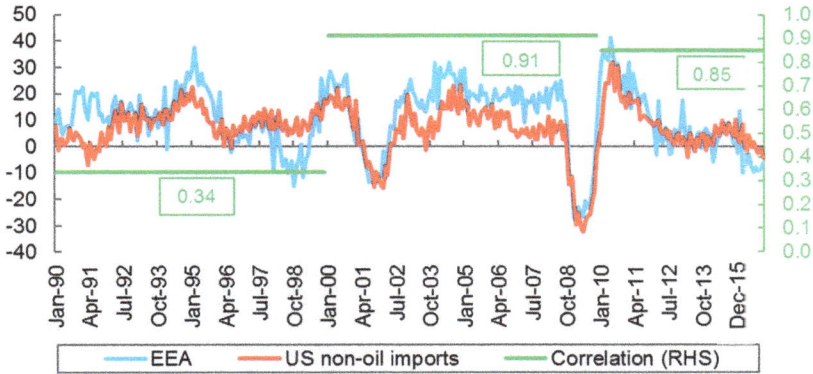

Figure 4.2: Correlation between growth in EEA exports and US non-oil imports

EEA = ASEAN–4 (Indonesia, Malaysia, the Philippines and Thailand); NIE (Hong Kong, China; the Republic of Korea; Singapore; and Taipei, China) and the People's Republic of China; RHS = right-hand side.

Note: Non-oil imports are calculated by subtracting crude oil imports from the total import of goods.

Source: Park (2017).

Underlying this strong linkage is the nature of intra-Asian trade, which is driven by the vertical integration of production chains, the final outputs of which are destined for markets outside the region. Figure 4.3 shows a breakdown of EEA exports based on exports destined for other countries within the region and those going elsewhere, based on the global value chain (GVC) database. The database was accessed from the multiregion input–output tables of the Asian Development Bank (ADB), using the methodology from Wang, Wei and Zhu (2014).[3] Intra-regional trade within EEA is then decomposed into production inputs and the region's final demand. A similar decomposition is made for trade with the rest of the world. For both decompositions, total final demand is derived for different regions, which takes into account the trade of intermediate goods in the production process for final demands. Based on our estimates, about 41.9 per cent of total EEA exports (instead of the about 29 per cent of total exports shown above) are eventually consumed by G3 countries.

---

3   The input–output tables of Bangladesh, Malaysia, the Philippines, Thailand and Vietnam were constructed by the ADB, while the rest of the input–output tables were sourced from the world input–output database. While both sets of tables have been constructed in a clear conceptual framework on the basis of officially published input–output tables in conjunction with national accounts and international trade statistics, level numbers are likely to remain different from those officially released by the respective economies.

The results show that G3 countries remain the main export destinations for final goods that leave EEA when taking into account the share of intermediate goods trade that is for assembly and production within the region, but which are eventually shipped out of the region as final goods.

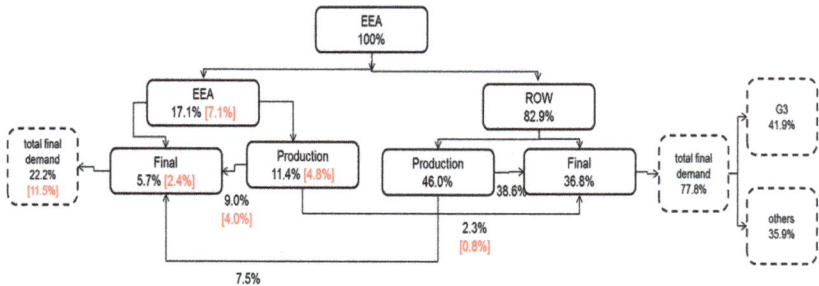

Figure 4.3: Value-added export decomposition—EEA, 2011

EEA = emerging East Asia; ROW = rest of world; G3 = US, EU and Japan; Value-added export decomposition = Domestic value-added + Returned domestic value. Values for the People's Republic of China are presented in red and in parentheses.

Source: Park (2017).

As a vast majority of intra-Asian trade stems from extra-regional demand, the growth of the intra-regional trade share in total emerging Asian exports does not necessarily indicate EEA's independence from an external demand shock. On the contrary, to the extent that intra-regional trade is driven by intra-industry processing and assembly through vertically integrated production chains, EEA exports remain highly sensitive to a shock from outside the region, especially one from the major advanced economies. The effect on Asian exports of the global slowdown, following the GFC, which originated from the US subprime mortgage sector and its ripple effects through the global financial system, was a vivid example of such sensitivity.

The United Nations Economic and Social Commission for Asia and the Pacific (UNESCAP, 2014) reported that strong growth in intra-firm and intra-industry trade through the vertical supply networks of multinational companies has boosted Asian trade both intra-regionally and inter-regionally. It suggested that regional production-sharing networks, allowing multinational companies to take advantage of specific local conditions and low-cost labour, may have contributed to the development of the intra-regional trade of intermediate goods destined for final consumption outside the region.

The PRC, as the region's main production base, has been at the centre of this growing intra-industry and intra-regional trade. In just two decades, between 1985 and 2015, the PRC's exports grew from US$27 billion to US$2,281 billion, while its imports grew from US$42 billion to US$1,602 billion. During this period of rapid growth, the pattern of PRC trade changed drastically. In the 1990s, the share of G3 markets steadily increased, reaching 50 per cent of total PRC exports by 2000, before declining gradually to around 35 per cent in 2015. Meanwhile, the PRC imported more than half of its total imports from Japan and EEA in the 1990s, although their collective share has fallen below 50 per cent in the past decade. However, from about 2000, the PRC has notably diversified its export and import partners, as the rest of the world takes up an increasing share of its total exports and imports (Figure 4.4).

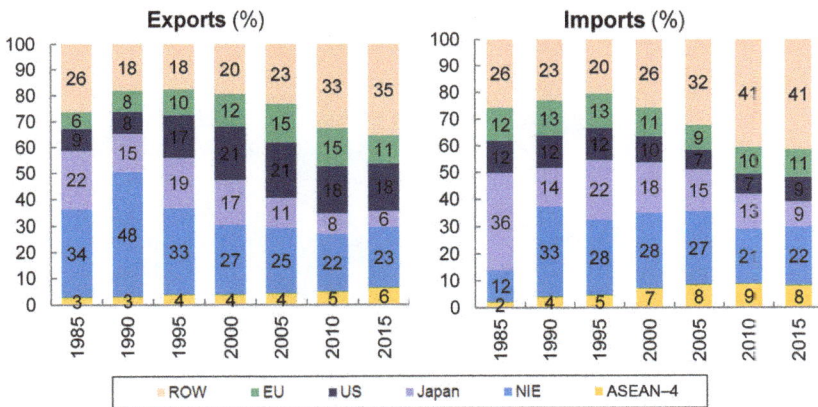

Figure 4.4: People's Republic of China export and import share, by trading partner

ASEAN–4 = Indonesia, Malaysia, the Philippines and Thailand; EU = European Union; NIE = Hong Kong (China), the Republic of Korea, Singapore, Taipei (China); ROW = rest of world; US = United States.

Source: Park (2017).

The basic pattern of the PRC's trade in the 1990s was characterised by the export of processed consumption goods to the US and EU, and the import of large volumes of processed intermediate and capital goods from regional economies. However, since the mid-2000s, the PRC has emerged as a major importer of primary commodities from the rest of the world, whereas processed intermediate and capital goods, rather than consumer goods, are leading its exports.

This changing trade pattern is well captured by the trend in the type of commodity exports and imports by the PRC (Figure 4.5). For example, about 70 per cent of the PRC's total imports consisted of primary and processed intermediate goods in the 1990s. By 2015, this rose to more than 75 per cent, with the share of primary intermediate goods expanding faster than that of processed intermediate goods, suggesting an increase in the PRC's self-production of intermediate goods. Most of the PRC's exports were processed consumption and intermediate goods in the 1990s, but the share of capital goods in the PRC's total exports increased from 17 per cent to about 30 per cent between 2000 and 2015, whereas processed consumption goods fell from 44 per cent to 30 per cent.

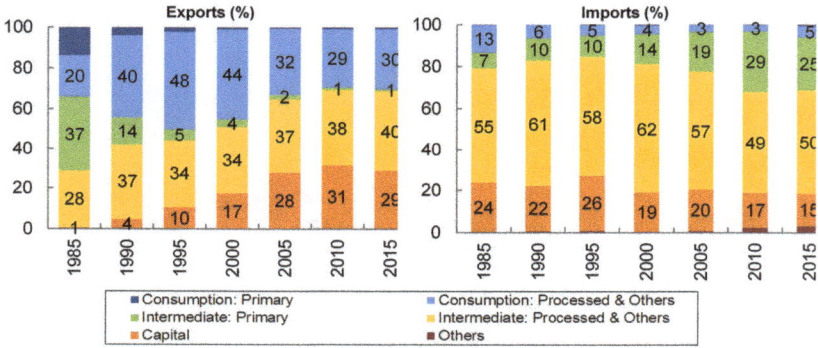

Figure 4.5: People's Republic of China export and import share, commodity groups

Note: Based on broad economic categories.
Source: Park (2017).

The analysis highlights a notable change in the pattern of the PRC's trade. There has been a gradual decline in the PRC's imports of processed intermediate goods from other Asian economies, whereas the PRC has increased imports of primary intermediate goods from the rest of the world. This suggests that the PRC has been increasingly internalising the manufacturing input supply in the GVC. The PRC also exports an increasingly large share of capital foods, suggesting that its manufacturing production is becoming more sophisticated and higher value-added. Athukorala and Ravenhill (2016) noted similar trends using the UN Comtrade data for PRC exports in different product categories. They observed that the PRC is deepening the domestic supply base for its exports, which may have reduced its import dependence on other Asian economies. Their study also noted that, although the PRC's exports have become much more geographically diversified, the US and EU remain important as export destinations.

The trade—FDI nexus: Global production sharing in Asia

FDI has played an important role in promoting intra-regional and inter-regional trade of host countries. The growth in inward FDI to EEA has been remarkable, rising from US$22 billion in 1990 to US$426 billion in 2015. Excluding the PRC, the region attracted US$290 billion in 2015, up from US$18 billion in 1990. The EEA region has been the largest recipient region in the world, attracting almost a quarter of global FDI.

The pattern of inward FDI to Asia reveals that firms' motivations for FDI are different to those for the rest of the world. Firms can enter the market (i) to avoid trade barriers and gain better access to local markets by undertaking the same production activities in multiple countries (horizontal FDI), or (ii) to lower production costs by relocating different stages of production to the country with the least cost (vertical FDI). More foreign affiliates in Asia established by FDI tend to be engaged in trade and investment for the purpose of re-exporting intermediate and final goods to countries outside the host country (vertical and export-platform FDI) than is the case in other developing regions.

Rapid expansion of FDI to EEA has been closely associated with the establishment of regional production networks by multinational companies, especially with the PRC as the region's main assembly and production hub, to create positive spillovers for the rest of the regional economies (Fukao, Ishido & Ito, 2003; Kawai & Urata, 2004; Eichengreen & Tong, 2005; ADB, 2006). Indeed, based on the number of foreign affiliates in Asia that both import and export, the PRC is the most popular host for vertical and export-platform FDI (Table 4.1) with various parent economies. By sector, inward FDI from trade-oriented firms is mostly concentrated in manufacturing, except in Hong Kong, China, where it mostly goes to business services (Table 4.2).

Table 4.1: Most common economy pairs for trade-oriented FDI firms

Destination	Origin	Number of FDI firms that import and export	% of total FDI firms
1. PRC	Japan	2,260	81
2. PRC	Hong Kong, China	1,314	76
3. PRC	US	646	74
4. PRC	Germany	625	76
5. PRC	Taipei, China	401	79
6. PRC	Korea, Rep. of	358	86

Destination	Origin	Number of FDI firms that import and export	% of total FDI firms
7. PRC	Singapore	337	71
8. Vietnam	Japan	306	72
9. Thailand	Japan	258	64
10. Indonesia	Japan	214	53
11. Taipei, China	Japan	212	74
12. PRC	France	177	77
13. Malaysia	Japan	175	78
14. Philippines	Japan	171	69
15. Singapore	Japan	164	54

PRC = People's Republic of China.
Source: ADB (2016).

Table 4.2: Inward FDI from trade-oriented FDI firms—EEA economies, by sector

Host economies	Mining	Manufacturing	Business services
PRC	0.005	0.980	0.014
Indonesia	0.005	0.796	0.200
Malaysia	0.020	0.955	0.022
Thailand	0.031	0.958	0.010
Vietnam	0.005	0.989	0.006
Hong Kong, China	0.008	0.311	0.674
Korea, Rep. of	0.035	0.930	0.030
Singapore	0.019	0.682	0.276
Taipei, China	0.027	0.918	0.055
India	0.012	0.587	0.399
Japan	0.014	0.784	0.201
Australia	0.053	0.828	0.114

PRC = People's Republic of China.
Note: Each row shows the fraction of foreign affiliates that export and import in country *i* in each sector. Rows may not exactly sum to one owing to statistical discrepancies.
Source: ADB (2016).

Table 4.3 highlights an important issue regarding the headquarters of parent companies and the activity of their foreign affiliates operating in EEA. Foreign affiliates with an EEA parent company, although limited in number, are much more likely to be engaged in international trade than are affiliates with non-East Asian parent companies. The effect arises from foreign affiliates of parent companies from high-income East Asian economies (known as NIE [newly industrialised economies]). However, even foreign affiliates of middle-income South-East Asian multinationals are more engaged in international trade than those belonging to multinationals from outside Asia.

Table 4.3: Number of FDI firms by parent economy

Parent economy/region	Total number of FDI firms	Proportion that imports & exports (%)
Emerging East Asia	47,057	36.2
PRC	31,298	31.6
ASEAN–4	2,788	30.4
NIE	12,971	48.4
Rest of world	183,073	9.9
India	52,009	11.2
Japan	104,066	6.3
US	3,369	41.4
EU	6,128	48.4

Note: Based on global ultimate headquarters.
Source: Based on data from Ramondo (2016).

Strong trade and FDI linkages can be a channel for shock transmission. As the PRC has emerged as an important hub for intra-industry and intra-regional trade and investment in Asia, it is likely that economic interdependence between the PRC and the rest of Asia has also increased.

Financial integration and spillovers

Financial integration, in theory, offers many benefits, including better consumption smoothing through international risk sharing, more efficient allocation of capital for investment and enhanced macro-economic and financial discipline (Park & Lee, 2011). However, in practice, tighter financial linkages also generate a higher risk of cross-border financial contagion, as illustrated by the episodes of financial crisis.

Financial market integration is another important channel for shock transmission and a determinant of business cycle synchronisation. Therefore, the degree of financial integration among EEA equity and bond markets is empirically investigated, in terms of both quantity and prices.

With greater capital account openness, the shares of international portfolio assets and liabilities held by Asian economies have increased. Figure 4.6 shows the trend of the cross-border portfolio asset holdings of AXC countries by region since 2001, based on the International Monetary Fund's (IMF) coordinated portfolio investment survey data.[4] The value of the region's foreign portfolio asset holdings surged from US$331.9 billion in 2001 (2.6 per cent of the world's total foreign portfolio assets) to US$2.6 trillion (5.6 per cent) in 2015. When the value is scaled by GDP, the size of AXC's foreign asset holdings increased from 26.3 per cent of GDP in 2001 to 67.7 per cent in 2015.[5]

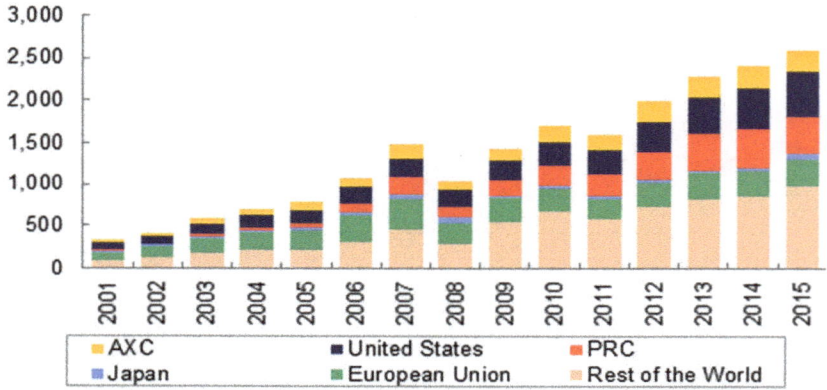

Figure 4.6: AXC's cross-border portfolio asset holdings (US$ billion)

AXC = emerging East Asia excluding PRC; PRC = People's Republic of China.

Note: AXC includes Hong Kong, China; Indonesia; the Republic of Korea; Malaysia; the Philippines; Singapore; and Thailand. The PRC is not included because it only commenced reporting portfolio holdings in the first half of 2015.

Source: Park (2017).

The data on the asset holdings of a country can be also interpreted as liabilities by the counterpart country. For example, the Republic of Korea's holding of financial assets in Thailand can be interpreted as Thailand's liability to Korea. Figure 4.7 illustrates EEA's financial liabilities by

---

4   The coordinated portfolio investment survey is a voluntary data collection exercise conducted under the auspices of the IMF that collects an economy's data on its holdings of portfolio investment securities. Data are separately requested for equity and investment fund shares, long-term debt instruments and short-term debt instruments.

5   The PRC began reporting portfolio holdings in the first half of 2015. If the PRC's data is included, the value of EEA's foreign portfolio asset holdings for 2015 is US$2.9 trillion (6.2 per cent of world foreign portfolio assets). When the value is scaled by GDP, the size of EEA's foreign asset holdings is 19.4 per cent in 2015.

their geographic destinations since 2001. The US and the EU comprise the major share of EEA's financial liabilities, which makes the region vulnerable to changes in their financial conditions. For example, during the GFC, tightening credit conditions in the US and the EU prompted repatriation of their investment funds in EEA.

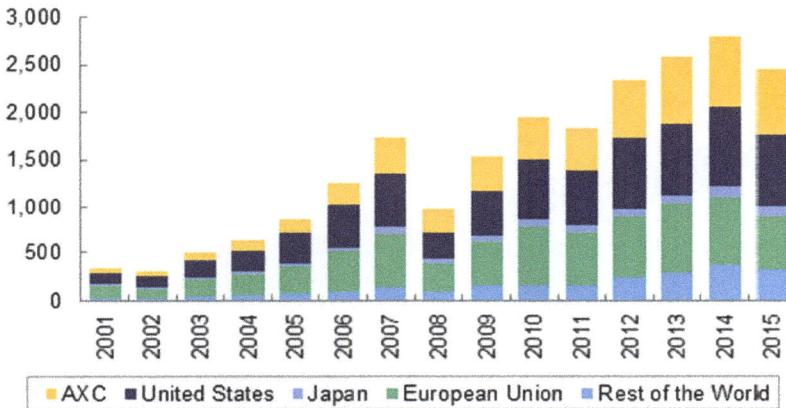

Figure 4.7: EEA's cross-border portfolio liabilities (US$ billion)

EEA = emerging East Asia; AXC = EEA excluding PRC; PRC = People's Republic of China.

Note: EEA includes the PRC; Hong Kong, China; Indonesia; the Republic of Korea; Malaysia; the Philippines; Singapore; and Thailand.

Source: Park (2017).

Hong Kong (China), the Republic of Korea and Singapore are the three largest investors among the EEA economies. In 2015, Hong Kong held international portfolio assets of approximately US$1.3 trillion, or 2.7 per cent of world total international portfolio assets, Singapore held US$962 billion and the Republic of Korea held US$236 billion. On average, an individual EEA economy held foreign portfolio assets worth US$359 billion in 2015, which is much lower than the US$738 billion average for an economy that is part of the EU.[6]

The EEA region's foreign portfolio asset holdings have become more geographically balanced since 2001. If EEA financial markets have become more regionally integrated, then a higher share of financial assets

---

6   EU member economies included in the database are Austria, Belgium, Bulgaria, Cyprus, Czech Republic, Denmark, Estonia, Finland, France, Germany, Greece, Hungary, Ireland, Italy, Latvia, Lithuania, Luxembourg, Malta, Netherlands, Poland, Portugal, Romania, Slovak Republic, Slovenia, Spain, Sweden and the UK. Data for Croatia are not available. Data for Ireland are not included because there are no data for 2015.

should be traded within the region and held by regional investors. The share of the EU and US economies as a percentage of EEA's total foreign assets has declined from 48 per cent in 2001 to 34.8 per cent in 2015 (32.8 per cent for AXC), whereas the share of the PRC and the rest of the world increased substantially during this period, from 34.8 per cent to 51.8 per cent (55.3 per cent for AXC). EEA's foreign portfolio assets are increasingly being invested in the region. Regional portfolio asset holdings increased from 14.7 per cent to 26.4 per cent from 2001 to 2015, with a large share invested in the PRC. Excluding the PRC, regional asset holdings are rather low and steady (they declined from 11.7 per cent of EEA's total foreign asset holdings in 2001 to 11.0 per cent in 2015).

The sharp increase in EEA's international portfolio asset holdings suggests a greater degree of financial openness and integration—both regionally and globally. However, the pace of financial integration in emerging Asia still lags behind that in Europe. The international portfolio asset holdings of an average EEA economy in 2015 were 19.4 per cent of its GDP, which is very low compared to the average EU country's holdings of 119 per cent of GDP. Moreover, the share of EEA's portfolio assets (both equities and debt securities) in the total international portfolio asset holdings of EEA in 2015 was much lower (26.1 per cent) than that of EU asset holdings of EU economies (61.4 per cent).

If financial markets are fully integrated, assets with similar risk characteristics should be priced similarly (after adjusting for risks). In other words, greater financial integration should be accompanied by the closer co-movement of financial asset prices. The data used to measure the degree of co-movement of financial asset returns comprise benchmark stock prices and bond return indexes, both sourced from Bloomberg. Correlations were computed between EEA and Japan and between the Eurozone and the US, as well as within EEA economies. For stock market returns, weekly log differences of benchmark stock price indexes were calculated to obtain continuously compounded weekly total returns from 1 January 1990[7] to 19 August 2016. For bond returns, the total return indices of the JP Morgan Asia Diversified[8] were used for EEA, and Bloomberg Barclays indices were used for G3 economies.

---

7   For Singapore and the Eurozone, the data series started from 31 August 1999 and 31 December 1996, respectively.

8   JP Morgan Asia Diversified is a suite of indices that tracks local currency government bonds issued by emerging and developed Asian countries (excluding Japan). See www.jpmorgan.com/country/PH/en/detail/1320549416493

Similarly to stock market returns, weekly log differences were computed for bond return indexes from 31 December 2004[9] to 31 August 2016. Using weekly—as opposed to daily—data can help to avoid the potential problem of non-synchronous data.

Table 4.4 presents the simple correlations in equity and debt markets computed over the full sample period, together with sub-samples that exclude crisis periods. Correlation coefficients of EEA stock markets' returns with advanced economies increased sharply following the AFC, and continued after the GFC. Intra-regional correlation among the EEA economies also increased. These results illustrate the significant spillover effects of the crisis on EEA markets and their increased financial integration with advanced economies after 1998. In particular, remarkable increases in financial market correlations are noted for AXC and the PRC. Correlation of EEA bond market returns for EEA and G3 economies also rose after the GFC, although both intra- and inter-regional correlations remained generally lower than those of the stock market.

To account for the time-varying dynamics[10] of financial market correlations, especially during episodes of financial crisis, we employ a simple model of dynamic conditional correlation (DCC).[11] The DCC model, developed by Engle (2002), Engle and Sheppard (2001) and Tse and Tsui (2002), is a dynamic specification based on conditional correlations within generalised autoregressive conditional heteroskedasticity (GARCH) or multivariate autoregressive conditional heteroskedasticity (ARCH) models. It is a recent method allowing simultaneous modelling of variances and conditional correlations of several series.

---

9   The data series for the Philippines started from 1 February 2008.

10   The descriptive statistics for the EEA economies indicate that the variances of the different series' returns neatly increased during the crisis. All series' returns are not normally distributed (Skewness $\neq 0$ and Kurtosis $\neq 3$).

11   The dynamic correlations are constructed as follows:

$$R_t = (1 - \alpha - 1)\bar{R} + \alpha\left(\varepsilon_{i,t-1}\varepsilon_{j,t-1}\right) + \beta R_{t-1}$$

where α and β are key scalar parameters to be estimated and R_t is the time-varying correlation matrix, the elements of which are defined as follows:

$$\rho_{i,j,t} = q_{i,j,t} \Big/ \sqrt{q_{ii,t}q_{jj,t}}$$

where $\bar{R}$ is the unconditional expectation of $\varepsilon_t\varepsilon_t'$; $\rho_{i,j,t}$ is the conditional correlation between the asset returns of countries i and j at time t and $q_{i,j,t}$ is the off-diagonal elements of the variance–covariance matrix.

Table 4.4: Simple correlations in financial asset returns

	Full sample	Pre-AFC	Pre-GFC	Post-GFC
Equity market returns				
EEA–EEA	0.39	0.23	0.36	0.53
AXC–PRC	0.12	0.02	0.08	0.31
EEA–JPN	0.36	0.16	0.36	0.45
EEA–Eurozone	0.44	0.22	0.38	0.52
EEA–US	0.39	0.20	0.36	0.57
Bond market returns				
EEA–EEA	0.23	–	0.10	0.28
AXC–PRC	0.13	–	-0.01	0.17
EEA–JPN	0.17	–	0.15	0.20
EEA–Eurozone	0.21	–	0.23	0.24
EEA–US	0.25	–	0.17	0.29

AFC = Asian financial crisis; GFC = global financial crisis; JPN = Japan; EEA = emerging East Asia; AXC = EEA excluding the People's Republic of China.

Note: Owing to data constraints, EEA countries' bond market returns only include Indonesia, Malaysia, the Philippines, Thailand, the Republic of Korea, Singapore and the People's Republic of China.

Source: ADB calculations, using data from Bloomberg LP.

The estimation consisted of two steps. First, the conditional variance of each variable was estimated using a univariate ARCH procedure. Second, the standardised regression residuals obtained in the first step were used to model those conditional correlations that vary through time. The analysis attempted to infer how the region's financial markets moved in relation to financial fluctuations in these systemic countries.

Figure 4.8 shows that the relationship between EEA equity returns and the three major economies' equity returns strengthened post-AFC and continued to do so pre-GFC. After the GFC, the relationship slightly weakened but it eventually recovered to pre-GFC levels. The results also show that conditional correlations among EEA economies, especially between AXC and the PRC, have visibly strengthened since the AFC. Figure 4.9 illustrates that the conditional correlations of EEA bond returns are generally lower than those of equity returns and that they have been relatively steady—although they increased slightly in the post-GFC period.

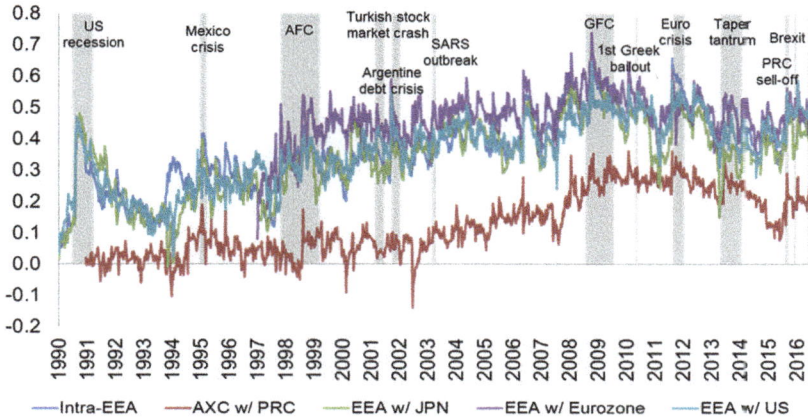

Figure 4.8: Dynamic conditional correlations of equity market returns—
EEA

EEA = emerging East Asia; AXC = EEA excluding PRC; PRC = People's Republic of China;
JPN = Japan; US = United States.

Source: Park (2017).

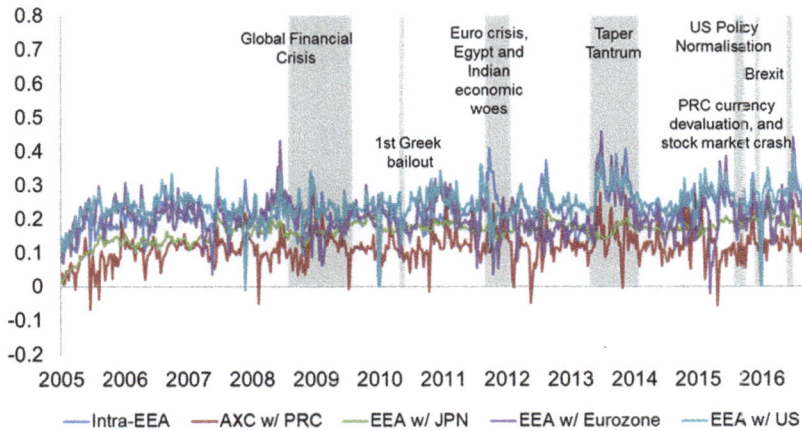

Figure 4.9: Dynamic conditional correlations of bond market returns—
EEA

EEA = emerging East Asia; AXC = EEA excluding PRC; PRC = People's Republic of China;
JPN = Japan; US = United States.

Source: Park (2017).

Business cycle synchronisation and macro-economic interdependence

It is likely that deepening trade and financial linkages will influence the degree of macro-economic interdependence. Business cycle synchronicity may change over time, subject to the effects of trade openness, financial liberalisation and institutional set-ups, such as regional trade and investment agreements. Hirata, Kose and Otrok (2013) suggested that business cycle movements are driven by a combination of global, regional and country factors, and that the strength of each component can influence the degree of business cycle synchronisation at global and regional levels. The recent trends in Asia's global and regional trade and financial linkages suggest a stronger influence of both global and regional components in driving its business cycle. However, the progress of regional trade, financial integration and regional institution building, especially in Asia, could facilitate business cycle synchronisation more at regional levels than at the global level.

Asia's business cycle correlations within and beyond the region

This section examines the evolution of business cycle co-movements between EEA, the PRC and major industrialised economies. Figure 4.10 illustrates the correlations of quarterly real business cycles in EEA with Japan, the EU and the US, as well as among sub-regional groupings within EEA, using 12-quarter (three-year) moving averages. For example, the correlation in 2015Q4 is calculated as the average correlation between EEA and the US over a 12-quarter period ending in 2015Q4. Figure 4.10 also presents the average of the bilateral correlations within EEA and between EEA and G3 economies in the sample over three periods: (i) pre-AFC (1985Q1–1997Q1), (ii) pre-GFC (1999Q1–2007Q3) and (iii) post-GFC (2009Q3–2016Q2) to separate out the effect of the crisis on the business cycle co-movements.

Pre- and post-GFC can be also grouped as post-AFC (see Figure 4.10). The correlation analysis shows that business cycle correlations between EEA and G3 economies increased visibly in the post-AFC period, but generally declined post-GFC. EEA's intra-regional business cycle correlations also increased in the post-AFC period, but decreased slightly post-GFC. The results also show that the co-movement between the business cycles of the PRC and the rest of EEA increased in the post-AFC period, but weakened in the post-GFC period.

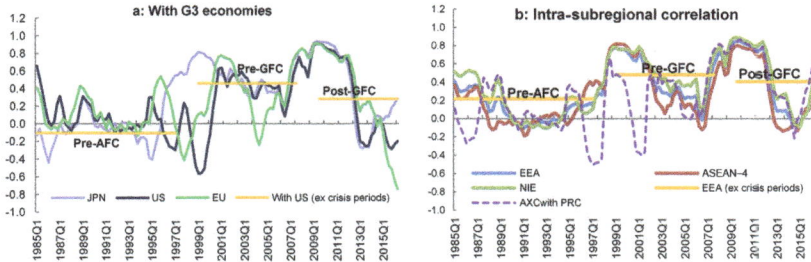

Figure 4.10: Business cycle correlations—EEA

AFC = Asian financial crisis; AXC = EEA excluding PRC; EEA = emerging East Asia; EU = European Union; GFC = global financial crisis; JPN = Japan; PRC = People's Republic of China; US = United States.

Note: EEA includes ASEAN–4 (Indonesia, Malaysia, the Philippines and Thailand), NIE (Hong Kong, China; the Republic of Korea; Singapore; and Taipei, China) and the PRC. Three-year moving correlations are based on cyclical Hodrick–Prescott filtered, seasonally adjusted gross domestic product at constant prices.

Source: Park (2017).

Instead of average three-year moving bilateral correlations, the instantaneous quasi-correlation measure is also employed to remove the lagged effects of the financial crises that occur in moving averages when correlations are calculated over rolling windows of three years.[12] This measure was first proposed by Abiad, Furceri, Kalemli-Ozcan and Pescatori (2013) and used in Duval, Cheng, Oh, Saraf and Seneviratne (2014). Using annual data on real GDP growth rates, quasi-correlations within EEA and between EEA and Japan, the EU and the US since 1985 are depicted in Figures 4.11 and 4.12.

Consistent with findings from similar studies, it was found that business cycle correlations increased sharply during crisis times (Figure 4.11). The largest spikes occurred around the AFC for the EEA region's

---

12 The instantaneous quasi-correlation measure of business cycle synchronisation is computed as:

$$QCORR_{ijt} = \frac{(g_{it} - g_i^*) * (g_{jt} - g_j^*)}{\sigma_i^g * \sigma_j^g}$$

where $QCORR_{ijt}$ is the quasi-correlation of the real GDP growth rates of countries i and j in year t; g_{it} denotes the output growth rate of countries i and j in year t; and g_i^* and g_j^* represent the mean and standard deviation of the output growth rate of country i, respectively, during the sample period. The growth rate is the first difference of the log of real GDP (see Abiad et al., 2013; Duval et al., 2014).

economies, with correlations increasing intra-regionally for EEA and between AXC and the PRC. The region's business cycle correlations with the EU and the US were largest during the GFC. During normal times (excluding the crisis period), the instantaneous quasi-correlations were much smaller in general.

However, Figure 4.12 shows an increase in instantaneous quasi-correlations between EEA and the PRC, Japan and the EU after the GFC. The instantaneous quasi-correlation with the US increased after the AFC but declined after the GFC. The intra-regional correlation declined after the AFC, although it climbed higher after the GFC. Among the sub-regional groupings of EEA, the high-income NIE economies show particularly high business cycle correlations both intra- and inter-regionally.

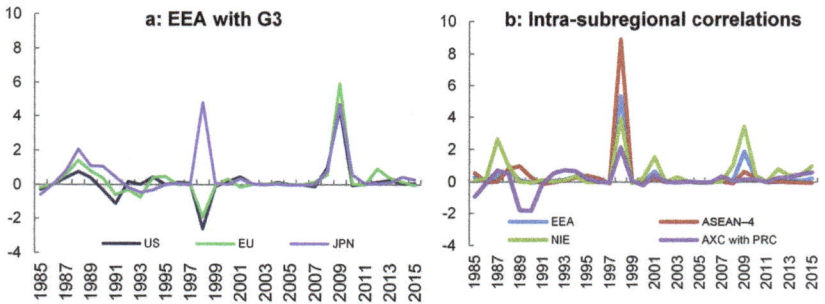

Figure 4.11: Median instantaneous quasi-correlations of real GDP growth rates—EEA

AXC = EEA excluding PRC; EEA = emerging East Asia; GDP = gross domestic product; PRC = People's Republic of China; EU = European Union; JPN = Japan; US = United States.

Note: AXC includes the ASEAN–4 (Indonesia, Malaysia, the Philippines and Thailand) and NIE (Hong Kong, China; the Republic of Korea; Singapore; and Taipei, China). Based on the methodology of Abiad, Furceri, Kalemli-Ozcan and Pescatori (2013).

Source: Park (2017).

Business cycle synchronicity may increase during crisis periods because economies are exposed to common shocks. However, shocks that originate in one economy could also transmit to other economies. The analysis of various correlation measures suggests relatively stronger business cycle co-movements within EEA and between EEA and G3 economies after the AFC compared with the pre-AFC period, which is in line with previous studies (see Helbling et al., 2007; Kose et al., 2008).

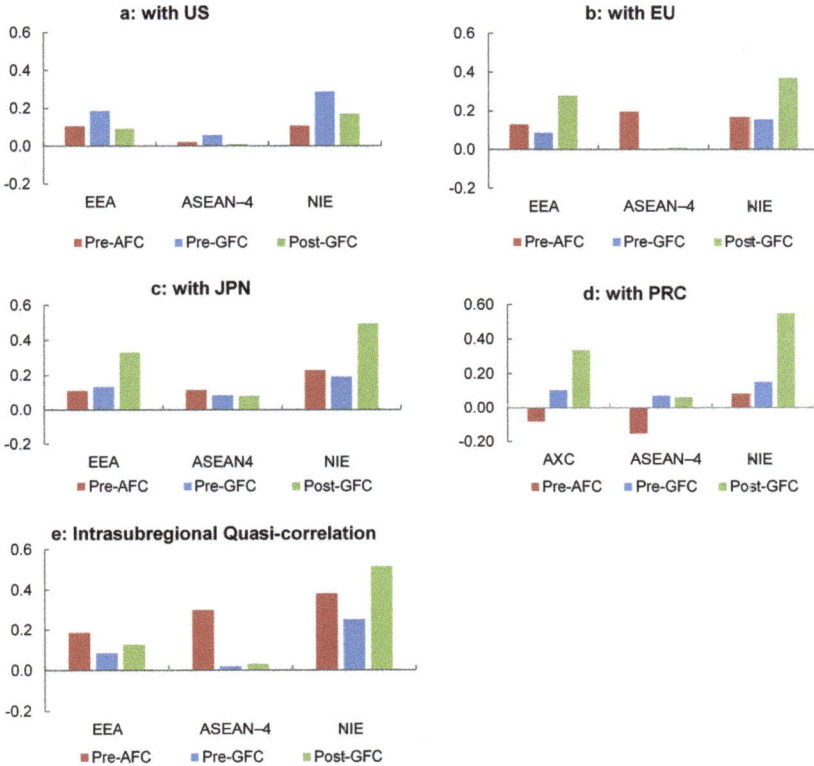

a: with US

b: with EU

c: with JPN

d: with PRC

e: Intrasubregional Quasi-correlation

Figure 4.12: Instantaneous quasi-correlations of real GDP growth rates—EEA (excluding crisis periods)

AFC = Asian financial crisis; AXC = EEA excluding the PRC; EEA = emerging East Asia; EU = European Union; GDP = gross domestic product; GFC = global financial crisis; JPN = Japan; PRC = People's Republic of China; US = United States.

Note: Pre-AFC covers 1985–96, pre-GFC covers 1999–2007 and post-GFC 2010–15. EEA includes ASEAN–4 (Indonesia, Malaysia, the Philippines and Thailand), NIE (Hong Kong, China; the Republic of Korea; Singapore; and Taipei, China) and the PRC. Based on the methodology from Duval, Cheng, Oh, Saraf and Seneviratne (2014) and Abiad, Furceri, Kalemli-Ozcan and Pescatori (2013).

Source: Park (2017).

The business cycle correlations declined somewhat in the 2000s, but increased again during the GFC. Our findings support the growing importance of regional components, especially of the PRC, in business cycle synchronicity. The correlations of the region's business cycles with those of the PRC increased following the AFC and were even more marked than those with the G3 after the GFC. International business cycle correlations are generally much higher for NIE countries, which are more open to international trade and finance. The results also indicate the growing economic influence of the region's major economies (the PRC and Japan) in recent years.

Vector auto-regression model and results

A VAR model is employed to examine the inter- and intra-regional macro-economic interdependence of EEA over three different sample periods, reflecting the ongoing changes in the region's trade, investment and financial linkages within and beyond the region. VAR models can identify the relevant structural shocks—including those arising from US output, global financial risk (as measured by the Volatility Index (VIX) of the Chicago Board Options Exchange[13]), global trade volume growth, PRC output (as a proxy for regional shock) and the output of individual AXC economies—and analyse the effects of each shock on an individual variable in a systematic way.

Assume that an economy, i (i=1, 2, … , 10), is described by the following structural form equation:

$$G(L)y_t^i = d^i + e_t^i, \tag{1}$$

where G(L) is a matrix polynomial in the lag operator Λ, y_t^t is an m′1 data vector, d^i is an m′1 constant matrix, m is the number of variables in the model and e_t^i denotes a vector of structural disturbances (Kim et al., 2011).

By assuming that structural disturbances are mutually uncorrelated, $var(e_t^i)$ can be denoted by Λ, which is a diagonal matrix, in which the diagonal elements are the variances of structural disturbances. The individual fixed effect, d^i, is introduced to control for the country-specific factors that are not included in the model. We are interested in examining the time-series relationship. Therefore, by including the individual fixed effects, we exclude the cross-sectional information in the estimation. We estimate the following reduced form VAR with the individual fixed effects:

---

13   VIX is the implied volatility of S&P 500 index options calculated by the Chicago Board Options Exchange. It is quoted in percentage points and translates, roughly, to the expected movement in the S&P 500 index over the next 30-day period, which is then annualised. Often referred to as 'the fear index', the VIX represents the market's expectation of stock market volatility. VIX is a registered trademark of the Chicago Board Options Exchange.

$$y_t^i = c^i + B(L)y_{t-1}^i + u_t^i, \tag{2}$$

where c^i is an m´1 constant matrix and B(L) is a matrix polynomial in the lag operator L.

There are several ways of recovering the parameters in the structural form equation from the estimated parameters in the reduced form equation. The identification schemes under consideration impose recursive zero restrictions on contemporaneous structural parameters by applying the Cholesky decomposition to the reduced form residuals, Λ, as in Sims (1980).

For each of the AXC economies, a five-variable VAR model is constructed, in which US denotes US output (a proxy for the output of advanced economies), VIX denotes the volatility index, wtrade denotes global trade volume growth, PRC denotes PRC output and AXC_i denotes the output of each East Asian economy, excluding the PRC. The contemporaneously exogenous variables are ordered first. The first three variables, US, VIX and wtrade, are included to examine the relationship among external factors, and the fourth variable, PRC, is a proxy for a regional shock. The last variable, AXC_i, is included to examine the effects of the local factors on the output of individual East Asian economies.

Some orderings of the variables can be regarded as more natural than others. US output, VIX, global trade growth and PRC output are treated as contemporaneously exogenous to each individual AXC country's output, which is far smaller than US or PRC output. US output, VIX and world trade growth are all global factors that should naturally be exogenous to AXC output. The PRC output is considered as a regional factor. The model assumes that the PRC output is unaffected by individual AXC economy output, but is affected by US output, global risk and world trade growth. In contrast, it is assumed that the three global factors are not affected by PRC output contemporaneously.

We use quarterly data and estimate the model for the period before the AFC (1987Q1–1997Q1) and after it (1999Q1–2016Q2). A constant term and four lags are assumed. Real GDP is used as the measure of output. As we are interested in business cycle phenomena, we exclude the trend from the data by applying a Hodrick–Prescott filter to give seasonally adjusted GDP at constant prices (Hodrick & Prescott, 1997).

Figure 4.13 reports the aggregate impulse responses of the external shocks on individual AXC business cycles for the periods pre- and post-crises (both AFC and GFC). The aggregate impulse responses are computed as the simple average of impulse responses across AXC economies.

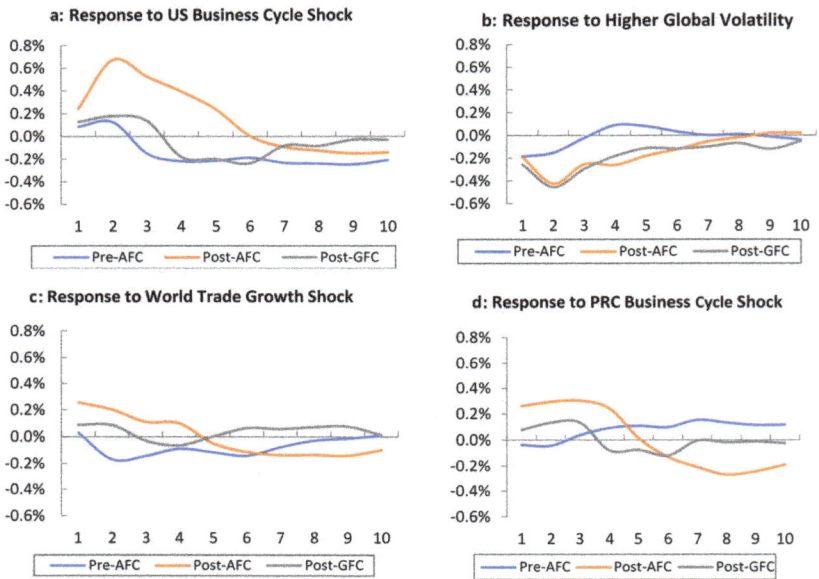

Figure 4.13: Impulse responses of AXC business cycles to external shocks (x-axis = number of quarters, y-axis = % change in GDP)

AFC = Asian financial crisis; AXC = emerging East Asia excluding PRC; PRC = People's Republic of China; US = United States.

Note: Pre-AFC covers 1987Q1–1997Q1. Post-AFC covers 1999Q1–2016Q2. US, PRC and individual AXC economy business cycles are based on the Hodrick–Prescott filtered seasonally adjusted GDP at constant prices.

Source: Park (2017).

The results show that the effects of a US shock on individual AXC economies are quite substantial. Higher US output creates a positive and persistent boost to AXC output, an effect that appears to strengthen considerably after the AFC, although it lessens in the period after the GFC. In response to a US output shock prior to the crisis, AXC output increases by 0.09 per cent on impact, peaks at 0.13 per cent after the second quarter, then decreases and returns to the initial level after three quarters. After the AFC, the effect is much higher—peaking at 0.68 per cent and remaining more persistent—after six quarters.

Higher global risks, as measured by higher levels of the VIX, exert a negative effect on AXC output. Again, the negative effect appears to be larger and longer after the AFC than before it. It lasts for around three quarters before the crisis and two years after.

The effect of higher world trade growth on AXC output becomes more significant and positive after the AFC, although, after the GFC, the effect softens but becomes more persistent. This reflects the region's strong trade growth and export-driven economic recovery following the AFC and GFC. After the AFC, the positive effect is higher—at around 0.2 per cent—and it dies down after a year. The pick-up in the expansion of global/regional value chains, together with the region's strong exports in the aftermath of the crisis, might explain this positive effect.

Finally, a positive shock to PRC output—after controlling for the effect of global factors—has different effects on AXC output before and after the AFC. Prior to the crisis, the effect is negative, although small, and it lasts for around three quarters. After the crisis, the effect is positive and substantial, at around 0.3 per cent, and it is more persistent, lasting for more than a year. This shift from negative to positive effects of a PRC output shock may reflect a shift in the PRC's role in the region's production value chain, as well as its growing investment and financial market influence. In the past two decades, the PRC has become increasingly more integrated into the regional value chain in the process of increasing its domestic production for the region's value chain supplies and final consumption imports.

Figure 4.14 shows the share of AXC output variances (the average share across 10 quarters) resulting from global, regional and domestic factors. It reveals that shocks to domestic factors tend to explain most of the output variance in the pre-AFC period, although the effect has weakened post-AFC, falling from 57.6 per cent to 40.8 per cent (Figures 2.14a, 2.14b). Of the four external factors, the shares of US output and PRC output—as a proportion of output variance—increased the most after the AFC. The share of US output increased from 12.2 per cent to 26.4 per cent over the two periods, and that of PRC output increased from 7.2 per cent to 12.7 per cent. Among individual AXC economies, the effects of a US output shock increased sharply for Hong Kong, Taipei, Singapore and Thailand (see Appendix A). The effects of a PRC output shock are also large for Hong Kong, the Republic of Korea, Malaysia and Taipei.

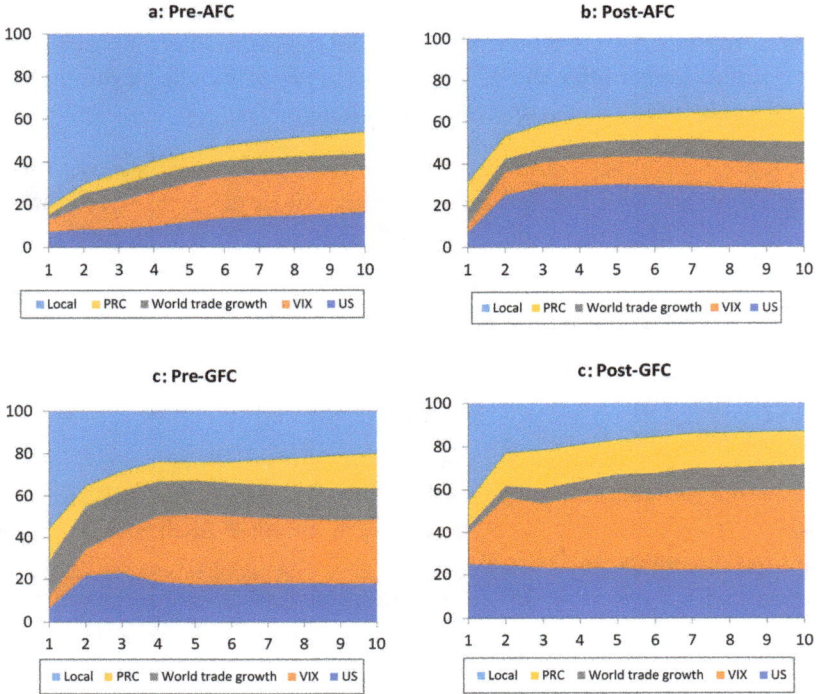

Figure 4.14: Share of AXC output variances resulting from external and local factors (%, x-axis = number of quarters)

AFC = Asian financial crisis; AXC = emerging East Asia excluding PRC; PRC = People's Republic of China; GFC = global financial crisis; US = United States.

Note: Pre-AFC covers 1987Q1–1997Q1. Post-AFC covers 1999Q1–2016Q2. Pre-GFC covers 1999Q1–2007Q3. Post-GFC covers 2009Q3–2016Q2. US, PRC and individual AXC economy business cycles are based on the Hodrick–Prescott filtered, seasonally adjusted GDP at constant prices.

Source: Park (2017).

When we separate the post-AFC period into pre- and post-GFC periods, the shares of global trade and financial shocks in AXC output variance become much more prominent (Figures 2.14c, 2.14d). In the pre-GFC period, the combined share of global financial volatility and world trade growth is 42.7 per cent (26.3 per cent and 16.4 per cent respectively). In the post-GFC period, the share is 41.8 per cent, with the share of global volatility at 33.2 per cent and that of world trade growth at 8.5 per cent. The share of US output increased from 17.6 per cent in the pre-GFC period to 23.0 per cent in the post-GFC period, and the corresponding shares of PRC output rose from 12.1 per cent to 15.8 per cent. However, the share of domestic factors declined from 27.6 per cent to 19.5 per cent. The influence of global volatility increased considerably in Indonesia, Malaysia, Taipei and Thailand in the post-GFC period (Appendix B).

Conclusion

Nearly two decades ago, a devastating financial crisis swept across South-East and East Asia. Today, EEA stands strong, with a remarkable record of high and sustained economic growth since the crisis. Its average annual growth in GDP reached 7.6 per cent over the past two decades. The strength of the region's exports, especially with the PRC at the centre of tight regional production networks, has underpinned this performance. The post-crisis economic recovery has been based on strong trade and financial openness, and deeper economic integration in EEA has led to an expectation that the region will gain greater macro-economic independence from the US economy and become an independent growth source for the world economy.

The findings of this study suggest that intra-regional trade and financial linkages are, indeed, strengthening, and that the actions of the PRC, in moving up in the GVC and increasing self-production of manufacturing inputs, may lead to a more independent source of global growth. However, the findings provide no supporting evidence for Asia's decoupling from the world economy from the current structural and cyclical viewpoints.

The expansion of Asia's trade and investment links is still driven by the region's structurally linked production network to global final demand. EEA has become more, not less, integrated with the global economy and, as a result, the effect of a global shock, whether related to trade or financial markets, will be greater. Further, deeper regional economic integration facilitates the transmission of shocks across the economies of the region.

The PRC exerts a growing influence on both regional and global economies with its sizeable economy, but its export-driven growth remains structurally linked to the demand from major industrial countries. To the extent that the PRC imports a large share of primary and processed intermediate goods to serve final demand in the G3 economies, a slowdown in the G3 could have a negative effect on the PRC's exports, which would, in turn, reduce the PRC's imports from the rest of Asia. At the same time, to the extent that FDI flows are related to intra-firm and intra-industry trade to serve external demand, FDI flows are likely to be responsive to the prospect of export growth. A sharp fall in exports and, subsequently, a reduction in FDI may harm the PRC's economy and then spill over to the rest of Asia.

Asian business cycles remain sensitive to external shocks. It is important that Asian countries maintain a stable macro-economic environment of low inflation and prudent fiscal balances, with modest levels of debt to allow room for policymakers to undertake macro-economic stabilisation measures whenever necessary. Greater macro-economic interdependence, through tighter trade and financial linkages, also requires greater cooperation in trade, finance and exchange rate policies—both regionally and globally. As economic and financial shocks travel more rapidly from a country to its trading partners through increased trade and financial linkages, it is in the common interest of all Asian countries to maintain prudent national macro-economic management, while strengthening regional policy cooperation. Synchronisation of real growth and inflation in the region should generate common interests to ensure close cooperation in macro-economic and exchange rate policies.

The rapid integration of the PRC into the regional and global economies presents the rest of Asia with challenges and opportunities. The PRC's growing economy will play an increasingly vital role in promoting regional growth through the expansion of intra-regional trade and financial flows. Although some Asian exporters may face non-negligible adjustment costs as they find their comparative advantages changing as a result of growing competition from the PRC economy, sound macro-economic management and comprehensive structural reform will ultimately contribute to higher economic efficiency and productivity and, therefore, to greater economic welfare.

Acknowledgements

The author wishes to thank Abigail Golena, Paul Mariano, Ana Kristel Molina and Mara Claire Tayag for their excellent research support.

References

Abeysinghe, T. & Forbes, K. (2005). Trade linkages and output-multiplier effects: A structural VAR approach with a focus on Asia. *Review of International Economics 13*, 356–375. doi.org/10.1111/j.1467-9396. 2005.00508.x

Abiad, A., Furceri, D., Kalemli-Ozcan, S. & Pescatori, A. (2013). Dancing together? Spillovers, common shocks, and the role of financial and trade linkages. In International Monetary Fund, *World Economic Outlook 2013* (pp. 81–111). Washington, DC: International Monetary Fund, October.

Are Asian economies decoupling from the US? (2008, 20 March). *Bloomberg Businessweek*. Retrieved from: www.bloomberg.com/news/articles/2008-03-20/are-asian-economies-decoupling-from-u-dot-s-dot-businessweek-business-news-stock-market-and-financial-advice

Asian Development Bank (ADB). (2006). Developing Asia and the world. *Asian Development Outlook 2006 Update*. Hong Kong, China: Oxford University Press for the Asian Development Bank.

Asian Development Bank (ADB). (2007). Uncoupling Asia: Myth and reality. *Asian Development Outlook 2007: Growth Amid Change*. Hong Kong, China: Asian Development Bank.

Asian Development Bank (ADB). (2016). Special theme: What drives foreign direct investment in Asia and the Pacific. In *Asian Economic Integration Report 2016*. Manila: Asian Development Bank.

Asian Development Bank (ADB). (n.d.). Multi-region input–output database. Retrieved November 2017 from: www.adb.org/data/icp/input-output-tables

Athukorala, P. & Ravenhill, J. (2016). China's evolving role in global production networks: The decoupling debate revisited. *Working Papers in Trade and Development, Working Paper No. 2016/12*. Canberra, ACT: Crawford School of Public Policy, The Australian National University.

Baxter, M. & Kouparitsas, M. (2005). Determinants of business cycle comovement: A robust analysis. *Journal of Monetary Economics 52*, 13–157. doi.org/10.1016/j.jmoneco.2004.08.002

Calvo, S. & Reinhart, C. M. (1996). Capital flows to Latin America: Is there evidence of contagion effects? In G. A. Calvo, M. Goldstein & E. Hochreiter (Eds.), *Private capital flows to emerging markets after the Mexican crisis* (pp. 151–71). Washington, DC: Institute for International Economics.

Claessens, S., Dornbusch, R. & Park, Y. C. (2001). Contagion: Why crises spread and how this can be stopped. In S. Claessens & K. J. Forbes (Eds.), *International financial contagion* (pp. 19–41). New York, NY: Springer. doi.org/10.1007/978-1-4757-3314-3_2

Clark, T. E. & van Wincoop, E. (2001). Borders and business cycles. *Journal of International Economics 55*, 59–85. doi.org/10.1016/S0022-1996(01)00095-2

Duval, R., Cheng, K., Oh, K. H., Saraf, R. & Seneviratne, D. (2014). Trade integration and business cycle synchronization: A reappraisal with focus on Asia. *IMF Working Paper 14*(52). Washington, DC: IMF. doi.org/10.5089/9781475522464.001

Eichengreen, B. & Tong, H. (2005). Is China's FDI coming at the expense of other countries? *NBER Working Paper No. 11335*. Cambridge, MA: NBER. doi.org/10.3386/w11335

Engle, R. (2002). Dynamic conditional correlation: A simple class of multivariate generalised autoregressive conditional heteroskedasticity models. *Journal of Business and Economic Statistics 20*, 339–50. doi.org/10.1198/073500102288618487

Engle, R. & Sheppard, K. (2001). Theoretical and empirical properties of dynamic conditional correlation multivariate GARCH. *NBER Working Paper No. 8554*. Cambridge, MA: NBER. doi.org/10.3386/w8554

Frankel, J. A. & Rose. A. K. (1998). The endogeneity of the optimum currency area criteria. *The Economic Journal 108*, 1009–1025. doi.org/10.1111/1468-0297.00327

Fukao, K., Ishido, H. & Ito, K. (2003). Vertical intra-industry trade and foreign direct investment in East Asia. *Journal of the Japanese and International Economies 17*, 468–506. doi.org/10.1016/j.jjie.2003.09.004

Heathcote, J. & Perri, F. (2004). Financial globalization and real regionalization. *Journal of Economic Theory 119*, 207–43. doi.org/10.1016/j.jet.2003.06.003

Helbling, T., Berezin, P., Kose, A., Kumhof, M., Laxton, D. & Spatafora, N. (2007). Decoupling the train? Spillovers and cycles in the global economy. In International Monetary Fund, *World Economic Outlook 2013* (pp. 121–60). Washington, DC: International Monetary Fund.

Hirata, H., Kose, A. & Otrok, C. (2013). Regionalization vs. globalization, *IMF Working Papers 13/19*. Washington, DC: International Monetary Fund.

Hodrick, R. & Prescott, E. (1997). Post-war US business cycles: An empirical investigation. *Journal of Money, Credit and Banking 29*, 1–16.

Imbs, J. (2004). Trade, finance, specialization and synchronization. *The Review of Economics and Statistics 86*, 723–34. doi.org/10.1162/0034653041811707

Imbs, J. (2006). The real effects of financial integration. *Journal of International Economics 68*, 296–324. doi.org/10.1016/j.jinteco.2005.05.003

Inklaar, R., Jong-A-Pin, R. & de Haan, J. (2008). Trade and business cycle synchronization in OECD countries—a re-examination. *European Economic Review 52*, 646–66. doi.org/10.1016/j.euroecorev.2007.05.003

International Monetary Fund (IMF). (n.d.-a). *Coordinated direct investment survey*. Washington, DC: International Monetary Fund. Retrieved September 2016 from: cpis.imf.org

International Monetary Fund (IMF). (n.d.-b). *Direction of trade statistics*. Washington, DC: International Monetary Fund. Retrieved October 2016 from: www.imf.org/en/Data

International Monetary Fund (IMF). (n.d.-c). *International financial statistics*. Washington, DC: International Monetary Fund. Retrieved October 2016 from: www.imf.org/en/Data

Kalemli-Ozcan, S., Sørensen, B. E. & Yosha, O. (2003). Risk sharing and industrial specialization: Regional and international evidence. *American Economic Review 93*, 903–18. doi.org/10.1257/0002828 03322157151

Kawai, M. & Urata, S. (2004). Trade and foreign direct investment in East Asia. In G. de Brouwer & M. Kawai (Eds.), *Exchange rate regimes in East Asia* (pp. 15–102). London, England: Routledge Curzon.

Kim, S. & Kim, S. H. (2013). International capital flows, boom–bust cycles and business cycle synchronization in the Asia Pacific Region. *Contemporary Economic Policy 31*, 191–211. doi.org/10.1111/j.1465-7287.2011.00285.x

Kim, S., Kim, S. H. & Wang, Y. (2003). International capital flows and boom–bust cycles in the Asia Pacific Region. *Korea University Working Paper 03-03*. Seoul: Korea Institute for International Economic Policy. Retrieved from: www.kiep.go.kr/eng/sub/view.do?bbsId=working& nttId=131735&searchIssue=&searchEngWrt=&pageIndex=14#

Kim, S. & Lee, J-W. (2008). Real and financial integration in East Asia. *ADB Working Paper Series on Regional Economic Integration No. 17*. Hong Kong, China: Asian Development Bank.

Kim, S., Lee, J-W & Park, C-Y. (2009). Emerging Asia: Decoupling or recoupling. *ADB Working Paper Series on Regional Economic Integration No. 31*. Hong Kong, China: Asian Development Bank.

Kim, S., Lee, J-W & Park, C-Y. (2011). Ties binding Asia, Europe and the USA. *China and the World Economy 19*(1), 24–46.

Kose, M. A., Otrok, C. & Prasad, E. S. (2008). Global business cycles: Convergence or decoupling? *IMF Working Paper 8*(143). Washington, DC: International Monetary Fund.

Kose, M. A., Prasad, E. S. & Terrones, M. E. (2003). How does globalization affect the synchronization of business cycles? *American Economic Review 93*, 57–62. doi.org/10.1257/000282803321946804

Kose, M. A., Prasad, E. S. & Terrones, M. E. (2007). How does financial globalization affect risk sharing? Patterns and channels. *IMF Working Paper 7*(238). Washington, DC: International Monetary Fund.

Kose, M. A. & Yi, K-M. (2002). The trade comovement problem in international macroeconomics. *Federal Reserve Bank of New York Staff Report No. 155*. New York, NY: Federal Reserve Bank of New York. Retrieved from: www.newyorkfed.org/research/staff_reports

Kraay, A. & Ventura, J. (2007). Comparative advantage and the cross-section of business cycles. *Journal of the European Economic Association 5*, 1300–33. doi.org/10.1162/JEEA.2007.5.6.1300

Moneta, F. & Ruffer, R. (2006). Business cycle synchronization in East Asia. *European Central Bank Working Paper Series No. 671*. Frankfurt am Main: European Central Bank. Retrieved from: www.ecb.europa.eu/pub/research/working-papers/html/index.en.html

Oxford Economics. (n.d.) *Global economic databank*. Oxford, England: Oxford Economics. Retrieved October 2016 from: www.oxfordeconomics.com/

Park, C.-Y. (2017). *Decoupling Asia Revisited*. Manila, Philippines: Asian Development Bank. doi.org/10.22617/WPS178597-2

Park, C-Y. & Lee, J-W. (2011). Financial integration in emerging Asia: Challenges and prospects. *Asian Economic Policy Review 5*(2), 176–98.

Ramondo, N. (2016). Factory Asia: The determinants of multinational activity in the context of global value chains. *Working paper, Asian Development Bank*. Retrieved from: aric.adb.org/pdf/events/aced2016/paper_nataliaramondo.pdf

Shin, K. & Wang, Y. (2004). Trade integration and business cycle co-movements: The case of Korea with other Asian countries. *Japan and the World Economy 16*, 213–30. doi.org/10.1016/S0922-1425(03)00028-8

Sims, C. A. (1980). Macroeconomics and reality. *Econometrica 48*, 1–48. doi.org/10.2307/1912017

The decoupling debate. (2008, 6 May). *The Economist*. www.economist.com/node/10809267

Tse, Y. K. & Tsui, A. K. C. (2002). A multivariate generalized autoregressive conditional heteroscedasticity model with time varying correlations. *Journal of Business & Economic Statistics 20*, 351–62. doi.org/10.1198/073500102288618496

United Nations Economic and Social Commission for Asia and the Pacific (UNESCAP). (2014). *Asia-Pacific trade and investment report 2014: Recent trends and developments*. Bangkok, Thailand: United Nations.

US Census Bureau. (n.d.). US international trade in goods and services report. Retrieved October 2016 from: www.census.gov/

Wang, Z., Wei, S-J. & Zhu, K. (2014). Quantifying international production sharing at the bilateral and sectoral levels. *NBER Working Paper No. 19677*. Cambridge, MA: NBER.

World Bank. (n.d.). *World integrated solution*. Retrieved October 2016 from: wits.worldbank.org/

Appendices

Appendix A. Share of output variances resulting from external and local factors—pre-AFC versus post-AFC (%, x-axis = number of quarters)

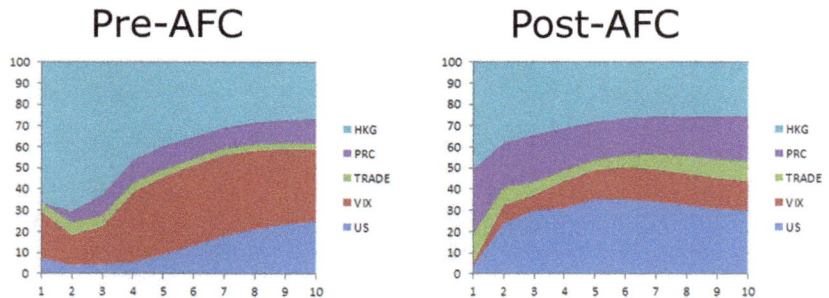

Figure A4.1: Hong Kong, China

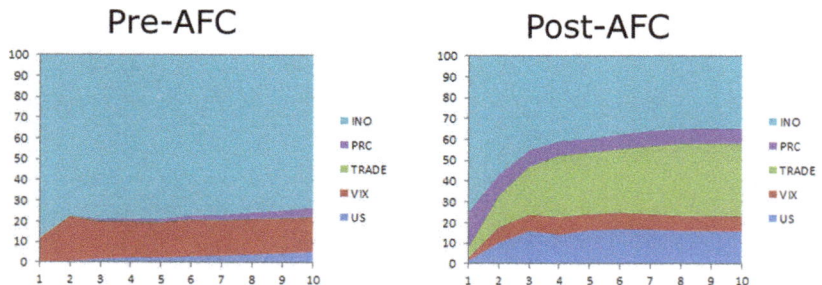

Figure A4.2: Indonesia

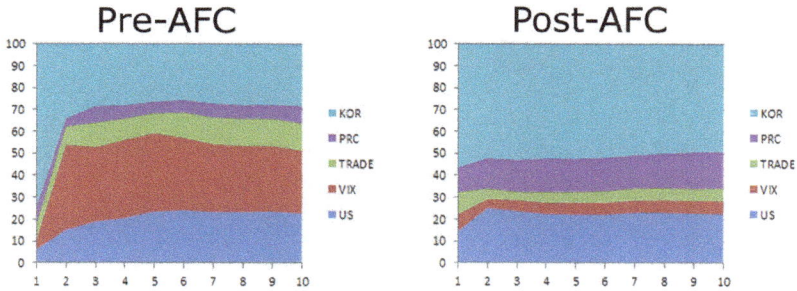

Figure A4.3: Republic of Korea

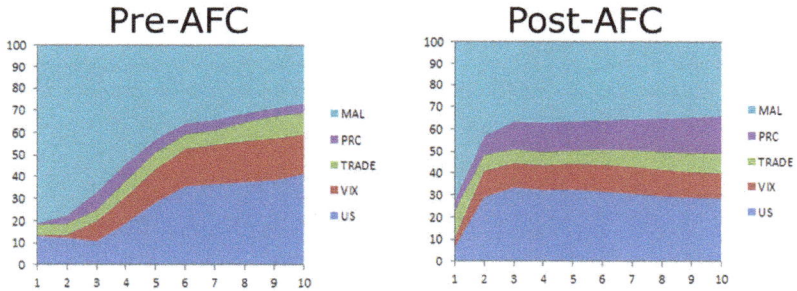

Figure A4.4: Malaysia

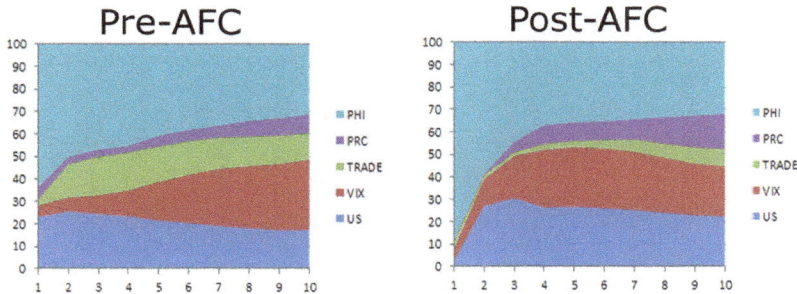

Figure A4.5: Philippines

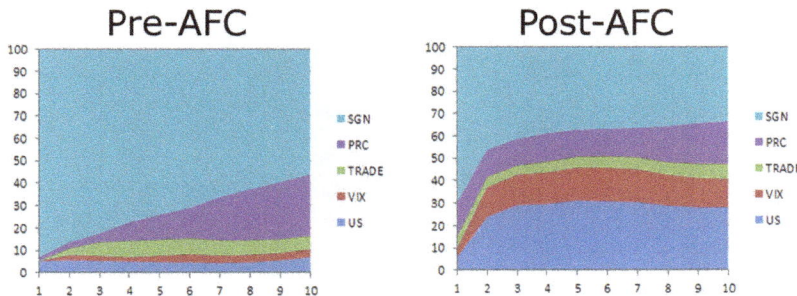

Figure A4.6: Singapore

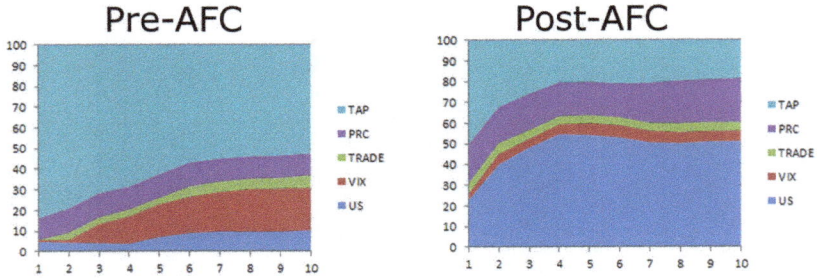

Figure A4.7: Taipei, China

AFC = Asian financial crisis; AXC = emerging East Asia excluding PRC; PRC = People's Republic of China; US = United States.

Note: Pre-AFC covers 1987Q1–1997Q1. Post-AFC covers 1999Q1–2016Q2. US, PRC and individual AXC economy business cycles are based on the Hodrick–Prescott filtered, seasonally adjusted GDP at constant prices. TRADE refers to world trade growth.

Source: ADB calculations using data from Bloomberg LP, IMF (n.d.-c) and Oxford Economics (n.d.).

Appendix B. Share of output variances resulting from external and local factors—pre-GFC versus post-GFC (%, x-axis = number of quarters)

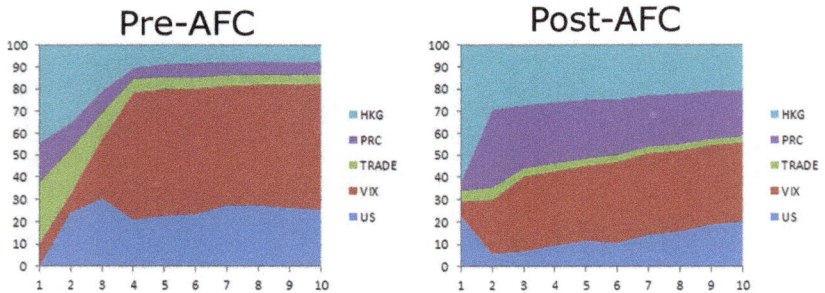

Figure B4.1: Hong Kong, China

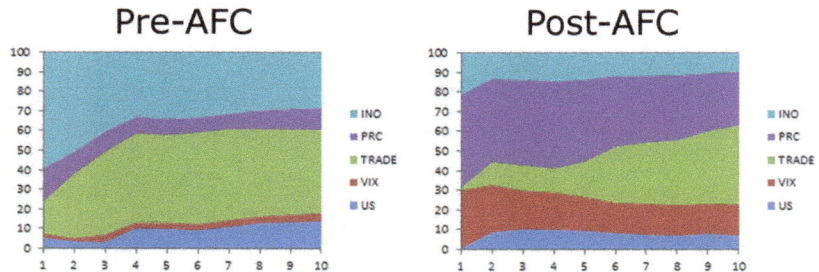

Figure B4.2: Indonesia

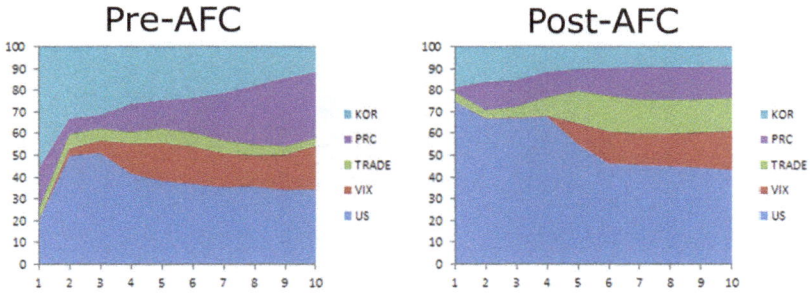

Figure B4.3: Republic of Korea

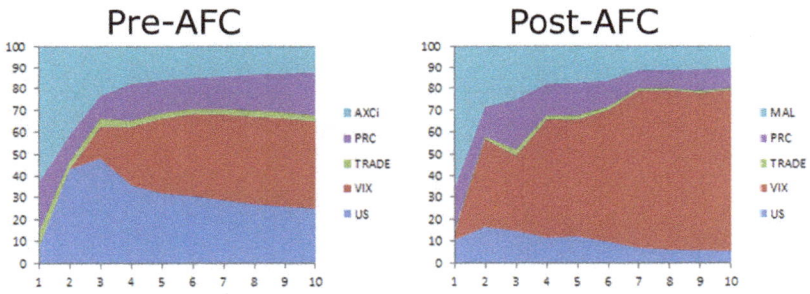

Figure B4.4: Malaysia

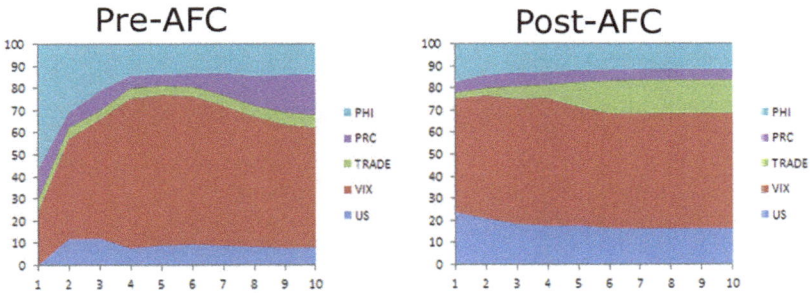

Figure B4.5: Philippines

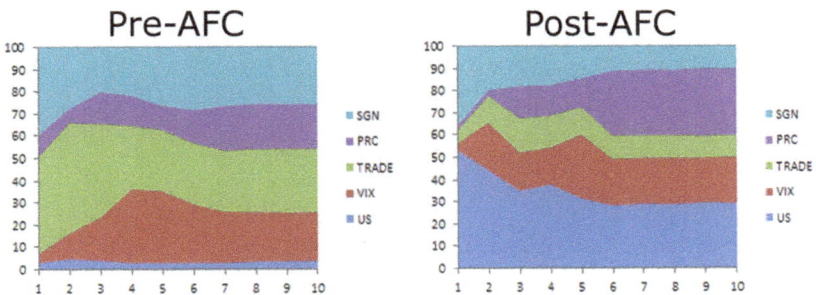

Figure B4.6: Singapore

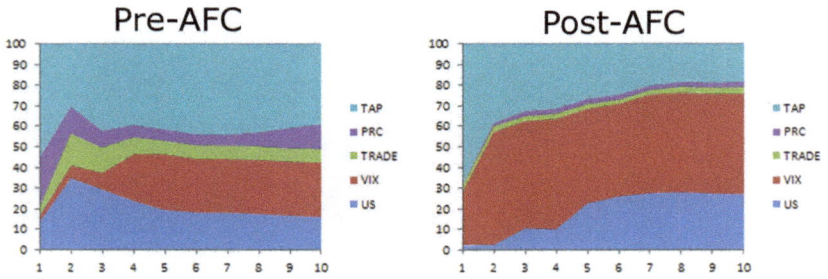

Figure B4.7: Taipei, China

AFC = Asian financial crisis; AXC = emerging East Asia excluding PRC; PRC = People's Republic of China; US = United States.

Note: Pre-AFC covers 1987Q1–1997Q1. Post-AFC covers 1999Q1–2016Q2. US, PRC and individual AXC economy business cycles are based on the Hodrick–Prescott filtered, seasonally adjusted GDP at constant prices.

Source: ADB calculations using data from Bloomberg LP, IMF (n.d.-c) and Oxford Economics (n.d.).

5

Financial liberalisation and trade: An examination of moving up value chains in the Asia–Pacific region

Wendy Dobson and Tom Westland

Introduction

Financial liberalisation, also known as domestic financial market development and opening, is, potentially, a fundamental factor in an economy's development and long-term growth. Financial market development and opening influences potential growth by accelerating capital accumulation and increasing economic efficiency through the mobilisation of resources and facilitation of cross-border economic exchange. Well-functioning financial institutions can play a critical role in this process through risk management and closing information gaps, reducing the risks faced by investors by pooling savings and distributing funds among many users. They also collect and evaluate information needed to make prudent and productive investment decisions and improve management and governance by evaluating the performance of borrowers.

The benefits of financial liberalisation in developing economies include a wider choice of financial services, faster economic growth owing to greater competition from foreign firms, access to better service channels (such as credit cards in developing countries), faster access to services and better credit assessment procedures and information-gathering techniques.

However, financial liberalisation also entails risks, especially if governments open their economies—thereby making themselves vulnerable to external shocks—but continue with outdated regulation and supervision of their financial systems. Modernising and strengthening domestic institutions is a priority so that regulators and supervisors are better able to evaluate and manage the risks in a more complex market-oriented system. Striking a balance between stability and efficiency can be difficult. The events of the 1997–98 Asian financial crisis (AFC) made clear the risks of promoting more open capital markets to increase efficiency; in times of crisis, markets would focus on national vulnerabilities and could reverse capital flows, causing costly real economy and banking system stresses. In response, emerging market economies, while continuing to deepen their integration into regional and global markets, began to build buffers against capital flow reversals by accumulating foreign exchange reserves.

Both the AFC and the global financial crisis (GFC) in 2008–09 prompted questions about the links between the performance of financial systems and the real economy in terms of national growth rates, job creation and inclusivity, and cross-border flows of trade and investment. Capital has flowed ever more freely across borders since the last century, as national governments have opened markets and deregulated finance. At the same time, market-based financial innovation and advances in information and communications technology have left national regulators and central bank governors scrambling to catch up. Recent writings by former Bank of England Governor Mervyn King and British economist John Kay, among others, have emphasised the growth of 'financialisation', a term applied to the shift in behaviour of financial institutions away from their primary purpose of supporting businesses and households in the real economy towards self-serving interactions among themselves (Kay, 2015; King, 2016). Part of this trend involves financial institutions using mathematical innovations that may be profitable to market participants but, arguably, serve no socially useful purpose. As a result, some, including King, have insisted that the system is broken and needs to be redesigned.

In the post-GFC environment, more than a decade after the AFC, there is concern regarding a 'new normal' for global growth, as slow rates of recovery have persisted in advanced countries long after the 2008 onset of the crisis. In Asia, growth rates are healthy but slower than expected. China's growth is strong but slowing, as its rebalancing strategy proceeds. It is moving away from the investment-driven export growth of the past and reallocating economic activity more towards domestic demand and consumption; it is also modernising its financial system to support the eventual use of the renminbi as a global reserve currency. India has more modest goals and is growing relatively strongly. Even so, the Asian Development Bank (ADB) predicted a possible new normal for potential growth in developing Asia (ADB, 2016), noting that the region's average potential growth declined by 2.2 percentage points during 2008–14 from its historical trend (and global potential growth dropped by 2.7 points). The ADB estimated that, in the context of China's strong trade and investment ties within the region, the moderation of growth in China is associated with a 0.5 per cent reduction in potential growth in other Asian economies (ADB, 2016). India is much less connected, although one focus of the Modi government is deepening regional integration.

David Lipton (2016), First Deputy Managing Director of the International Monetary Fund (IMF), has pointed out that, in the face of continued capital market volatility, countries are responding with greater accumulation of reserves and stronger current account positions, which have procyclical effects. He recommended a collective response, involving several elements to support growth and globalisation:

- a reliable financial safety net in which emerging market economies have an equal voice in setting and applying the rules
- collective assessment of supervisory frameworks and tax systems in countries from which capital flows originate to reduce incentives for short-term debt flows to emerging market economies
- reassessment of tax policies with respect to their debt bias
- permission for greater transfer of technology to include property rights protection that goes beyond traditional tariff reductions to open up to foreign direct investment (FDI).

Owing to the magnitude of debts and the roles played by banks in the GFC, there have been concerted efforts to tighten banking rules and reduce the likelihood of future financial crises. At both the Bank for

International Settlements and the Financial Stability Board, regulators from the major economies have taken a number of measures that some critics see as fighting the complexity of the pre-crisis system with more complexity. Banks' capital requirements have been raised and stress tests of bank balance sheets have become more onerous. In addition, banks' liquidity requirements have been increased to strengthen their ability to withstand high demands for liquidity to repay debts or meet depositors' demand in the event of a bank run. Banks designated as systemically significant financial institutions because of the complexity and scale of their operations have been required to produce living wills, or plans for how they would wind up their complex operations in the event of a financial crisis. Resolution mechanisms to enable troubled banks to continue services while they deal with crises or wind up have also been improved. In the US and UK, moves have been made to restore the separation of basic retail banking, which only serves households and businesses, from the more complex trading activities of investment and shadow banking.

Although there is evidence of greater market discipline in the reduced sizes of previously very large banks in the US, UK and Europe, and in the reduction of investment banking operations, more radical plans have also been proposed to ensure financial stability. Moral hazard remains pervasive in the current system, which is backed by central banks as lenders of last resort. King (2016) advocated breaking the banks' links with money creation by preventing central banks from lending to banks without collateral. Among other things, this requirement would force banks to hold more equity on their balance sheets.

This chapter focuses on the links between financial liberalisation and a particular aspect of the real economies in developing Asia, specifically export upgrading, or moving up the value chain. Dependent as the region is on innovation and higher value-added production to assist in raising real incomes, moving up the value chain is a significant goal in many Asia–Pacific economies. The remainder of this chapter is organised as follows. First, we measure and assess financial liberalisation in the region, particularly in China and India, the region's largest markets. Second, we examine empirical evidence for links between financial liberalisation and export upgrading as complementary parts of governments' economic and financial sector reform strategies. Third, we assess the implications of these links.

Financial liberalisation in East Asia

Prior to the AFC, many economies had opened capital accounts, even though their financial systems were bank dominated and their regulatory and legal infrastructures were underdeveloped. In the wake of the AFC, national financial reforms have proceeded apace. ASEAN+3, which consists of the Association of Southeast Asian Nations (ASEAN), the People's Republic of China, Japan and South Korea (i.e. the +3), has created the ASEAN+3 Macroeconomic Research Office as a regional institution that carries out macro-economic surveillance of members. The largest economies in ASEAN+3 are now also members of the Group of Twenty (G20).

The crisis-affected economies have strengthened their domestic financial systems and recognised that their heavy reliance on debt in bank-dominated systems requires the development of more complex, diverse and transparent financial systems that allow savers and investors to interact with confidence with borrowers and issuers who are unknown to them. Capital market institutions, such as Thailand's Securities and Exchange Commission, have been created to diversify the supply of financial instruments that can help withstand external shocks. It has also been acknowledged that governments should rely more on market discipline in financial markets to reduce moral hazards. Requirements on foreign firms seeking market entry in Korea and Thailand have been eased; it is understood that these entrants can help recapitalise weak financial institutions, introduce modern financial instruments and provide management skills and training. Governments have permitted more exchange rate flexibility; both Japan and Korea have flexible exchange rates, although their governments have intervened periodically to influence the values. Malaysia, Indonesia and the Philippines allow their currencies to float. However, India and China lag behind on such reforms.

Among the crisis-affected countries, Korea appears to have made significant progress in restructuring and opening; Hong Kong and Singapore, as international financial centres, are, of course, further advanced. As Park and Patrick (2013) have aptly summarised:

> Japan and Korea have learned that financial intermediation is best based on competitive financial markets, control over inflation, macroeconomic stability, and appropriate institutional framework and structure, and effective prudential regulation for institution and system safety. (p. 11)

Measuring financial liberalisation

Documenting the depth and nature of financial liberalisation is no easy task. There is no consensus in the literature on whether *de jure* or *de facto* measures of liberalisation are more useful, and why some measures are more popular. In the discussion that follows, we rely on the dataset of Abiad, Detragiache and Tressel (2008), which offers *de jure* measures of financial reform on several dimensions for a broad panel of countries from 1970 to 2005. Abiad et al.'s dataset is a broad panel of 91 economies with annual observations on a set of financial regulation indicators from 1973 to 2005. It is an attempt to codify existing literature on *de jure* government intervention in financial markets across seven broad areas: 1) regulations on the direction of credit to priority sectors and excessively high reserve requirements of over 20 per cent; 2) interest rates controls, both for deposit and lending rates, including the imposition of rates by fiat and the bands within which interest rates are permitted to fluctuate; 3) barriers to new entrants in the financial system; 4) state ownership of banks; 5) restrictions on capital account transactions, including multiple exchange rates, transaction taxes and outright bans on financial flows, either inward or outward; 6) prudential regulation and supervision, as measured by the Basel I risk-based capital adequacy ratios, the independence of the supervisory agency, the number of institutions exempt from supervision and the effectiveness of examinations of banks; and 7) security market policy.

We also use the World Bank's World Financial Development Database (WFDD), another panel dataset with wide coverage, and the widely used Chinn–Ito index of capital account liberalisation (Chinn & Ito, 2006).

Figure 5.1 summarises the historical relationship between *de jure* financial liberalisation and per capita income in the countries studied, using a simple bivariate regression of the Abiad et al. (2008) aggregate financial reform index on per capita gross domestic product (GDP), estimated separately for each year from 1973 to 2005. The correlation between income and financial liberalisation peaked in the late 1980s and, by 2005, poor countries were beginning to catch up to the richer ones. Significant financial liberalisation occurred in low- and middle-income countries in the 1990s.

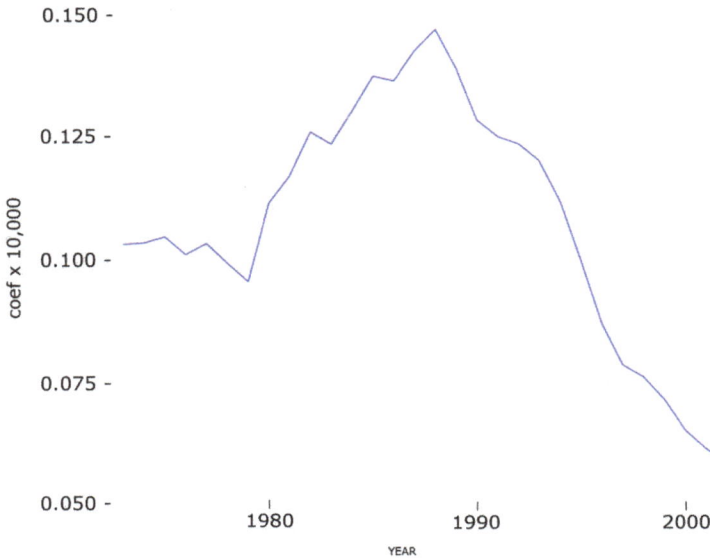

Figure 5.1: Regression coefficients, 1973–2005 (bivariate ordinary least squares regression of financial liberalisation aggregate index on annual per capita income)
Source: See Appendix B.

In Figure 5.2, the evolution of financial deregulation in three of developing Asia's most important economies, China, India and Indonesia, can be observed. In the 1990s, Indonesia was ahead of both China and India on several domestic reform measures. However, it has lagged behind on banking supervision; although not a measure of liberalisation, banking supervision does indicate the maturity of the regulatory environment. China and India had overtaken Indonesia in this area by 2005. Another example of financial reform is the liberalisation of interest rate controls, a key component of reform in Asia. The Abiad et al. (2008) sub-index on interest rate controls varies from zero to four; a value of four indicates that both deposit interest rates and lending interest rates are determined in competitive financial markets, a value of zero indicates that both deposit and lending rates are set by governments and intermediate values indicate partial liberalisation. On this metric, Indonesia's interest rates were fully controlled until 1982, resulting in a score of zero; the same was true of India until 1992 and China until 2002.

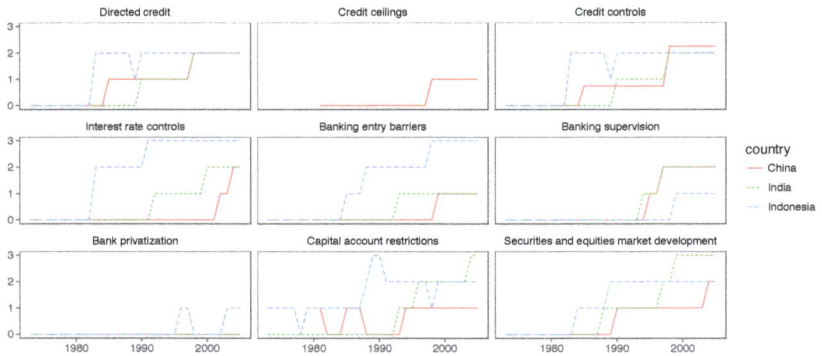

Figure 5.2: Indices of financial liberalisation, selected countries (1972–2005)

Source: Compiled by authors using data from Abiad et al. (2008).

China and India

A more detailed analysis of financial systems in China and India indicates that more financial liberalisation and market opening lies ahead. The Chinese financial system remains largely state-controlled, but renminbi internationalisation has become a high-profile rationale for modernising and opening the economy. Government policy and administrative guidance is extensive, and directed lending was heavily used in the depths of the GFC to offset the effects of external volatility and uncertainty. Since then, bad loans have been piling up on banks' books. China's overall debt/GDP ratio is estimated to be 237 per cent. The IMF, which estimates corporate debt/GDP at 145 per cent, has raised concerns about a possible financial crisis (Wildau, 2016). There are many possible scenarios that could result, ranging from bank failures that paralyse credit markets, to a Japanese-style malaise caused by distressed borrowers whose reduced appetites for risk-taking and investment reduce growth.

A structural concern is the fact that banks are accustomed to the riskless income generated by the generous spread between deposit and lending rates and many lack the expertise needed to manage risk. Banks' main depositors are household savers, who receive low returns and, in the absence of efficient bond and equity markets, have few other savings vehicles beyond housing investments. Many banks have wealthy customers engaged in shadow banking transactions that do not appear on their balance sheets. These transactions include informal lending and off–balance sheet lending by non-bank financial institutions, including trust companies, informal lenders and bond trading outside the banks.

Some have argued that these concerns are overstated because the debt build-up is mostly held within China, where the savings rate is very high (Lardy, 2016). One estimate is that loans plus banks' off–balance sheet assets are roughly equal to deposits. The required reserve ratio imposed on China's banks is 17 per cent, which is very high. In addition, some banks have been writing off their non-performing loans (NPLs) and others have adequate provisions. Even so, loans to state-owned enterprises (SOEs) are around 30 per cent of the total, and many of them are to 'zombie' companies, which are chronically unprofitable. There is political resistance to greater discipline. Whether the government has become more serious about managing these issues will become evident only when banks are required to accelerate write-offs and securitise underperforming bank assets (Lardy, 2016).

This reservation reflects the fundamental policy contradictions in China between the party's call for a 'decisive role' for market forces, the role of the state and the party's preference for stability. The cost of stability can be high. For instance, banks' growing stocks of NPLs can be off-loaded to asset management corporations, as occurred in the 2000s. Government can recapitalise the banks and asset management companies by issuing bonds, in effect socialising the debt, or the banks can roll over the loans or convert debt to equity. However, these practices are associated with increased financial system uncertainty, which has international consequences given China's growing economic clout in the world, and consequences for China's real economy.

There is no debate about the huge effects that China's ongoing financial reforms and its goal for renminbi internationalisation will have in terms of China's international footprint in trade and investment. Some predict that these reforms will trigger massive capital flows in and out of the Chinese economy. These capital flows already include FDI flows. While inflows continue to be restricted to industries considered of strategic importance, onerous approval requirements on outward FDI have been eased. The slowing economy and factors such as the government's encouragement for corporations to 'go out' are associated with a surge of deals, involving both mergers and acquisitions and green field investments by corporate China.

The surge in outward investment by corporate China has signalled some of the problems and risks associated with deeper Chinese financial integration. Since 2012, reported Chinese mergers and acquisitions activity in the US and Europe has risen at very rapid rates. US investments increased threefold between 2010 and 2015, according to the Rhodium Group's China Investment Monitor (China Investment Monitor, n.d.). Some of the enterprises initiating these transactions are large indebted enterprises, such as SOE ChemChina's successful US$44 billion bid for Swiss-owned Syngenta. Not only is ChemChina highly leveraged, but it is also far from clear that it has the capabilities to manage a large, complex and innovative company like Syngenta. The offer was an all-cash one, with CITIC Securities supplying US$30 billion in financing (suggesting a government role) and HSBC loaning US$20 billion. Reportedly, ChemChina is planning to sell equity shares in Syngenta and issue long-term debt. Larger questions remain about the role of the Chinese government in the transaction, reflecting China's strategic quest for security of food supplies (Kynge, Mitchell & Massoudi, 2016; Lardy, 2016).

In sum, China is sequencing the domestic reforms necessary to support financial integration into regional and global markets, with full capital account convertibility as its ultimate goal. Domestic financial market development is a work in progress; market forces, rather than the State Council and central bank, determine interest and (to an extent) exchange rates. As yet, there are no signs that the state will reduce its ownership (and with it, directed lending and moral hazard in the system) of the five large banks, which have potential losses on their corporate loan portfolios estimated by the IMF to be 7 per cent of GDP. The recent introduction of deposit insurance will mitigate moral hazard to some extent.

With respect to integration, foreign ownership of financial services remains controlled, but it is subject to gradual reform and opening beyond wealth management. Portfolio investment remains restricted. However, if the renminbi is to become a reserve currency, a deep, liquid and sound bond market will be essential. Until recently, China's inter-bank bond market has largely been closed to outside investors, except those with a quota under the Qualified Foreigner Institutional Investors (QFII) scheme. However, in June 2016, China signalled that it would open its onshore bond market to foreign investment by granting authorisation to a British investment management company, Insight Investment, to enter the market. Remaining restrictions on foreign financial institutions in the inter-bank bond market and through the QFII and the Qualified Domestic Institutional Investor programs will also have to be lifted.

The surge in outward direct investment is integrating China into the world economy as China negotiates bilateral investment treaties with a large number of countries. US negotiations have been particularly protracted, as a result of US insistence that China shrink its negative list of excepted sectors. However, progress may resume as President Xi Jinping signalled that China will further liberalise the FDI regime in his address to the World Economic Forum in January 2017.

The recent surge in China's international flows is not without risks. One risk is the potentially distorting consequences of state subsidies and guarantees for Chinese enterprises. Another risk relates to the asymmetries in implementing the many bilateral investment treaties that give foreigners less access in China than the Chinese have abroad. A third risk relates to the uncertainties associated with Chinese banks' huge debt loads and whether they will be written off or securitised in a timely manner. If not, concerns raised include whether there will be defaults that spill over borders, or a confidence crisis in China that causes stagnation or slow growth.

In India, financial liberalisation is moving at a slow pace. One reason for this is that India passed through the GFC relatively unscathed, owing to its capital controls and the small extent of its external linkages, which has slowed the impetus for reform and opening. Foreign investing firms continue to face restrictions in most of the traditional industries. However, in the past two years, foreign investment permissions have been eased in some areas. In the insurance and defence sectors, caps on foreign shares have been raised to 49 per cent, up from 26 per cent. Foreign invested enterprises may be wholly owned in some policy priority areas, including marketing Indian food products, high-tech and capital-intensive activities in railways; coffee, rubber and other foodstuffs; medical device manufacturing; the e-commerce marketplace; and non-bank ATMs (Panagariya, 2016).

Domestic financial development is lagging, with state-owned banks still accounting for as much as 70 per cent of loans. India's financial system remains a hybrid system, with market forces permitted but continuing high levels of government intervention and state ownership. India's domestic preoccupations are reflected in the requirement that all banks invest in public sector bonds; the state directs lending and requires that 40 per cent of bank loans go to 'priority sectors', including agriculture. The corporate bond market is heavily regulated and very small in size. In contrast, equity markets are open and well regulated, but capital controls continue to govern the flow of foreign funds into the debt market. By market capitalisation, India's biggest lender, HDFC, a private bank, is ranked number 63 globally. Since 2014, banking licences have been issued to 23 new players, nearly half of which are small finance banks. However, it is difficult to make money, and private and foreign banks look for investment and corporate banking for profits. Mobile banking is much talked about, but it has not taken off in India.

India's corporates have an advantage in international markets in that their home base market environment, despite government regulation, resembles the advanced countries and developing countries in Africa, in which they invest. India's equity markets are well developed and governed but their focus is largely domestic. An offsetting disadvantage is the small size of India's saving pool relative to China. Corporates have smaller assets and are largely on their own in international merger and acquisitions and FDI transactions.

Other key restrictions on the supply side remain to be tackled, including land acquisition laws and the successful introduction of a national goods and services tax. Highly restrictive labour laws have limited firm size and formal sector employment. However, four states have now liberalised such laws, and bankruptcy laws are also being modernised. Recently, the Reserve Bank of India conducted an audit of NPLs in the banking sector, which is a modestly encouraging sign that Indian institutions are committed to a process of reform in the domestic financial sector. However, the utility of the Scheme for Sustainable Structuring of Stressed Assets to facilitate the conversion of 'unsustainable' corporate debt into equity remains to be seen.

In summary, the two largest economies are gradually integrating into the regional and world economies as financial liberalisation proceeds. Domestic financial development continues, also at a gradual pace, because of domestic development priorities. Without deep, sound and liquid capital markets and a sound, well-regulated banking system, China would be ill-advised to fully open its capital account. India's economic modernisation priorities extend well beyond the financial sector to the real economy.

Empirical analysis of the effects of financial liberalisation on upgrading Asia–Pacific trade

Having provided a background on the two largest economies, we now turn to an empirical analysis of the relationship between financial liberalisation, financial integration and trade. Our specific focus is on countries moving up the value chain, as innovations increase productivity and the sophistication of goods exports. Understanding how the financial sector connects to the export sector can help to better understand the linkages between the financial reform agendas of East Asian governments and their economic integration strategies. We do not undertake this exercise to advocate for financial liberalisation as a potential influence on merchandise export sophistication. Rather, our goal is to determine whether financial reforms and efforts to move up regional value chains in trade can form complementary parts of a coherent economic policy reform strategy for governments in the region. As is made clear by the Chinese and Indian cases outlined above, maintaining the momentum of economic reform in developing countries requires movement on several fronts; financial sector reforms cannot be pursued in isolation to those occurring in the real sector. Therefore, it is important to understand the *connections* between policy strategies, which explains the focus of our analysis on the relationship between financial reform and export sophistication.

A deeper understanding of this relationship is timely, especially given the concerns about slowing global growth expressed in the IMF's April 2016 *World Economic Outlook,* entitled 'Too Slow for Too Long' (IMF, 2016). Asian growth can contribute to global growth through upgrading productive capacity, as China emphasises rebalancing its economy by encouraging innovation and productivity growth. Productivity performance is particularly important in increasing the sophistication of goods exports. In the analysis that follows, we measure this sophistication.

Measuring trade sophistication and upgrading

A useful way to measure the sophistication of a country's export basket is the export sophistication (EXPY) index developed by Hausmann, Hwang and Rodrik (2007). These authors derived an index for individual product sophistication, called PRODY, that, for each good x, is an average of the per capita income of each country that exports x, weighted by the country's revealed comparative advantage in x. Then, the EXPY index for a country i is an average of the PRODYs for each good x exported by i. More formally, we compute:

$$PRODY_k = \sum_j \frac{(x_{jk}/X_j)}{\Sigma_j \left(\frac{x_{jk}}{X_j}\right)} Y_j$$

and

$$EXPY_i = \sum_k \left(\frac{x_{ik}}{X_i}\right) PRODY_k$$

where x denotes exports of a particular good, X denotes total exports from a country, i and j index countries and k indexes individual goods. Thus, the EXPY index provides an indication of the per capita GDP that we would *predict* a country to have, given what we know about its export basket (and what we know about the per capita GDPs of countries that export the same goods).

One of the problems with using the EXPY and PRODY indices is that, so far, they have relied upon the use of gross trade flows, rather than value-added data. As some countries are more heavily involved in processing trade than others, these measures may convey the appearance that some countries have very sophisticated export baskets, when in fact they may only supply a small fraction of the value added to the final goods. This objection has been raised to counter the authors' claim that China is an outlier in exporting goods that are much more sophisticated than its per capita GDP would suggest (Wang & Wei, 2010). Using value-added data would alleviate this problem, but such data are only available for a limited number of countries and for a limited number of years. However, progress is being made on this front. Another possible way to address the concern about value-added data would be to remove countries that are heavily specialised in processing trade from the sample; however, this is a highly ad hoc solution. As such, we make no special adjustment for this particular problem at this stage.

Increasing export sophistication in Asia

Initially, we construct a dataset of EXPY values for 201 countries in each year from 1962 to 2014. For our bilateral disaggregated trade data, we use the Observatory of Economic Complexity's trade values dataset.[1] For our PRODY values, we use an average of the PRODYs in years 2003–07— that is to say, we use time-invariant PRODYs. We take per capita GDP values from the Penn World Tables.[2]

We first describe the database and some of the trends and patterns that we observe in it, with a particular focus on Asian countries. In general, we observe that, globally, export sophistication convergence is occurring. Countries with unsophisticated export baskets have higher growth in export sophistication, on average, than countries with sophisticated export baskets (with a correlation coefficient of –0.26). The Asian economies examined—Bangladesh, China, India, Indonesia, Malaysia, the Philippines, Thailand and Vietnam—all have much higher EXPY values than their per capita GDPs might lead us to predict (see Figure 5.3). However, given the orientation of Asian economies towards manufacturing exports, this is not surprising. With the exception of Bangladesh and, possibly, Indonesia, these economies showed reasonably steady growth in EXPY values up to the time of the GFC.

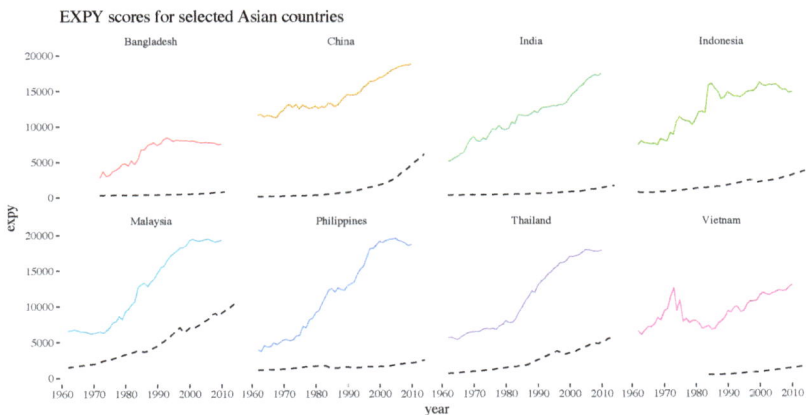

Figure 5.3: Trade indices and per capita income, selected Asian countries (1962–2014)

Note: Export sophistication index (solid lines); per capita income indices (dashed lines).

Source: See Appendix B.

---

1   atlas.media.mit.edu/en/resources/data/.

2   www.rug.nl/ggdc/productivity/pwt/.

Export sophistication and per capita income for the Asian countries is presented in Table 5.1. In 2010, the Philippines's export basket was roughly as sophisticated as Malaysia's, but its per capita income was less than a quarter of Malaysia's. India and Vietnam have the most sophisticated export baskets relative to their per capita income. However, all countries in this small sample display significantly more sophisticated export structures than might be expected, based solely on per capita income.

Table 5.1: Export sophistication and per capita income in selected Asian countries, 2010

	Per capita income, 2010	EXPY ('predicted' per capita income from export basket)	EXPY as a % of per capita income
Bangladesh	$760	$5,713	751
China	$4,515	$17,949	398
Indonesia	$3,125	$12,269	393
India	$1,387	$13,214	952
Malaysia	$9,069	$15,501	170
Philippines	$2,145	$14,733	687
Thailand	$5,112	$15,467	302
Vietnam	$1,334	$10,927	819

Source: See Appendix B.

Financial liberalisation and increasing export sophistication

There are various ways in which underdeveloped financial markets might impede a country's efforts to increase export sophistication. Exporting products, rather than simply selling them in home markets, requires firms to pay large fixed costs for market exploration and development. Other substantial costs include those for marketing and logistical services. 'Sophisticated' products, in our definition, are those produced primarily by richer (and, usually, capital-abundant) countries. This definition tends to imply that producers in poorer countries may struggle to enter markets dominated by firms in richer countries because they lack ready access to finance to cover the initial costs of entering the export market. Therefore, we might expect that only very profitable firms, or firms with secure access to financial markets, would be likely to enter sophisticated export markets. Moreover, domestic markets may offer insufficient economies of scale for firms to ever profitably produce sophisticated goods. It is intuitive that the more sophisticated the good, the larger the fixed costs of entry are likely to be, because such products are likely to be more capital intensive.

In this sense, developed financial markets can be considered as somewhat analogous to factor endowments in trade, and it is likely that countries with sophisticated, liquid financial markets will have a comparative advantage in producing and exporting goods for which access to credit is more important (Beck, 2002; Rajan & Zingales, 1998). Thus, we might expect that, all other things being equal, countries with better developed financial systems will export more sophisticated products (Carluccio & Fally, 2008). It is likely that a more developed and privately owned banking system will direct credit to firms with products that align with the country's comparative advantage, whereas a state-owned banking system might encourage different firms. Jaud, Kukenova and Strieborny (2012) found this to be the case in countries with competitive banking systems. In those countries, firms that export products that are *not* in line with national comparative advantage are more likely to exit foreign markets than are firms producing products that conform with comparative advantage. In countries where banking systems are not yet well developed, exporting firms do not exhibit such behaviour (Jaud et al., 2012). The market discipline that comes with financial development might have different effects on different countries' export sophistication, depending on whether these countries have a natural comparative advantage in sophisticated exports (for example, as a result of large endowments of labour or land). In other words, financial reform influences export sophistication in two ways, which may work in opposite directions depending on the specific country. There is a 'comparative advantage concentrating' effect and a 'comparative advantage upgrading' effect. This hypothesis, while an interesting one, is not tested in this chapter, and is left for future work.

Despite the theoretical relevance of financial liberalisation to trade structure, widely used empirical trade models do not always incorporate financial constraints or, indeed, any kind of financial sector. However, a substantial recent theoretical literature has linked financial constraints with trade flows. Chaney (2016) made a crucial contribution by adapting the Melitz model of heterogeneous firms in international trade and adding an exogenous liquidity constraint to test the effect of financial imperfections on the extensive margin of trade. His model predicted that firm-level liquidity constraints are a key determinant of whether individual firms do or do not export.[3] Meanwhile, Goksel (2012) has shown that similar predictions can be derived from a Krugman New Trade Theory–style model.

Empirical testing by Manova (2008) demonstrated that equity market liberalisation has a positive effect on exports in sectors that possess financial vulnerabilities—that is to say, sectors in which firms require relatively more outside finance, or in which firms possess relatively fewer assets as collateral. Berman and Héricourt (2008) have shown that, when firms lack adequate access to financial markets, they tend to restrict exporting at the extensive margin more than at the intensive margin; in other words, a lack of financial development prevents firms from exporting at all (i.e. anything) more than it prevents existing exporters from exporting more of the same kind of product. Some of the literature has explored the mechanisms that drive these more aggregate-level results by exploring more detailed data. Firm-level data has been used to examine the effect of financial liberalisation on the propensity of Indian firms to import capital goods to upgrade technology. Bas and Berthou (2011) showed that private and foreign banks are more likely to encourage technological upgrading in industrial firms than nationalised banks. Egger and Kesina (2013) provided similar results for a panel of Chinese firms, and Manova, Wei and Zhang (2015) found that, in China, removing restrictions on FDI has helped to alleviate exporters' credit constraints arising from underdeveloped domestic financial markets. Manova and Yu (2016) showed why firms that struggle to obtain finance in the domestic formal sector in China choose to enter the processing trade sector rather than pursue higher value-added activities—processing trade typically requires less access to external finance. This literature suggests that financial reform can play a potentially major role in facilitating economic diversification and upgrading productive capacities in these economies.

What about the sequence of financial reform? As we have argued above, it is generally accepted that for reasons of macro-economic stability, it is preferable to open the capital account only as the domestic financial system is strengthened and modernised. One of the reasons that sequencing of regulatory reforms governing domestic and international financial flows may be important for export sophistication is that such sequencing could affect the ability of financial institutions to allocate credit to high-productivity firms. Theoretically, opening the capital account with a relatively uncompetitive domestic financial sector could

---

3   An unpublished 2005 version of the paper is often cited.

have both positive and negative effects on export sophistication. On the one hand, such liberalisation provides new sources of capital for exporters who have difficulty accessing domestic sources of credit (or firms that did not previously export but would have in the absence of such credit constraints), and allows savers to diversify their portfolios, lowering the cost of capital. Exporting firms tend to have more 'international collateral' than do non-exporting firms, in the form of future export revenues (Caballero & Krishnamurthy, 2001), so capital account liberalisation might be expected to disproportionately help exporters. Conversely, by facilitating the flow of external credit to firms in the non-tradeable sector, capital account liberalisation may encourage a reallocation of resources (such as skilled labour) from the traded goods sector to the non-traded goods sector; in this sense, it may harm rather than help efforts to increase the sophistication of exported goods.

Episodes of financial reform and export sophistication growth in Asia

Is this relationship between export sophistication and financial development visible in the data? In Figure 5.4, we plot the evolution of export sophistication relative to the introduction of major financial reforms in India (1991), Indonesia (1983), Malaysia (1987), South Korea (1991) and Thailand (1992). We plot the export sophistication indices for these countries, showing how they changed after each set of reforms. The dashed line is a linear time trend fitted to the seven years *before* the event. This trend is manually extended to the 10 years following the event to give a very rough idea of what might have been expected to happen to export sophistication in the absence of policy changes (such as financial sector reform) or other exogenous changes in the economic environment.

In Indonesia, there was a substantial jump in export sophistication after the reforms of 1983, but this declined in the latter part of the decade. Some of the initial increase was the result of the increase in liquefied petroleum gas (LPG) production in 1984. LPG is considered a relatively sophisticated export, according to the PRODY index, because it is mostly exported by richer countries. It is unlikely that financial reform had much to do with the LPG boom. However, there were also changes in Indonesia's export basket that indicated signs of vigorous growth in more traditional industrial sectors. Indonesia's 1983 reforms were substantially domestically oriented, with a particular focus on liberalising interest rates. After India's 1991 liberalisation, EXPY growth was more or less unchanged until about seven years after the reforms, when it grew quite strongly. As we will see below, there is some evidence that financial reforms are associated with higher export sophistication about seven years after implementation of the reforms. India's reforms were also domestically oriented, but more gradual than Indonesia's. If there is a causal link between export sophistication and financial liberalisation, this may explain why export sophistication also responded with a lag to the 1991 reforms.

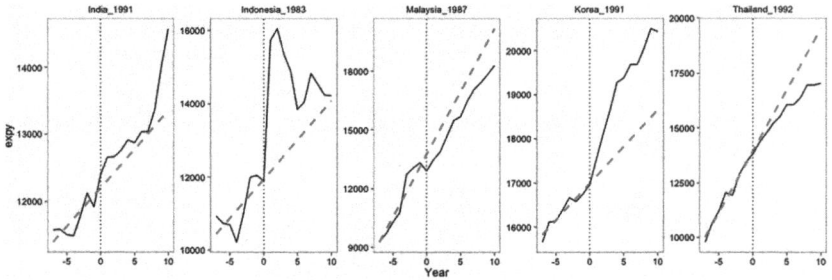

Figure 5.4: Export sophistication index before and after substantial financial reform events in India, Indonesia, Malaysia, South Korea and Thailand

Note: The year of the event, indicated in the title of each panel, has been set to '0'. The graph shows EXPY from seven years prior to the reform event to 10 years following the reform event, as well as an ordinary least squares trend for the first seven years of the x-axis, extended over the entire sample.

Source: See Appendix B.

Malaysia's EXPY growth was slightly less strong after the reforms of 1987 than before. Our dataset shows that the major reform in this year was a renewed commitment to interest rate liberalisation after an aborted effort earlier in the decade due to the weak global economic environment. Malaysia is distinguished from India and Indonesia because its capital account was already very open prior to the substantial reforms of the late 1980s. Indeed, from 1973 until the AFC, Malaysia imposed very few restrictions at all on foreign capital movements (see Manap & Ghani, 2012). The increase in South Korea's export sophistication after its 1991 financial reforms, domestic and international, was quite impressive. Bank lending rates and other interest rates were liberalised and restrictions on FDI were substantially loosened, although other controls on capital movements remained. The 1990s were a time in which the South Korean economy reoriented itself towards highly sophisticated exports in the micro-electronics, bioengineering and aerospace sectors. Firm evidence of a causal link between financial sector reforms and growth in export sophistication remains to be examined in depth.

Thailand's post-reform export sophistication growth, like Malaysia's, seemed to be slightly less impressive than before the reforms. Thailand opened its capital account before modernising its banking sector regulation. However, as entry into the sector was substantially blocked, the banks faced little competition. As Okabe (2006) argued, the lack of competition meant that the banks had little experience with financial intermediation. Hence, bank credit primarily involved short-term loans to the real estate and other services sectors, rather than long-term export-oriented manufacturing, which had been declining in profitability (although industrial firms did rely on short-term credit to increase their investment dramatically just prior to the crisis) (Dollar & Hallward-Driemeier, 2000). Thus, we might expect that poorly sequenced liberalisations might be less effective for increasing export sophistication, because of their contribution to speculative bubbles or other unproductive investments.

In the next section, we examine a possible causal connection between financial sector reform and export sophistication in a more rigorous econometric setting.

Evidence for the relationship between financial liberalisation and export upgrading

Before laying out our results, we begin by describing our empirical strategy. As our dependent variable, we use the EXPY variable, constructed as above. To test the robustness of our results, we also replicate each regression using the share of high-tech exports in manufactured exports from the World Bank (TECH) rather than EXPY as the dependent variable.

We include several control variables. Following the literature on export sophistication, we include per capita GDP and population (taking the natural log of both) plus a measure of trade openness, the imports share of GDP plus the exports share of GDP. To test our hypothesis about financial development aiding export sophistication, we test two commonly employed measures of the state of financial development: the ratio of liquid liabilities to GDP and the ratio of domestic credit to private sector firms to GDP. In regressions (7)–(10), we interact our measure of financial openness with the Chinn–Ito capital account openness measure, standardised so that the maximum value is one (this renders it a relative measure of capital account openness; that is to say, it measures a country's openness relative to the rest of the world) (Chinn & Ito, 2006).

Our empirical results are set out in Appendix A, Table A5.1. Our findings are as follows. The coefficients on the control variables are signed as expected and are mostly significant. The exception is our measure of trade openness, which is significant in regression (8) only. Three of the specifications are of note: (1), (8) and (10). In regression (1), we test the hypothesis that financial development, measured by domestic credit to the private sector as a proportion of GDP, will influence the share of manufactured exports that are classified as high technology; the regression does indeed suggest a positive relationship. This relationship is *not* found to exist with the EXPY variable when we test the equivalent hypothesis in regression (2). However, in regression (8), we allow for an interaction term between domestic credit to GDP and capital account openness, and we find that, although domestic credit to GDP *is* positively associated with higher EXPY, higher capital account openness relative to the rest of the world reduces this effect. The same phenomenon can be observed when using the liquid liabilities/GDP measure of financial development, as in regression (10). Regressions (8) and (10), which allow the effect of financial development on export sophistication to vary, depending on the openness of the capital account, are our preferred specifications. Regressions (2)–(6), which simply test the relationship between the two measures of export sophistication and the two measures of financial development, show no significant relationship. Regressions (7) and (9), in which the dependent variable is the high-technology exports variable, and which include the interaction with capital account openness, show no significant results either.

We interpret these regression results as suggesting that there is some evidence that financial reforms can be helpful for countries seeking to move into more sophisticated or more technologically advanced export markets. However, some caution should be exercised when opening the capital account, as there is evidence that it may hamper efforts to move up the value chain in manufactured exports. This result should not be taken as suggesting that capital account openness is necessarily a bad thing; the data we have used merely average out the historical experience of countries that have opened their capital account hastily and others that have taken a more measured and prudent approach. Our results are consistent with the following message for policymakers: developing the capacity and sophistication of domestic financial markets can yield positive results in terms of upgrading export baskets to more sophisticated, higher value-added product lines. A solid degree of capital account openness as a medium-term policy objective is supported by the literature. However, policymakers should proceed carefully, as there is a potential for such openness to influence the export sector.

Capital account reform and sequencing

To further examine the proposition that the sequencing of financial reforms matters, we run regression (11), in which export sophistication is regressed, as before, upon population and per capita income, as well as on a set of dummy variables that characterise the state of financial regulation in a country. These analyses separately consider the effect of domestic regulation (measuring controls on credit and interest rates, as well as banking sector rules) and regulation on cross-border financial flows. Details on the construction of these dummy variables and other aspects of the regression are found in Appendix A. Again, we find that population and per capita income are positively associated with export sophistication in the goods sector. We find that countries with significant restrictions on both domestic and international financial transactions tend to have lower export sophistication than do countries that have relatively few of either kind of restriction, even when controlling for per capita income and population. We find that countries that have liberalised their domestic financial markets, but *not* cross-border flows, show no signs of having significantly more or less sophisticated export sectors than countries with fully liberalised financial sectors. We find that countries that have substantially liberalised cross-border flows, but which retain significant domestic financial restrictions, have, on average, a lower export sophistication score than do countries that have liberalised both domestically and internationally; however, the difference is significant only at the 10 per cent level.

In a cross-sectional sense, then, it appears as if the sequencing of financial reforms does matter—or, to put it slightly differently, that the financial *system* matters, where 'system' refers to the combination of capital account openness and domestic market liberalisation. Even when we control for per capita income, countries that open capital accounts without first developing their domestic markets seem to have lower export sophistication than do countries that have liberalised *both* domestic and international financial controls. Unfortunately, the regression does not establish the direction of causality; however, in light of the many case studies of the causes of the AFC, it seems intuitively obvious. It is possible that countries with more sophisticated exports relative to their per capita income are more likely to have liberalised domestic financial markets and open capital accounts, but this seems less intuitive than an explanation in which the causality runs from financial deregulation to export sophistication.

Our empirical work, taken as a whole, suggests a possible connection between financial development and export sophistication, which is of interest to policymakers in Asian countries seeking to climb regional value chains. More work on this question is clearly desirable. Expanding the analysis to consider services as well as merchandise trade would be of great interest, but the available data is insufficiently disaggregated so far. It would also be interesting to test more disaggregated measures of capital account openness that distinguish between regulatory controls on different kinds of financial flows. However, although such disaggregated datasets exist, the time periods they cover are quite short and they do not allow us to adequately test the medium-term relationships between trade and finance that we test in our empirical work.

Our analysis suggests a relationship between the sequencing of financial liberalisation and export sophistication. Even when controlling for population and per capita GDP, the least sophisticated exporters are those that have only liberalised their capital account, without substantial domestic market development. Countries that have liberalised neither domestic financial markets nor international capital flows also have lower export sophistication than do countries that have liberalised in both senses. These results suggest to us that correctly sequencing future reform could be of assistance to China and India as they seek to move into markets with higher domestic value added and, hence, climb regional value chains.

Implications

Based on our export sophistication data, we recommend that China and India sequence domestic financial markets reforms as necessary precursors of capital account opening. The ambition of both countries to climb regional value chains by exporting higher value-added goods can be aided by correctly sequenced financial reform. As we have already emphasised, China's financial reform effort is proceeding gradually and methodically, with full capital account convertibility regarded as the end point.

More work on the connection between the channels through which financial reform influences real growth is needed, and export sophistication is, broadly speaking, a promising channel for further exploration. In addition, the use of more fine-grained measures of capital account openness could be helpful in determining whether certain kinds of capital controls are more harmful (or advantageous) than others for countries wishing to move into more sophisticated export lines. For example, future work in this area could focus separately on the role of the regulation of inward and outward flows of FDI in driving increased export sophistication in the domestic economy. Further analysis that includes services sectors is also desirable, but is seriously hampered by the paucity of disaggregated data.

Conclusion

The world economy is still recovering from the GFC and, although growth in many Asian economies is quite strong, the Asia–Pacific region is not immune to the problems of weak global demand and slower trade growth. Therefore, policymakers in the region are understandably eager to devise ways to lift domestic growth rates, and financial market reform and opening is a major part of the overall reform agendas of the governments of China and India, among other Asian economies. The composition and sequencing of these reforms is of considerable importance to their success. The evidence provided in this chapter of linkages between financial reform and opening and export sophistication establishes that a relationship exists, and that further investigation using better data is required. As China, India and other Asian economies pursue policies encouraging producers to move up global value chains and to produce and export higher value-added goods, they should consider coordinating such strategies with their financial reform objectives to maximise the real economy gains from these reforms.

References

Abiad, A., Detragiache, E. & Tressel, T. (2008). A new database of financial reforms. *IMF Working Paper No. 2008-2266*. Washington, DC: International Monetary Fund.

Asian Development Bank (ADB). (2016). *Asian Development Outlook 2016*. Hong Kong, China: Asian Development Bank. Retrieved 1 June 2016 from: www.adb.org/publications/asian-development-outlook-2016-highlights

Bas, M. & Berthou, A. (2011). Financial reforms and foreign technology upgrading: Firm level evidence from India. *European Trade Study Group Working Paper.*

Beck, T. (2002). Financial development and international trade: Is there a link? *Journal of International Economics 57* (1), 107–31.

Berman, N. & Héricourt, J. (2008). Financial factors and the margins of trade: Evidence from cross-country firm-level data. *Documents de Travail du Centre d'Economie de la Sorbonne no 50. Paris.* Retrieved from: halshs.archives-ouvertes.fr/halshs-00321632

Caballero, R. J. & Krishnamurthy, A. (2001). International and domestic collateral constraints in a model of emerging market crises. *Journal of Monetary Economics 48*(3), pp. 513–48. doi.org/10.1016/S0304-3932(01)00084-8

Carluccio, J. & Fally, T. (2008). Global sourcing under imperfect capital markets. *Paris School of Economics Working Paper No. 2008-69.* Retrieved from: halshs.archives-ouvertes.fr/halshs-00586005/document

Chaney, T. (2016). Liquidity constrained exporters. *Journal of Economic Dynamics and Control 72*, 141–54. doi.org/10.1016/j.jedc.2016.03.010

China Investment Monitor. (n.d.). Retrieved from: rhg.com/interactive/china-investment-monitor

Chinn, M. D. & Ito, H. (2006, October). What matters for financial development? Capital controls, institutions, and interactions. *Journal of Development Economics 81*(1), pp. 163–92. doi.org/10.1016/j.jdeveco.2005.05.010

Dollar, D. & Hallward-Driemeier, M. (2000). Crisis, adjustment, and reform in Thailand's industrial firms. *The World Bank Research Observer 15*(1), 1–22. doi.org/10.1093/wbro/15.1.1

Egger, P. & Kesina, M. (2013). Financial constraints and exports: evidence from Chinese firms. *CESifo Economic Studies 59*(4), 676–706. doi.org/10.1093/cesifo/ifs036

Goksel, T. (2012). Financial constraints and international trade patterns. *Economic Modelling 29*(6), 2222–25. doi.org/10.1016/j.econmod.2012.06.040

Hausmann, R., Hwang, J., & Rodrik, D. (2007). What you export matters. *Journal of Economic Growth 12*(1), 1–25.

International Monetary Fund (IMF). (2016). Too slow for too long. *World Economic Outlook April 2016*. Washington DC: International Monetary Fund.

Jaud, M., Kukenova, M. & Strieborny, M. (2012). Finance, comparative advantage and resource allocation. *World Bank Policy Research Working Paper 6111*. Washington, DC: World Bank.

Kay, J. (2015). *Other people's money: The real business of finance*. New York, NY: Public Affairs.

King, M. (2016). *The end of alchemy: Money, banking and the future of the global economy*. London, England: Little Brown.

Kynge, J., Mitchell, T. & Massoudi, A. (2016, 11 February). M&A: China's world of debt. *Financial Times*. Retrieved from www.ft.com/content/4c9642f6-d0a9-11e5-831d-09f7778e7377

Lardy, N. (2016, 2 June). No need to panic, China's banks are in pretty good shape. *Financial Times (UK)*, p. 11.

Lipton, D. (2016, 24 May). *Can globalization still deliver? The challenge of convergence in the 21st century*. Presented at the Stavros Niarchos Lecture, Peterson Institute for International Economics. Retrieved from: www.imf.org/en/News/Articles/2015/09/28/04/53/sp052416a

Manap, T. A. A. & Ghani, G. M. (2012). Malaysia's time varying capital mobility. *Economics Bulletin 32*(2), 1361–68.

Manova, K. (2008). Credit constraints, equity market liberalizations and international trade. *Journal of International Economics 76*(1), 33–47. doi.org/10.1016/j.jinteco.2008.03.008

Manova, K. Wei, S-J. & Zhang, Z. (2015). Firm exports and multinational activity under credit constraints. *Review of Economics and Statistics 97*(3), 574–88. doi.org/10.1162/REST_a_00480

Manova, K. & Yu, Z. (2016). How firms export: processing vs. ordinary trade with financial frictions. *Journal of International Economics 100*, 120–37. doi.org/10.1016/j.jinteco.2016.02.005

Okabe, Y. (2006). *The political origins of financial crises of the 21st century: Path dependence of financial systems in Korea, Thailand and Mexico.* Paper presented at the International Political Science Association World Congress, Fukuoaka, Japan. Retrieved from: paperroom.ipsa.org/papers/paper_5124.pdf

Panagariya, A. (2016, 18 May). Two years of reform: Substantial progress has been made towards restoring economic momentum. Much remains to be done. *The Indian Express.* Retrieved from: indianexpress.com/article/opinion/columns/pm-narendra-modi-2-years-of-modi-govt-bjp-two-year-anniversary-pradhan-mantri-krishi-sinchai-yojana-2804219/

Park, Y. C., & Patrick, H. (Eds.). (2013). *How finance is shaping the economies of China, Japan, and Korea.* New York, NY: Columbia University Press.

Rajan, R. & Zingales, L. (1998). Financial dependence and growth. *American Economic Review 88*, 559–86.

Wang, Z. & Wei, S-J. (2010). What accounts for the rising sophistication of China's exports? In Feenstra, R. C. & Wei, S.-J. *China's growing role in world trade* (pp. 63–104). Chicago: University of Chicago Press.

Wildau, G. (2016, 13 June). IMF sounds warning on China corporate debt. *Financial Times (UK)*, p. 7.

Windmeijer, F. (2005). A finite sample correction for the variance of linear efficient two-step GMM estimators. *Journal of Econometrics 126*(1), 25–51. doi.org/10.1016/j.jeconom.2004.02.005

Appendices

Appendix A: Regressions

Table A5.1: Regressions (1)–(10)

Regression	(1)	(2)	(3)	(4)	(5)	(6)	(7)	(8)	(9)	(10)
Dependent variable	TECH	EXPY	TECH	EXPY	TECH	EXPY	TECH	EXPY	TECH	EXPY
Lagged high tech	0.503*** (4.79)		0.490*** (4.55)		0.637*** (5.53)		0.507*** (4.89)		0.489*** (4.64)	
Lagged EXPY		0.465*** (6.23)		0.510*** (5.43)		0.467*** (6.16)		0.460*** (5.91)		0.507*** (5.22)
Per capita GDP	0.622* (2.12)	0.141*** (7.03)	1.106** (3.11)	0.131*** (5.11)	0.932** (2.76)	0.141***	0.651*	0.140***	1.143** (3.06)	1.14 (5.00)
Population	0.644* (2.56)	0.037*** (4.39)	0.797** (3.23)	0.0371*** (3.79)	0.556* (2.50)	0.0374*** (4.48)	0.580* (2.45)	0.0403*** (4.67)	0.753** (3.13)	0.0412** (4.04)
Trade/GDP	0.0213 (1.03)	0.000460 (1.85)	0.0245 (1.28)	0.000351 (1.31)	0.0199 (1.27)	0.000473 (1.81)	0.0194 (0.97)	0.000527* (2.01)	0.0233 (1.28)	0.000482 (1.87)
Credit to private firms/GDP	1.312** (3.08)	-0.00188 (-0.20)	0.717 (1.14)	0.00464 (0.33)			0.787 (0.72)	0.0456* (2.11)		
Liquid liabilities to GDP									1.067 (0.91)	0.0741** (2.99)

Regression	(1)	(2)	(3)	(4)	(5)	(6)	(7)	(8)	(9)	(10)
Capital account (KA) openness					-0.0838 (-0.12)	-0.0146 (-0.46)	-0.203 (-0.26)	-0.00211 (-0.06)	-0.0642 (-0.08)	-0.00892 (-0.29)
Credit × KA openness							0.658 (0.51)	-0.0646* (-2.46)		
Liquid liabilities × KA									-0.611 (0.24)	-0.0961* (-2.97)
Constant	-13.73* (-2.34)	3.153*** (6.51)	-20.03*** (-3.67)	2.833*** (4.90)	-15.29** (-2.68)	3.148*** (6.49)	-12.83* (-2.27)	3.171*** (6.26)	-19.47 (-3.40)	2.803*** (4.79)
A–B AR(1)	-3.109	-4.042	-3.049	-3.533	-3.233	-4.061	-3.120	-4.011	-3.055	-3.506
A–B AR(2)	0.416	0.821	0.387	1.603	0.615	0.828	0.418	0.815	0.402	1.604

Note: The t statistics are presented in parentheses. The symbols *, ** and *** denote p-values of <0.05, <0.01 and <0.001, respectively. A–B indicates the Arellano–Bond tests for autocorrelation of types AR(1) and AR(2).

Source: See Appendix B.

Regressions (1)–(10)

Regressions (1)–(10) employ the generalised method of moments two-step estimator with standard errors that have been corrected using the technique of Windmeijer (2005). The equations estimated are of the following form:

$$Export\ sophistication = \beta_0 + \sum_{j=1}^{c} \beta_j ControlVar_{itk} + \sum_{k=1+c}^{f} \beta_k FinancialVars_{itk} + \varepsilon_{it}$$

with variables instrumented by their own one-period lags in this level equation and by two-period lags in the first-differenced version of the above equation. We conduct the standard Arrellano–Bond tests for autocorrelation of type AR(1) and AR(2) in the errors of the first-differenced equation. We also perform Sargan–Hansen J-tests for overidentifying restrictions. None of these tests indicate any cause for concern in our regressions.

Regression (11)

In this regression, five-year averages of all variables are taken. Following the results of the Hausmann test, a fixed rather than random effects estimator is used; standard errors are clustered at the country level. The state of financial liberalisation in a country i at period t is characterised by four variables: *neither, both, capital_only* and *domestic_only*. We consider that a country's financial system is relatively un-liberalised if the mean of the Abiad et al. (2008) variables measuring directed credit, credit controls, interest rate controls, entry barriers and privatisation variables is less than two (with the highest possible score being three). The capital account is considered relatively open if a country scores higher than two out of three on the variable indicating international capital movements.

Table A5.2: The effect of reform sequencing on export sophistication

Regression (11)	
Population	19.52*** (4.91)
Per capita income	0.15*** (4.39)
Capital account liberalisation only dummy	−714.72* (−176)

Regression (11)	
Domestic financial liberalisation only dummy	63.04 (0.1652)
Neither capital account nor domestic financial liberalisation	−888.4** (−2.96)
N = 272 R² = 0.28	

Note: The t statistics are presented in parentheses. The symbols *, ** and *** denote p-values of <0.05, <0.01 and <0.001, respectively.

Source: See Appendix B.

Appendix B: Data sources

Variable	Source	Notes
EXPY	Product-level trade data from the Centre d'études prospectives et d'informations internationales BACI database; GDP data from World Development Indicators (WDI)	EXPY constructed as outlined in text above from time-invariant PRODYs
TECH	WDI	n/a
Population	WDI	n/a
Per capita GDP	WDI	n/a
Trade openness	WDI	Imports/GDP + Exports/GDP
Liquid liabilities to GDP	WFDD	n/a
Domestic credit to private sector	WFDD	n/a
Capital account openness	web.pdx.edu/~ito/Chinn-Ito_website.htm	KAO_OPEN (standardised) variable is used
Capital account liberalisation dummy (regression 11)	Abiad et al. (2008)	0 if continuous variable <2; 1 otherwise
Domestic financial liberalisation dummy (regression 11)	Abiad et al. (2008)	Described above; 0 if composite index <2; 1 otherwise

6

Evolution of production networks in the Asia–Pacific region: A vision in value-added and employment dimensions

Hubert Escaith, Satoshi Inomata and Sébastien Miroudot

Introduction

As production activities are increasingly being fragmented and relocated across borders, a number of people have started to use the expression 'global value chain' (GVC), yet often without knowing what it really encompasses. The concept of GVCs was first elaborated through the discussions of the Global Value Chains Initiative (2000–05) sponsored by the Rockefeller Foundation, and further crystallised in the seminal paper of Gereffi, Humphrey and Sturgeon (2005). Since then, substantial effort has been invested in empirical studies that attempt to capture the nature of global production sharing. Thanks to the successful development of the trade in value-added (TiVA) database by the Organisation for

Economic Co-operation and Development (OECD) and the World Trade Organization (WTO),[1] 'mapping GVCs' has now become one of the key research agendas in the relevant academic fields.[2]

Given this context, we aim to present empirical evidence on the key features of GVCs in the Asia–Pacific region using a multi-country input–output model as a principal drawing tool. The structure of the chapter is as follows. The first section provides a brief overview of empirical challenges for GVC studies and shows how the method of input–output analyses can complement the traditional approach. The second section presents a general picture of global production networks, with a particular focus on the evolution of vertical production system among countries. The third section demonstrates the development of value-added flows across countries in relation to major trade agreement schemes. The fourth section considers the effect of firms' global activities on domestic employment, which has been a central subject of political debates over time. The final section concludes the chapter.

An overview of empirical challenges for mapping GVCs

The early challenges involved in developing quantitative descriptions of GVCs are exemplified by the studies that utilise firm-specific business records. They generally aim to identify the structure of production processes and/or the sales networks of some particular products, based on the data provided by the manufacturers themselves or the 'teardown reports' of private consulting companies (Sturgeon, Nielsen, Linden, Gereffi & Brown, 2013).

Pioneering research in this area includes the work of Dedrick, Kraemer and Linden (2008) who conducted an analysis of the value-added structure of four representative products—Apple's iPod and video iPod, and Hewlett Packard's and Lenovo's laptop computers—using the information from business reports. Among other findings, the study revealed that a video

---

1   Hereafter, the OECD–WTO TiVA database.
2   However, note that the main objective of Gereffi et al. (2005) is to examine the governance structures of organising cross-border production networks by focusing on a particular relationship between a lead firm and a service supplier. Hence, the scope of the empirical analyses introduced in the present chapter is somewhat different from their original motivation. See Inomata (2017) for a survey of various analytical frameworks for GVC studies.

iPod with a retail price of US$299 in 2005 was associated with a breakdown of US$144 for the product's factory cost, US$75 for distribution margins and US$80 for the profit of the lead firm (Apple); of the overall factory cost, only US$3.86 was attributable to assembly services in the People's Republic of China (PRC).

These product-level approaches are useful in illustrating the structure of production chains because they directly utilise the data provided by individual firms rather than resorting to any forms of statistical inference. However, there are a number of weaknesses associated with this approach.

First, the approach has limited applicability to the consideration of macro-economic issues, such as trade policies, because the analytical focus is only on a particular product and/or the activity of a few firms. Moreover, it is unable to capture aggregate flows of value added in the broader national context. Second, as pointed out by Dedrick et al. (2008), the majority of firm data does not explicitly identify the compensation of employees, an important component of value-added items in the national accounting framework, but merges it with other types of production costs. Third, as values are generated at every point of the production process, the value-added analysis should be able to trace all the production stages along the entire supply chain. However, the product-level approach only considers the value-added structure of direct input suppliers (the first-tier suppliers), but leaves the rest of the value-added stream untracked. For example, a hard disk drive in an iPhone contains various sub-parts produced in different countries; therefore, it requires further decomposition of the value-added sources.

Given the limitations of this first approach, increasing attention is being directed to the use of statistical tables called multi-country input–output tables (MCIOTs). An MCIOT provides a comprehensive map of the international transactions of goods and services. This massive dataset combines national input–output tables of various countries at a given point in time. As the tables contain information on supply–use relations between industries and across countries, which are totally absent from foreign trade statistics, it is possible to identify the vertical structure of international production sharing. Further, in contrast to the product-level approach, input–output analysis covers the entire set of industries that comprise an economic system, which enables researchers to capture cross-border value flows at the level of a country or region. Theoretically, it has the capacity to track the value-added generation process of every product in every country at every production stage.

GVC studies using input–output tables have become increasingly prominent in the last decade, yet their origin can be traced back to the beginning of the century, when Hummels, Ishii and Yi (2001) introduced the concept of vertical specialisation (VS). The VS metric is defined as the amount of imported intermediate inputs used for the production of an exported good or, put differently, the import content of exports, which is presented as a measurement of international production sharing.

The idea was brought into the value-added context by Chen, Cheng, Fung and Lau (2009) who were the first to investigate the statistical distortions that arise from ignoring the presence of processing trade and measuring international trade in gross terms. Here, the long-debated issue of US–PRC trade imbalances was fully considered in a value-added perspective. The approach is further developed and methodologically formalised in Koopman, Wang and Wei (2012), in which the PRC's national input–output matrices are separated into two components, one for the export processing sectors and one for the rest of the economy.

Whereas these empirical exercises relied on individual country national input–output tables, Daudin, Monperrus-Veroni, Rifflart and Schweisguth (2006) utilised the database of the Global Trade Analysis Project (GTAP) and constructed an MCIOT of 70 countries and their composite regions for the calculation of the domestic value-added content of exports, alongside indices of VS and regionalisation. Johnson and Noguera (2012) calculated the ratio of value-added exports to gross exports (referred to as the VAX ratio) as a metric of international production sharing, again using the GTAP database. This study extensively discussed the effect of production sharing on the scale of bilateral trade balances with respect to a myriad of countries and regions. In relation to the US trade deficit with the PRC, it determined that the deficit fell by 30–40 per cent when calculated in terms of value added compared with the traditional calculation.

Geometry of GVCs

A network approach to mapping value chains

Graphs are the most intuitive approach for mapping trade networks. Despite their apparent simplicity, graphs can be subjected to more advanced analysis that enables measurement of the pivotal role that trade partners play (Escaith, 2014). A trade network is best described as directed graphs, or digraphs, because it is made of directed edges (imports from, exports to) connecting vertices (trade partners).

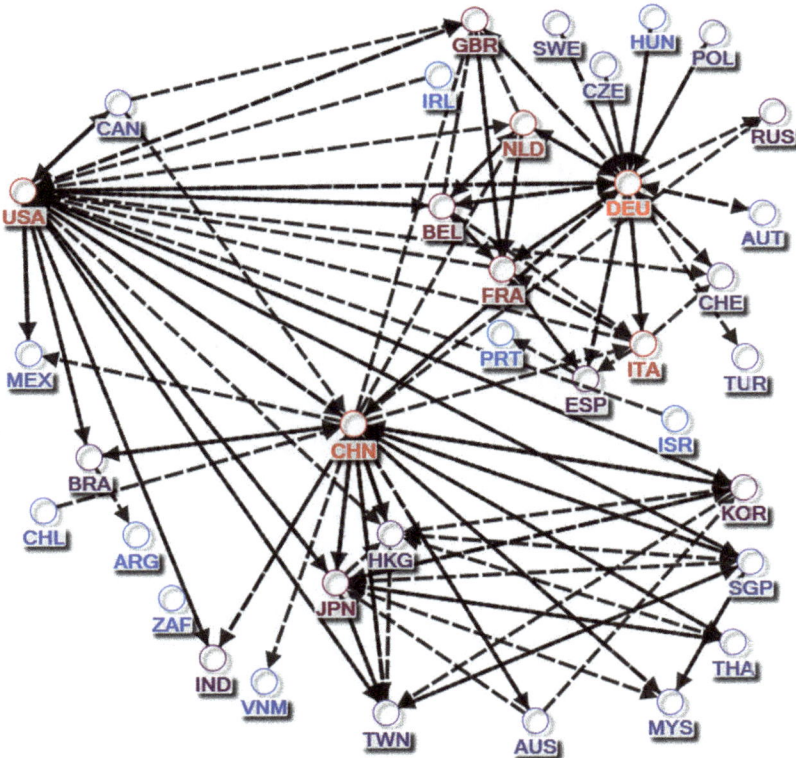

Figure 6.1: Network of trade in intermediate inputs, 2011

Note: Graph based on the 62 OECD–WTO TiVA economies and the value of their bilateral gross trade flows. The figure shows only the most important flows (over US$100 million). The colour-coding indicates the node's centrality, ascending from blue to red.

Source: Based on UN COMTRADE data, excluding oil.

Trade in intermediate goods and services are of particular importance for mapping international supply chains. Those flows of intermediate products represent 'business to business' interactions that closely track the extent of inter-industrial relationships between countries and sectors. Figure 6.1 shows international trade in intermediate products for the economies included in the OECD–WTO TiVA database. To simplify the graph, only the most relevant trade flows are shown; that is, only those trade flows greater than US$100 million are shown with a solid arrow.

There are several interesting features of this graph. First, global supply chains are organised in sub-regions, each one of which is organised around one or several hubs. The European value chains have Germany as the main hub, with the UK and France as sub-centres. (The roles of Belgium and the Netherlands are also important, but more for their strategic sea-shipping logistic situation than for their industrial leadership.) The Asia–Pacific region (the south-west part of the graph) has two poles: the PRC and the US, with Japan and South Korea as secondary hubs. (Hong Kong and Singapore play the roles of logistic platforms.)

The US plays a key role in the GVC network, as it is the main linkage between the European, Asian and North and South American countries. In the language of network analysis, the US ranks high in terms of its 'centrality'. The centrality indicator used in Figure 6.1 (page rank) is a measure of influence. The intuition behind its calculation is that if a trade partner (a node or a vertex in network analysis) 'influences just one other node, who subsequently influences many other nodes (who themselves influence still more others), then the first node in that chain is highly influential' (Borgatti, 2005, p. 61). In our graph, the colour-coding indicates the node's centrality, ascending from blue to red.

Therefore, a player's centrality is not only a function of its own importance in the world economy, but is also a function of the centrality of the trade partners with which it is associated. In Europe, the most influential country is Germany, followed by Italy. This may not seem intuitive, but Italy plays an important role connecting the northern part of the EU with southern economies. In the Asia–Pacific region, the two most central economies are the PRC and the US.

Evolutionary perspective of production networks in the Asia–US region

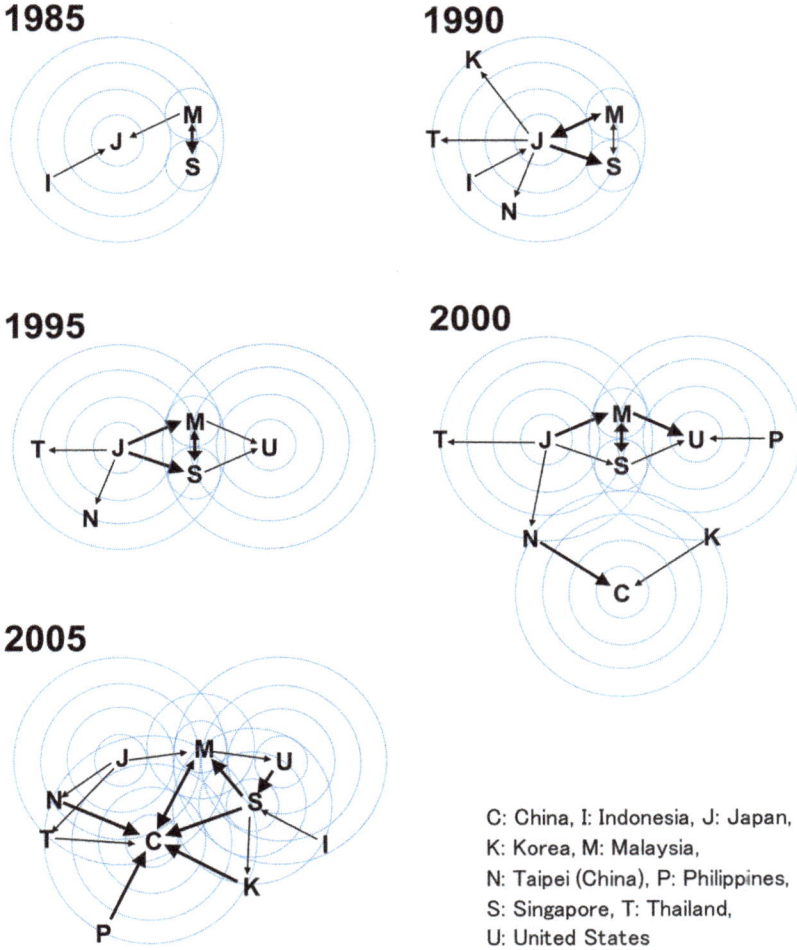

1985

1990

1995

2000

2005

C: China, I: Indonesia, J: Japan,
K: Korea, M: Malaysia,
N: Taipei (China), P: Philippines,
S: Singapore, T: Thailand,
U: United States

Figure 6.2: Evolution of regional supply chains in East Asia, 1985–2005
Source: Escaith and Inomata (2013).

Figure 6.2 traces the evolution of production networks in the Asia–US region from 1985 to 2005.[3] The visualisation of the calculation results is based on the method presented in Dietzenbacher, Romero and Bosma (2005),

---

3   Note that, in contrast to the other sections of this chapter, the analysis here does not cover the Latin American countries.

with some graphical elaboration as developed by Inomata (2008). Arrows represent the selected supply chains among the countries of the region, with the direction of arrows corresponding to flows of intermediate products. Each arrow has two features: thickness and length. The thickness indicates the strength of linkages between industries, whereas the length, as measured against the ripple in the background, is given by the average propagation length (APL), developed in Dietzenbacher et al. (2005).[4] The number of circles that an arrow crosses represents the rounded value of the APL, the average number of production stages and the level of technological fragmentation and sophistication of that particular supply chain.

The study uses the Asian International Input–Output Tables for 1985, 1990, 1995, 2000 and 2005 covering 10 economies: PRC (C), Indonesia (I), Japan (J), Korea (K), Malaysia (M), Philippines (P), Singapore (S), Thailand (T), Taipei, China (N) and the US (U).

In 1985, there were only four key players in the region: Indonesia (I), Japan (J), Malaysia (M) and Singapore (S). The basic structure of the production network was that Japan built up supply chains from resource-rich countries, such as Indonesia and Malaysia. In this initial phase of regional development, Japan drew on a substantial amount of natural resources from neighbouring countries to feed its domestic industries.

By 1990, the number of key players had increased. In addition to the four countries already mentioned, Japan had extended its supply chains for intermediate products to Korea (K), Taipei, China (N) and Thailand (T). While continuing to rely on the productive resources of Indonesia and Malaysia, Japan began to supply products to other East Asian economies, particularly to the group known as the newly industrialised economies (NIEs) of Hong Kong, Korea, Singapore and Taiwan. During this phase, the relocation of Japanese production bases to neighbouring countries was accelerating, triggered by the Plaza Accord in 1985. The development of strong linkages was observed between core parts suppliers in Japan and assembly platforms in foreign countries.

In 1995, the US (U) came into the picture. It drew on two key supply chains originating in Japan, one via Malaysia and the other via Singapore. These two countries came to bridge the supply chains between East Asia and the US. The length of the arrows between Malaysia and Singapore

---

4   See Technical Note 6.1 in Appendix A.

should be noted. Compared with the other arrows, their shortness indicates that the supply chains involve fewer production stages, suggesting that the degree of processing is relatively low. Thus, the product flows between these countries are distributional rather than value adding.

In the year 2000, on the eve of its accession to the WTO, the PRC began to emerge as the third regional giant. The country entered the arena with strong production linkages to Korea and Taipei (China), and gained access to Japanese supply chains through the latter. The US also brought a new supply chain from the Philippines (P). This completed the basic structure of the tri-polar production network in the Asia–US region.

Thereafter, the regional production networks showed dramatic development. By 2005, the centre of the network had completely shifted to the PRC, pushing the US and Japan to the periphery. The PRC became the core market for products of the region from which final consumption goods were produced for export to the US and European markets. The nature of the supply chains that the PRC developed with other countries are also noteworthy. The length of the arrows surrounding the PRC indicates that the supply chains extending towards the PRC were characterised by a high degree of fragmentation and sophistication, incorporating substantial amounts of value added from each country involved in the production networks. Therefore, the competitiveness of Chinese exports was attributable not only to its cheap labour force, but also to the sophisticated intermediate products that the country received from other East Asian economies, as embedded in goods labelled 'Made in China'.

The APL method can also be used to identify the relative position of countries within the global production system. Updating the methodology proposed by Inomata (2008), Figure 6.3 presents the changes of countries' positions in the Asia–US region between 1985 and 2005 with respect to forward and backward APLs.

Reading the diagram along the top-right/bottom-left diagonal, the entire length of the supply chains that each country participates in is represented. Most economies have moved towards the top-right corner, meaning that they increased the length of their supply chains between 1985 and 2005. In particular, the PRC demonstrated an outstanding increase in the length of its supply chains. The interlinking of its domestic supply chains with overseas production networks was accelerated by the country's accession to the WTO in 2001, as suggested by the big leap in the value from 1985 to 2005.

In contrast, the top-left/bottom-right direction shows the relative position of each economy within regional supply chains, as determined by the ratio of forward and backward APLs. The US and Japan, the most advanced economies in the region, are located in the upstream position, although they reduced their 'upstreamness' during the period and the US, in particular, has swapped its position with Korea. The PRC has remained in the downstream segment of regional supply chains, which reflects the country's dominant position as a final assembler of regional products.

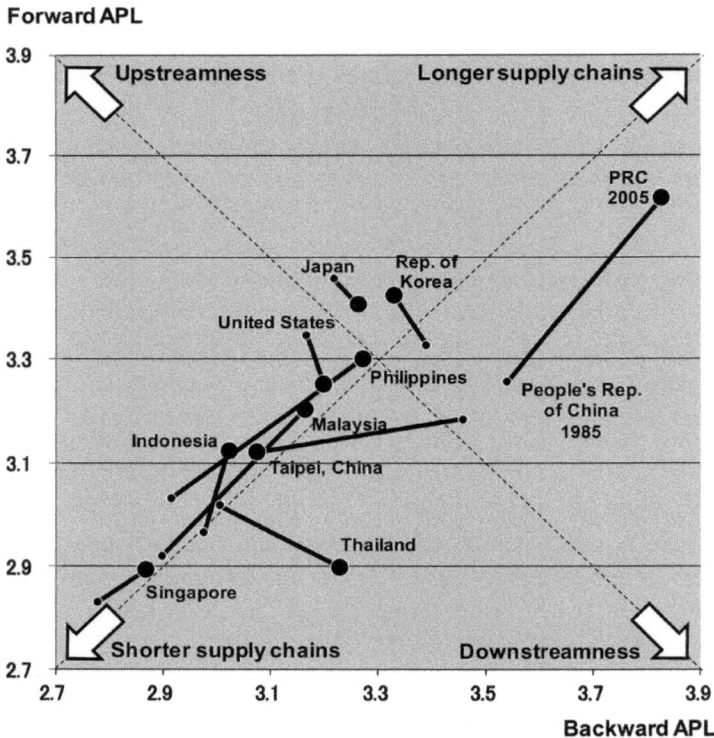

Figure 6.3: Changes in the relative positions of countries in the regional supply chains, 1985–2005
Source: Escaith and Inomata (2013).

The other economies remain more or less in the middle range, although with two notable changes: Taipei (China) moved up into the middle cluster and Thailand moved downstream to a large extent. These changes clearly reflect the development of the roles of the two economies in the region. Taipei (China) significantly increased its electronics manufacturing services and became a major parts supplier to big computer multinationals, whereas Thailand invited and accommodated a massive inflow of Japanese car assembly plants, leading to it being named the 'Asian Detroit'.

Figure 6.4 maps the previous diagram into a one-dimensional schematisation of the relative position of countries within regional supply chains. From 1985 to 2005, the upstream economies have been more or less clustered together, whereas the PRC and Thailand became downstream standalones. Bipolarisation between parts suppliers and final assemblers can be observed during this period.

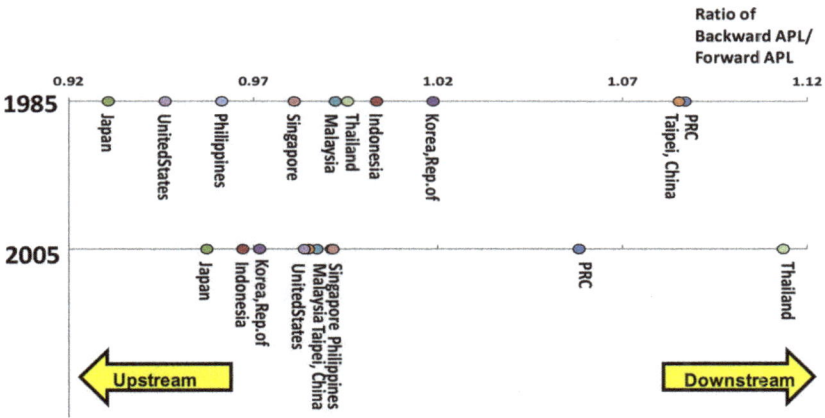

Figure 6.4: One-dimensional schematisation of the countries' relative positions, 1985–2005

Source: Authors' drawing.

Cross-national transfer of value added

The organisation of international production networks is, so far, mostly regional, with production taking place in a given region and the goods sold to consumers in the same region. This is especially the case in Europe, with Western Europe absorbing the manufacturing produced in Eastern Europe. It is somewhat the case in North America, but to a lesser extent, as the main source of final demand is the US.

Asia presents a slightly different picture. The supply part of the networks are regionally concentrated, yet on the demand side the networks are fairly global (across the Pacific Ocean and the Eurasian continent). This configuration originates from the early days of Japan's export-led growth strategy in the second half of the twentieth century, followed by that of the NIEs in the 1970s. The evolution took a dramatic turn with the PRC's accession to the WTO in 2001, resulting in the insertion of 700 million Chinese workers into the global economy. This was made possible through an increase in offshoring capabilities, which, in turn, was made possible by the rapid development of communication technology and transportation systems. Both of these had a tremendous effect on the PRC's comparative advantage in the region (and beyond).

Figure 6.5 presents cross-national transfers of value added in 1995 and 2011 in relation to the country coverage of major regional trade agreements (RTAs), using the OECD–WTO TiVA database (see Technical Note 6.2 in Appendix A).[5] Flow values are rounded into five increments according to thresholds indicated in the figures; the size of a black spot in each cell represents the magnitude of value-added flows for a particular pair of countries, where rows are countries of origin and columns are countries of destination.[6]

---

5   For a general description of the data, see www.oecd.org/sti/ind/tiva/tivasourcesandmethods.htm
6   Owing to the layout requirements of the tables, India and Cambodia are circumscribed within the Asia–Pacific Economic Cooperation (APEC) frame, but it should be noted that these economies were not APEC members at the time of writing this article in 2016. Also, the following economies are not included in the relevant RTA frames because the database does not cover their national data: Laos, Myanmar for ASEAN and Regional Comprehensive Economic Partnership (RCEP); Peru for Trans-Pacific Partnership (TPP); and Peru and Papua New Guinea for APEC.

From 1995 to 2011, we observe the following three developments:

1. Overall, value-added flows became busier.
2. Three regional clusters of value-added flows in North America, Europe and Asia can be identified throughout the period.
3. However, the regional value-added intensities became less prominent in 2011 as the US and PRC continued to extend their value chains beyond their respective regions, both in terms of origin and destination of value added.[7]

Zooming into the constituent countries of the regional clusters, in 1995, the US value chains with Canada and Mexico were particularly impressive, following the establishment of the North American Free Trade Agreement in 1994. In Europe, Germany and France are the regional centres of value flows. By 2011, US value chains penetrated all over the world, whereas the European countries, other than Germany and France, also increased their contribution to regional value flows. In Asia, in contrast, value-added trade is mostly concentrated within the trio of the PRC, Japan and the Republic of Korea. Other economies, including the Association of Southeast Asian Nations (ASEAN) economies, did not register their presence in regional value networks. In view of regional agreements, the influence of the US over Asian countries is quite evident in any form of RTA frameworks.

---

7   A parallel argument from a different perspective is given in Miroudot and Nordstrom (2015).

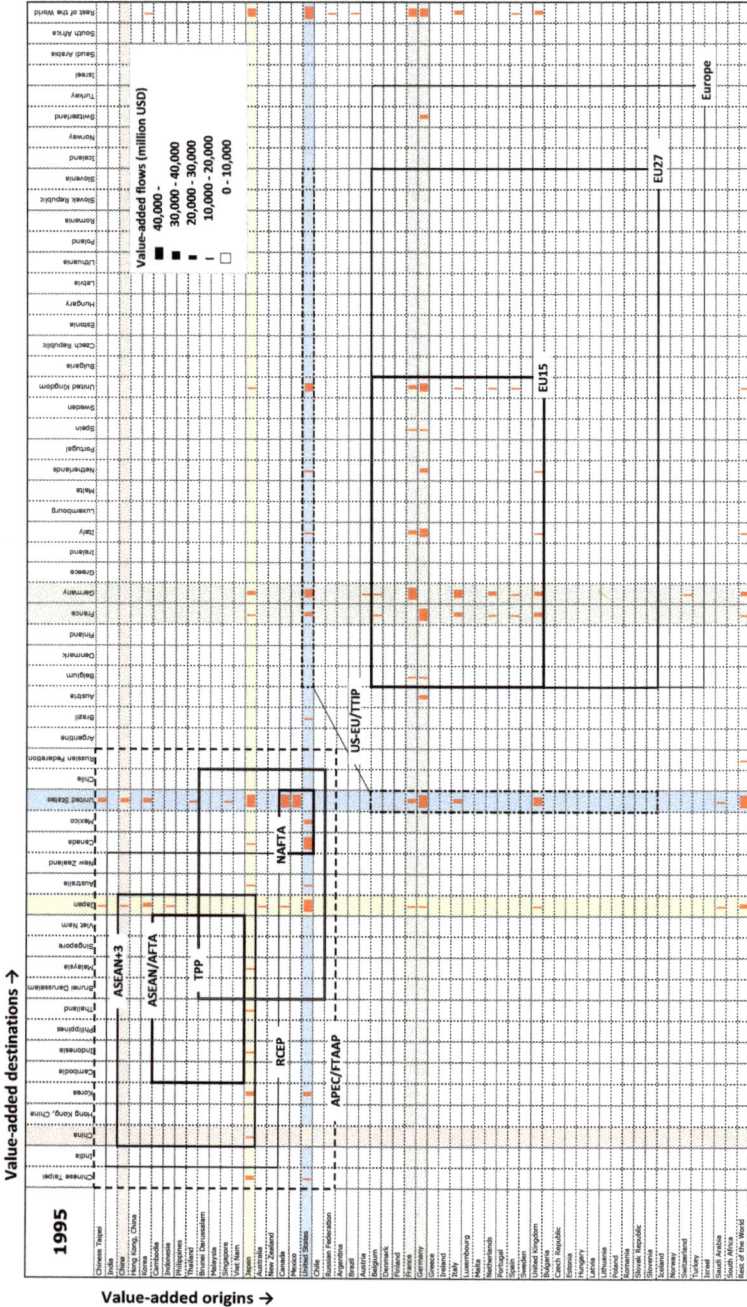

Figure 6.5a: TiVA from a regional perspective, 1995
Source: Authors' design, based on the OECD–WTO TiVA database.

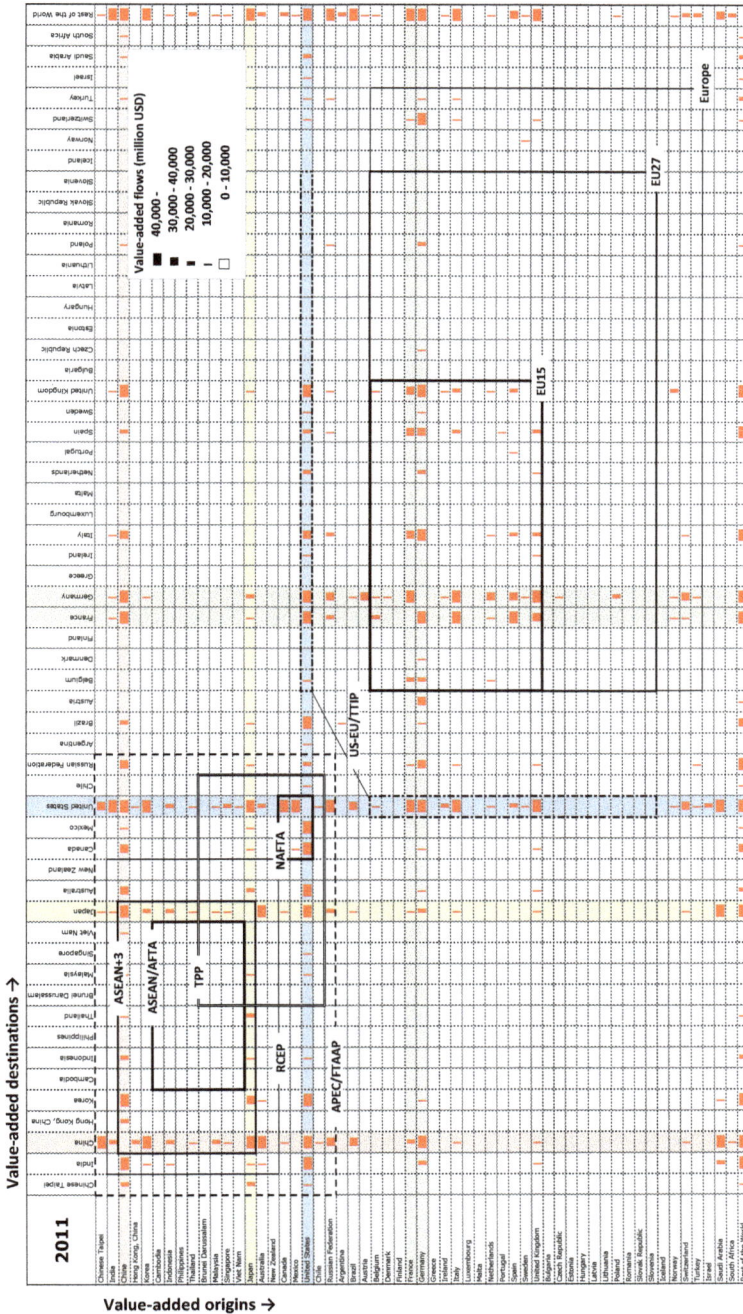

Figure 6.5b: TiVA from regional perspective, 2011

Source: Authors' design, based on the OECD–WTO TiVA database.

Table 6.1 summarises the amount of value added captured by each RTA framework. Based on the recognition that the expansion of membership assumes non-trivial costs to the scheme,[8] the column of the country averages indicates the 'efficiency' of respective RTAs in terms of capturing value added. The table shows that the most efficient RTA is, potentially, the Trans-Pacific Partnership (TPP), followed by the Free Trade Area of the Asia–Pacific (FTAAP).

Table 6.1: Numeric summary of TiVA from the Asia–Pacific regional perspective, 1995–2008

Regional trade agreement/ Free trade area	No. of member economies	Intra-regional trade in value added	Million USD Average per economy
ASEAN/AFTA	8	1,399,015	174,877
ASEAN+3	11	14,173,082	1,288,462
ASEAN+6/RCEP	14	17,408,587	1,243,471
TPP	11	22,924,391	2,084,036
APEC/FTAAP	18	34,249,601	1,902,756

Note: ASEAN = Association of Southeast Asian Nations; AFTA = ASEAN Free Trade Area; APEC = Asia–Pacific Economic Cooperation forum; RCEP = Regional Comprehensive Economic Partnership.

Source: Authors' calculation, based on the OECD–WTO TiVA database.

Effect of GVCs on employment

In view of the high rate of unemployment affecting many open economies, the net effect of GVCs on employment was the subject of heated debate in the years following the global crisis of 2008–09. A recent review from the World Bank (Farolle, 2016) pointed out that the issues are mainly concentrated in developed countries, where lower-skilled workers are exposed to higher chances of job loss, whereas countries with large labour surpluses and low wages have observed relatively strong job growth following their GVC integration.

8   In addition to the bureaucratic costs of plurilateral negotiation, an accompanying risk is having to give up the embodiment of some 'deeper' rules in exchange for term settlement among the larger number of parties, with different levels of institutional development.

Promoting labour standards in GVCs is often considered a win–win situation for all concerned, as workers in developing countries benefit from improved working conditions and exporting firms experience productivity gains that assist them to remain competitive. However, this positive viewpoint is not unanimously accepted. Economic success may not always be accompanied by higher wages and social upgrading, and some authors have pointed to the existence of regressive upgrading patterns, especially in textile and apparel industries.[9]

In the present chapter, we adopt a sectoral approach and link the OECD–WTO TiVA database with sectoral employment statistics by skill levels. The method developed for measuring the generation and cross-border transfers of value added also enables researchers to map the job content of imports and exports (see Technical Note 6.3 in Appendix A).[10] Figure 6.6 indicates that an increasing number of jobs are related to export activities over the period from 1995 to 2011. Here, we count jobs in exporting industries plus employment generated indirectly through domestic supply chains (the nexus of suppliers of intermediate goods and services). The increase, relative to the situation in 1995, is particularly pronounced in India (plus 6 percentage points, or a 67 per cent increase relative to 1996), Japan (5 percentage points and a 60 per cent increase) and the PRC (4 percentage points and a 41 per cent increase).[11]

---

9   For example, Bernhardt and Milberg (2011) found considerable variations in economic and social upgrading across countries and industries using micro-data on four sectors: horticulture, apparel, tourism and mobile telephones.

10   However, this approach has two caveats. The first one is to blur the heterogeneity that exists between different firms belonging to the same industrial sector in the same country. By definition, outsourcing and GVC insertion involve a strategic decision taken by individual firms and not all enterprises may implement the same strategy. Second, it is probable that the employment impacts that we measure are overestimated. The firms that are active in international trade are usually large firms, which are more productive than smaller ones and employ fewer workers per unit of output. Because our estimates are based on sectoral averages mixing small and large firms that are oriented to serving the domestic market or active in international trade, the relationship between trade in value added and underlying employment is probably overstated. On efforts to overcome these problems, see Koopman, Wang and Wei (2012); Tang, Wang and Wang (2014); and Ma, Wang and Zhu (2015).

11   However, it is erroneous to understand these figures as net job creation. Some of the jobs created in one country to satisfy final demand in another country may displace the domestic labour in the latter. Competition from cheap labour forces abroad has often been identified as a cause of stagnant or even declining demand for low-skilled workers in the US. In this light, the frequently asked questions are: What would have happened if emerging countries had been less successful in their industrialisation? What would happen to manufacturing employment if US firms re-shored the tasks they had outsourced to developing countries? Such thought experiments are useful in their own right, but it is difficult to find evidence to determine answers because some of the tasks performed by human hands in developing countries could be substituted by the work of robots in developed countries.

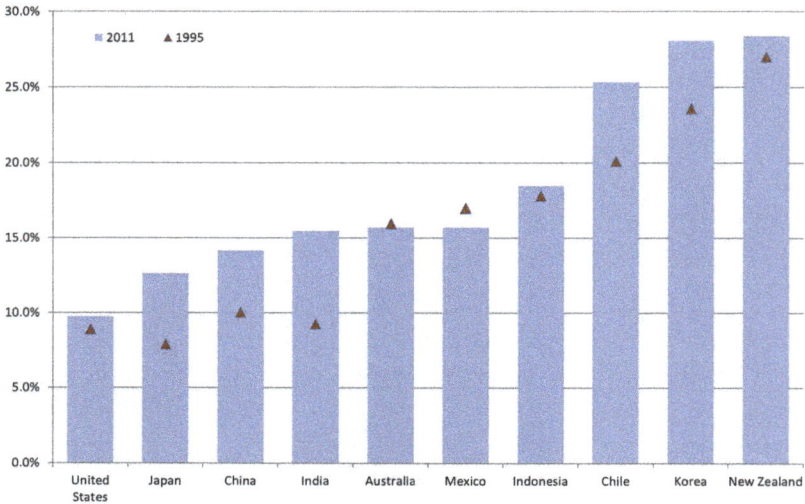

Figure 6.6: Share of domestic employment directly and indirectly created by exports, 1995–2011
Source: Based on OECD (2016).

The industrial origin of jobs created by exports varies from country to country (see Figure 6.7). Developed countries, shown on the left-hand side of Figure 6.7, specialise in services, particularly R&D or business services, in which they have so far maintained their comparative advantage. Conversely, countries rich in natural resources create more employment opportunities in their primary sectors. This is particularly the case in Indonesia, but also in the PRC and India. Australia, despite being a developed economy, has a strong primary-based export sector. It may seem surprising that Chile, the world's largest exporter of copper, does not reflect its gross export specialisation in the number of jobs related to its large mining sector. This apparent paradox reflects the fact that modern mining industries are highly capital-intensive and, thus, generate a relatively low amount of employment. By contrast, most of the jobs indirectly related to extracting operations are supporting activities, such as maintenance, energy supply and transportation, classified under the service sector rather than the mining sector per se.

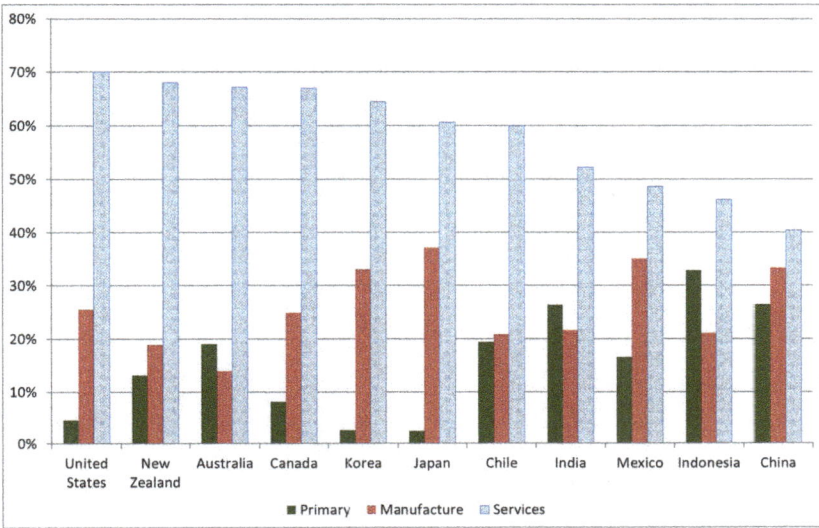

Figure 6.7: Sectoral share of employment directly and indirectly created by exports (2011)

Source: Based on OECD (2016).

When it comes to considering the performance of non-exporting sectors, some firms may indirectly participate in export efforts by providing intermediate products to lead exporting firms. This mode of GVC participation is particularly important for providers of services (which are traditionally considered as 'non-tradeable') or for small- and medium-sized firms that do not have the capacity to engage in global market operations. Compared with the previous import-substitution industrial policies that privileged the development of large-scale, full-set industries, the utilisation of more flexible networks of efficient, second-tier suppliers is one of the distinctive features of the new mode of industrialisation.[12]

In Figure 6.8, the shares of direct and indirect job creation by exports are relatively balanced across countries. Mexico and the PRC present contrasting pictures. Exports account for 10 per cent of direct employment

---

12   Indeed, the most distinctive feature of GVC-based industrial policies is simply the recognition that some inputs or tasks are better being imported or offshored than being sourced at home. The motto 'capture as much value added as you can' that underlines many GVC-related researches is a viable remedy for industrial failure and a waste of resources. GVC governance is not a zero-sum game like that of the mercantilist approach but a win–win strategy that opens up opportunities for many (although it should be recognised that there could be also losers from the process, whose situation needs to be addressed by public authorities).

in Mexico, while in PRC this figure is only half that, at about 5 per cent. This seems counterintuitive in the case of the PRC, especially when recalling the example of electronic products assembly, involving a very low level of integration with the domestic economy. However, it should be noted that the PRC's exports are also concentrated within the heavy industries (e.g. steel and metal products) that purchase bulk inputs from the rest of the economy (energy, raw material, transportation services and so on), thereby forming strong domestic linkages all over the country. Conversely, Mexico, owing to its geographical proximity to the US, exports more services than does the PRC.

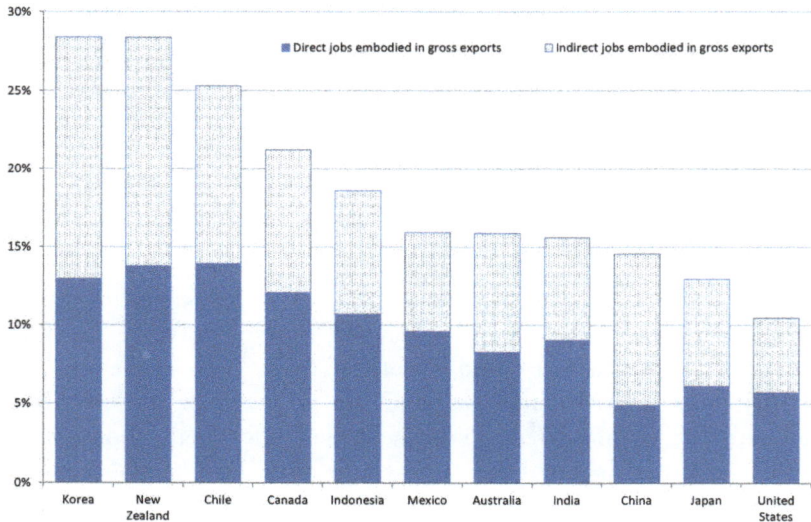

Figure 6.8: Direct vs indirect job creation by exports (2011)
Source: Based on OECD (2016).

Another important aspect of globalisation is the polarisation of income resulting from a switch in demand towards labour with higher qualifications. Despite a growing interest in this issue, it is not easy to test empirically whether offshoring activities create or destroy domestic jobs in different ways for different levels of qualification, particularly because most of the structural changes in labour markets are triggered by technological innovations or changes in consumer demand.

Figure 6.9 shows that the countries that have experienced a significant shift from low- and medium-skills towards higher qualifications are not mature economies, but mainly middle-income, developing economies.

Indeed, the US experienced the smallest structural change in labour demand. Curiously, the PRC, after the US, has been quite stable in the distribution of export-related demand for jobs by skill levels.[13]

Irrespective of development status, the export-related demand for low-skilled jobs has fallen in all countries, whereas demand for higher-skilled ones is on the rise. The most salient change is the profile of medium-skilled jobs in countries competing for relative advantages on the export markets. Three countries (Korea, Canada and the US) registered a drop in the relative demand for medium-skilled workers, whereas other countries had positive demand (although sometimes only on a small scale, such as the case of Japan). Mexico is prominent among the countries promoting medium-skilled tasks that are related to exports. A possible explanation for this is that Mexico, facing tough competition with the PRC for its traditional *maquiladora* (low-cost assembly) exports to the US, may have striven to achieve a significant industrial upgrading, shifting from producing low value-added products using cheap labour force to higher value-added products that employ more medium-skilled workers.

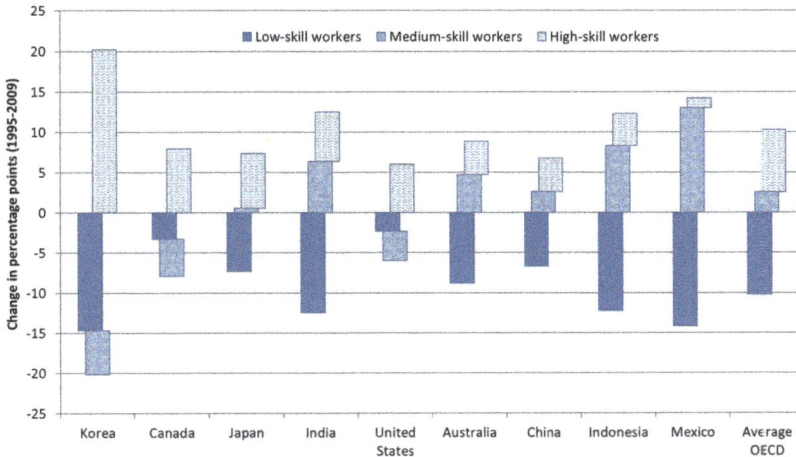

Figure 6.9: Structural change in export-related employment by skills (1995–2009)
Source: Based on OECD (2016).

---

13 Measuring the differential through standard deviation, the US has the lowest dispersion (5.2), followed by China (5.9), which was much lower than the OECD average of 9.2 or Korea's high mark of 18.1.

Conclusions

The concept of GVCs has reshaped our understanding of comparative advantage and international economics. As a result of progress in statistics as well as methodological advancement in input–output analyses and graph theories, we are now in a position to map and visualise international production networks by tracing supply–use relations of goods and services between industries and across borders.

This chapter has provided some evidence about the nature of GVCs in the Asia–Pacific region, with particular attention to cross-national transfers of value added and employment opportunities. We have provided a numeric description of the structure of the production networks, using the multi-country input–output table as a principal analytical tool.

Following a brief overview of prior empirical works, we examined the evolution of regional production networks in the Asia–US region. From 1985 to 2005, the inter-industrial network moved from a simple hub and spokes cluster, centred on Japan, to a much more complex structure following the emergence of the PRC that involved various countries as secondary pivots. We also identified the relative position of countries within the regional production networks, which revealed the role and specialisation of each economy in the region's vertical production system.

Comprehensive utilisation of the OECD–WTO TiVA database elucidated some key features about the configuration of GVCs. The cross-national transfer of value added was highly regionalised at the outset of economic globalisation, with North America, Europe and Asia operating as three value chain clusters. However, this gradually changed, as the US and the PRC continued to expand their production networks all over the world.

In this process, reorganisation of production systems based on cross-country comparative advantages took place, which had a significant effect on the relative demand for labour by skill levels. The demand for low-skilled jobs went down, whereas the demand for high-skilled tasks increased, and this was the case across both developed and developing Asian–Pacific economies. However, depending on the country's status of economic development, the demand for medium-skilled workers involved considerable variation.

The increasing complexity of production networks that we observe today requires a very careful treatment of the statistical assets that are available because analytical results become more and more sensitive to the ways that the relevant information is handled. While MCIOTs assist greatly in understanding production networks, the model remains at an early stage of development and considerable effort must be invested in upgrading the database to capture the full implications of economic globalisation for our societies.

References

Bernhardt, T. & Milberg, W. (2011). Economic and social upgrading in global value chains: Analysis of horticulture, apparel, tourism and mobile telephones. *Working Paper No. 6, Capturing the Gains Project.* Manchester, England: University of Manchester.

Borgatti, S. (2005). Centrality and network flow. *Social Networks, 27*(1), 55–71. doi.org/10.1016/j.socnet.2004.11.008

Chen, X., Cheng, L., Fung, K. C. & Lau, L. (2009). The estimation of domestic value-added and employment induced by exports: An application to Chinese exports to the United States. In Y. W. Cheung & K. Y. Wong (Eds.), *China and Asia: Economic and financial interactions*. London, England: Routledge.

Daudin, G., Monperrus-Veroni, P., Rifflart, C. & Schweisguth, D. (2006/ French version, 2009/English version). Who produces for whom in the world economy? *OFCE Document de travail* No. 2009-18. Paris: Observatoire Francais des Conjonctures Economiques.

Dedrick, J., Kraemer, K. & Linden, G. (2008). Who profits from innovation in global value chains? A study of the iPod and notebook PCs. *Industry Studies 2008*. Irvine, CA: Personal Computing Industry Center.

Dietzenbacher, E., Romero, I. & Bosma, N. S. (2005). Using average propagation lengths to identify production chains in the Andalusian Economy. *Estudios de Economia Aplicada, 23*, 405–22.

Escaith, H. (2014). Mapping global value chains and measuring trade in tasks. In B. Ferrarini & D. Hummels (Eds.), *Asia and global production networks: Implications for trade, incomes and economic vulnerability.* Cheltenham, UK: Asian Development Bank and Edwards Elgar Publishing. doi.org/10.4337/9781783472093.00015

Escaith, H. & Inomata, S. (2013). Geometry of global value chains in East Asia: The role of industrial networks and trade policies. In D. Elms & P. Low (Eds.), *Global value chains in a changing world.* Geneva, Switzerland: Fung Global Institute, Nanyang Technological University and World Trade Organization.

Farolle, T. (2016, August). Do global value chains create jobs? *IZA World of Labor,* 291. doi.org/10.15185/izawol.291

Gereffi, G., Humphrey, J. & Sturgeon, T. (2005). The governance of global value chains. *Review of International Political Economy, 12*(1), 78–104. doi.org/10.1080/09692290500049805

Hummels, D., Ishii, J. & Yi, K-M. (2001). The nature and growth of vertical specialization in world trade. *Journal of International Economics, 54*(1), 75–96. doi.org/10.1016/S0022-1996(00)00093-3

Inomata, S. (2008). Average propagation lengths: A new concept of the 'distance' between industries, with an application to the Asia–Pacific Region. *Sangyo-Renkan, 16*(1) (in Japanese).

Inomata, S. (2017). Analytical frameworks for global value chains: An overview. In *World Bank, Global Value Chain Development Report 2017* (Chapter 1). Washington, DC: The World Bank Group.

Johnson, R. C. & Noguera, G. (2012). Accounting for intermediate production sharing and trade in value added. *Journal of International Economics, 86,* 224–36. doi.org/10.1016/j.jinteco.2011.10.003

Koopman, R. B., Wang, Z. & Wei, S. J. (2012). Estimating domestic content in exports when processing trade is pervasive. *Journal of Development Economics, 99*(1), 178–89. doi.org/10.1016/j.jdeveco.2011.12.004

Ma, H., Wang, Z. & Zhu, K. (2015). Domestic content in China's exports and its distribution by firm ownership. *Journal of Comparative Economics, 43,* 3–18.

Miroudot, S. and Nordstrom, H. (2015). Made in the world? *Robert Schuman Centre for Advanced Studies Research Paper* No. RSCAS 2015/60. Florence, Italy: European University Institute.

Organisation for Economic Co-operation and Development (OECD). (2016, June). Global value chains and trade in value added: An initial assessment of the impact on jobs and productivity. *OECD Paper TAD/TC/WP (2015)10/FINAL.* Paris, France: OECD.

Sturgeon, T. J., Nielsen, P. B., Linden, G., Gereffi, G. & Brown, C. (2013). Direct measurement of global value chains: Collecting product- and firm-level statistics on value added and business function outsourcing and offshoring. In A. Mattoo, Z. Wang & S-J. Wei (Eds.), *Trade in value added: Developing new measures of cross-border trade* (pp. 289–320). Washington, DC: The World Bank.

Tang, H., Wang, F. & Wang, Z. (2014). The domestic segment of global supply chains in China under state capitalism. *Working Paper No. 186.* Dallas, Texas: Federal Reserve Bank of Dallas Globalization and Monetary Policy Institute.

Appendix A: Technical notes

Technical Note 6.1: Calculation of APL

The conventional input–output approach to supply chains analyses generally focuses on measuring interconnectedness, or the strength of linkages among industries, based on the traditional demand-pull or cost-push impact models. The increasing complexity of production systems requires measurement, not just of the strength, but also of the 'length' of linkages for mapping production networks.

The length dimension of production linkages was first addressed by the input–output model of APL developed by Dietzenbacher, Romero and Bosma (2005). The APL represents the average number of production stages lining up in every branch of production networks. Therefore, it effectively measures an industry's level of fragmentation.

Suppose that there is an n-sector economy with a production structure defined by the input coefficient matrix A, as shown in Figure A6.1a. Input coefficients a_{ij} are calculated from an input–output table by dividing input values of goods and services used in each industry by the industry's corresponding total output, that is, $a_{ij} = z_{ij}/X_j$, where z_{ij} is the value of good/service i purchased for the production of industry j, and X_j is the total output of industry j. Then, the coefficients represent the direct requirement of inputs for producing just one unit of output of industry j.

$$A = \begin{bmatrix} a_{11} & a_{12} & a_{13} & \cdots & a_{1n} \\ a_{21} & a_{22} & a_{23} & \cdots & a_{2n} \\ a_{31} & a_{32} & a_{33} & \cdots & a_{3n} \\ \vdots & \vdots & \vdots & \ddots & \vdots \\ a_{n1} & a_{n2} & a_{n3} & \cdots & a_{nn} \end{bmatrix}$$

Figure A6.1a: An input coefficient matrix

One-step path

$$Ind3 \xrightarrow{a_{13}} Ind1$$

Two-step path

$$Ind3 \xrightarrow{a_{23}} Ind2 \xrightarrow{a_{12}} Ind1$$
$$Ind3 \xrightarrow{a_{33}} Ind3 \xrightarrow{a_{13}} Ind1$$
$$\vdots \qquad\qquad \vdots \qquad\qquad \vdots$$

and   so on

Figure A6.1b: Impact delivery paths

The vertical sequence of production propagation can be understood using Figure A6.1b, described as follows. Let us consider the effect of extra demand for 100 units in sector 3 upon the output of sector 1. The simplest form of all is given by the direct linkage [3→1], which is calculated as a product of multiplying 100 units by input coefficient a_{13}. This is because a_{13}, by definition of an input coefficient, represents the immediate amount of good 1 required for producing just one unit of good 3. Alternatively, there is a two-step path going through another industry, say, [3→2→1]. This is derived by two-stage multiplication, that is, 100 units by a_{23}, and then by a_{12}. Alternatively, there could be a two-step path going through the same sector, such as [3→3→1] or [3→1→1], which would be derived respectively as [100 x a_{33} x a_{13}] or [100 x a_{13} x a_{11}] (see Figure A6.1b).

The exercise reveals that the impact of any two-step path, whatever the sequence of sectors, can be given by reinjecting a set of direct impacts back into the input coefficient matrix, that is, A^1 x $A = A^2$. Similarly, the impact of three-step paths is given by A^2 x $A = A^3$, that of four-step paths by A^3 x

$A = A^4$ and so on, which is evident from $[A^2]_{ij} = \Sigma_k a_{ik} a_{kj}$, $[A^3]_{ij} = \Sigma_k \Sigma_h a_{iz} a_{kh} a_{hj}$, and so on. The amount of impacts shown in each layer of A^ks (k = 1, 2, 3,…,) are a result of the initial demand injection passing through all k-step paths. They capture the effect of every direct and indirect linkage that undergoes exactly the k-steps of the production process with k segments of production stages.

Meanwhile, it is mathematically known that a Leontief inverse matrix L, which shows the total amount of goods and services required for the production of one unit of output, can be expanded as an arithmetic series, that is, $L = (I - A)^{-1} = I + A + A^2 + A^3 + A^4 + …$, where I is an identity matrix (with one in diagonal elements and zero elsewhere). From the above, it is immediately clear that the equation represents the decomposition of the total impact on output into its constituent impact layers according to the number of production stages involved. I is an initial demand injection, and the following A^ks are regarded as progressive impacts of the initial demand when production chains are sliced at the kth stage of the production process.

With this preliminary understanding, APL is defined as:

$$v_{ij} = 1 * a_{ij}/(l_{ij} - \delta_{ij}) + 2 * [A^2]_{ij}/(l_{ij} - \delta_{ij}) + 3 * [A^3]_{ij}/(l_{ij} - \delta_{ij}) + \cdots$$

$$= \sum_{k-1}^{\infty} k \left[[A^k]_{jj} \Big/ \sum_{k-1}^{\infty} [A^k]_{jj} \right]$$

where A is an input coefficient matrix, a_{ij} is its element, l_{ij} is a Leontief inverse coefficient, δ_{ij} is a Kronecker delta, which is δ_{ij} = 1 if $i=j$ and δ_{ij} = 0 otherwise, and k is the number of production stages along the path. We also define that v_{ij} = 0 when $(l_{ij} - \delta_{ij})$ = 0.

The first term on the right-hand side of the upper equation shows that the impact delivered through one-step paths (k = 1), that is, the direct impact, amounts to an $a_{ij} / (l_{ij} - \delta_{ij})$ share of the total impact given by the Leontief inverse coefficient (less unity for diagonal elements because of δ_{ij}).

Similarly, two-step paths (k = 2) contribute an $[A^2]_{ij} / (l_{ij} - \delta_{ij})$ share, and three-step paths (k = 3) an $[A^3]_{ij} / (l_{ij} - \delta_{ij})$ share of the total impact. This is evident from $L = I + A + A^2 + A^3 + …$, which is rearranged as $L - I = A + A^2 + A^3 + …$, and hence $(L - I)_{ij} = A_{ij} + [A^2]_{ij} + [A^3]_{ij} + …$

That is, APL is formulated as a weighted average of the number of the production stages that an impact from industry j goes through until it ultimately reaches industry i, using the share of impact at each stage as a weight. It represents the average number of production stages lining up in every branch of all the production chains or, in short, an industry's level of fragmentation.

Technical Note 6.2: Calculation of TiVA

A value-added export from country r to country s is calculated as:

$$TiVArs = \mathbf{v}^r \cdot \mathbf{L} \cdot \mathbf{f}^{\cdot s} \qquad (r \neq s)$$

where $\mathbf{v}^r$ is a value-added rate vector (row) of country r, $\mathbf{L}$ is an international Leontief inverse matrix and $\mathbf{f}^{\cdot s}$ is a final demand vector (column) of country s. $\mathbf{L} \mathbf{f}^{\cdot s}$ on the right-hand side of the equation gives the amount of each country's sectoral output induced, directly and indirectly, by the final demand of country s (both for domestic and imported products). As a value-added rate represents the amount of value added generated by one unit of production, multiplying country r's rate by the amount of the induced output, as given above, produces the value added of country r generated by the final demand of country s, which is understood as the value-added export from country r to country s.

In the two-country, two-product setup, the value-added export from country r to country s will be:

$$TiVA^{rs} = \begin{bmatrix} v_1^r & v_2^r & 0 & 0 \end{bmatrix} \begin{bmatrix} l_{11}^{rr} & l_{12}^{rr} & l_{11}^{rs} & l_{12}^{rs} \\ l_{21}^{rr} & l_{22}^{rr} & l_{21}^{rs} & l_{22}^{rs} \\ l_{11}^{sr} & l_{12}^{sr} & l_{11}^{ss} & l_{12}^{ss} \\ l_{21}^{sr} & l_{22}^{sr} & l_{21}^{ss} & l_{22}^{ss} \end{bmatrix} \begin{bmatrix} f_1^{rs} \\ f_2^{rs} \\ f_1^{ss} \\ f_2^{ss} \end{bmatrix}$$

and the value-added export from country s to country r is given as:

$$TiVA^{sr} = \begin{bmatrix} 0 & 0 & v_1^s & v_2^s \end{bmatrix} \begin{bmatrix} l_{11}^{rr} & l_{12}^{rr} & l_{11}^{rs} & l_{12}^{rs} \\ l_{21}^{rr} & l_{22}^{rr} & l_{21}^{rs} & l_{22}^{rs} \\ l_{11}^{sr} & l_{12}^{sr} & l_{11}^{ss} & l_{12}^{ss} \\ l_{21}^{sr} & l_{22}^{sr} & l_{21}^{ss} & l_{22}^{ss} \end{bmatrix} \begin{bmatrix} f_1^{rr} \\ f_2^{rr} \\ f_1^{sr} \\ f_2^{sr} \end{bmatrix}$$

Technical Note 6.3: Calculation of employment content of trade

The method introduced above for the measurement of TiVA can be applied to the calculation of the employment content of trade by simply swapping the value-added rate vector $\boldsymbol{v}^r$ for the employment rate vector $\boldsymbol{w}^r$, which represents the number of workers required to produce one unit of output. That is:

$$TiEmprs = \boldsymbol{w}^r \cdot \boldsymbol{L} \cdot \boldsymbol{f}^s \qquad (r \neq s)$$

7

The ASEAN Economic Community and the East Asian agenda[1]

Somkiat Tangkitvanich and Saowaruj Rattanakhamfu

The gap in East Asian integration

Economic integration through international trade and foreign direct investment (FDI) brings about economic prosperity by enabling the greater division of labour, which, in turn, facilitates more efficient resource allocation and improves productivity through competition.

The level of economic integration in East Asia is quite high—nearly half (47.2 per cent) of all the trade and over half (53.9 per cent) of all outward FDI in East Asia is intra-regional (see Figure 7.1). The two sub-regions of East Asia, North-East Asia and South-East Asia, are closely linked to each other through trade and direct investment. In fact, the linkages between the two sub-regions are stronger than those within the sub-regions.

---

1   A draft version of this paper was presented at the 38th PAFTAD Conference in November 2016 and revised in January 2017. Some details may have changed due to events between the time of writing and the time of publication.

(a) Trade   (b) Outward FDI

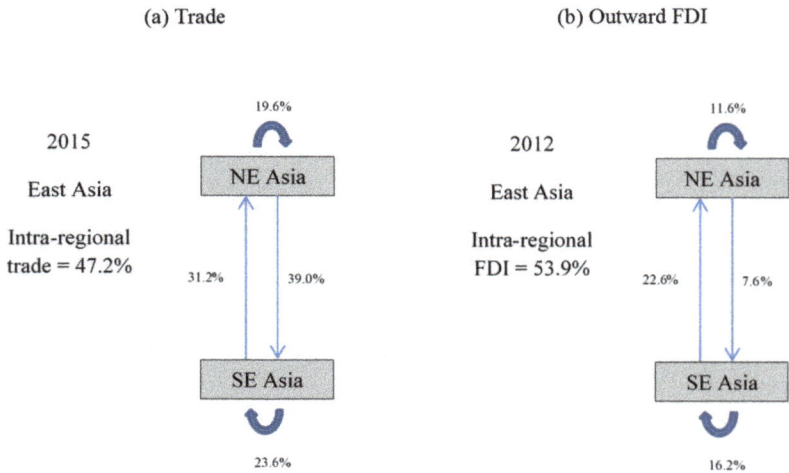

Figure 7.1: Intra-regional trade and foreign direct investment in East Asia (unit: per cent of total)

Source: Authors. Data from the Asian Development Bank's Asia Regional Integration Center.

From a broader perspective, the level of intra-regional trade in East Asia (as a share of total regional trade) is lower than that of the EU but higher than that of North America (the US and Canada). Adjusted for the different trade volumes of each region, the intra-regional trade intensity index for East Asia was 1.66 in 2015, lower than those for the EU (1.98) and North America (1.78).[2] This reflects two important facts.

First, East Asia not only trades intra-regionally but also maintains strong linkages with the rest of the world. Although the intra-regional trade share in East Asia increased slightly during 1995–2015 from 45.0 to 47.2 per cent, the region maintains strong trade linkages with the outside world via a well-known triangular trade structure (see Figure 7.2); production occurs within the region but final goods are then exported out of the region.

---

2   The intra-regional trade intensity index is the ratio of the intra-regional trade share to the share of world trade with the region, calculated using trade data. It is computed as $(T_{ii}/T_i)/(T_j/T_w)$, where T_{ii} is exports of region i to region i plus imports of region i from region i, T_i is total exports of region i to the world plus total imports of region i from the world, T_j is total exports of region j to the world plus total imports of region j from the world and T_w is total world exports plus imports. The index determines whether trade within the region is greater or smaller than should be expected on the basis of the region's importance in world trade. An index of more than one indicates that trade flow within the region is larger than expected, given the importance of the region in world trade (for more details, refer to aric.adb.org/integrationindicators/technotes).

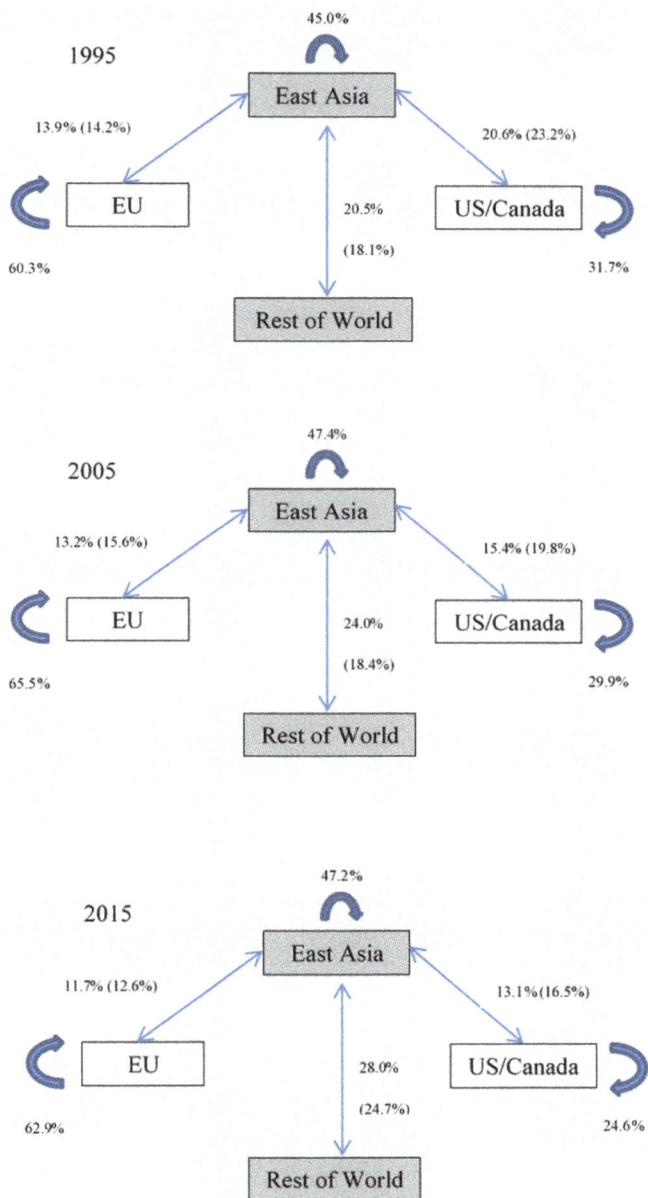

Figure 7.2: Shares of intra-regional trade in East Asia and inter-regional trade linkages between East Asia and the world

Note: The numbers in parentheses are trade shares from the perspectives of East Asia's trading partners.

Source: Authors. Data from the Asian Development Bank's Asia Regional Integration Center.

Second, if East Asia reduces trade barriers within the region, it will provide more room for intra-regional trade expansion. Without further progress on liberalisation through the World Trade Organization, the only option to expand trade in the region is through unilateral, bilateral or regional action with other countries in the region. East Asia is still in the early stages of forming free trade agreements (FTAs); therefore, there is great potential for intra-regional trade expansion.

North-East Asia still has only one FTA, the China – South Korea FTA. China became South Korea's largest trading partner in 2004, but the FTA only came into effect in late 2015 and it is still viewed as rather shallow (Schott & Jung, 2015). The negotiations for a trilateral FTA between China, Japan and South Korea, launched in 2012, have made minimal progress because of political tensions between Japan and the other two countries.

South-East Asia appears to have made more progress on FTAs, including through the Association of Southeast Asian Nations (ASEAN) Free Trade Area (AFTA), which was implemented in 1993, and the AEC, which was officially launched in late 2015. However, the AEC implementation is behind schedule, as discussed in the next section.

A mega-FTA negotiation launched in 2013 under the name of the Regional Comprehensive Economic Partnership (RCEP) involves an effort to integrate North-East Asia, South-East Asia and three other major trading partners. RCEP negotiations were scheduled to be finalised by 2016 but the negotiation progress is lagging far behind schedule. Meanwhile, the Trans-Pacific Partnership (TPP), which encompasses 12 countries in East Asia and the Pacific, was concluded in late 2015. However, it is unlikely to come into effect under Donald Trump's Presidency in the US.

The delay in formally integrating East Asia through FTAs means that a large portion of intra-regional trade occurs outside the preferential treatment and protection offered by FTAs, exposing it to existing barriers and possible future protectionism. Table 7.1 provides a rough estimate of the ratio of intra-regional trade uncovered by any FTAs for the ASEAN+3 and the ASEAN+6 regions. The estimation, shown in column (3), is obtained by subtracting the ratio of intra-regional trade covered by FTAs, proxied by the ratio of trade between existing FTA partners in column (2), from the ratio of intra-regional trade in column (1).

Table 7.1: Intra-regional trade with free trade agreement partners and non-partners to total trade in 2015

Region/ country	Intra-regional trade to total trade (1)	Intra-regional trade with FTA partners to total trade (2)	Intra-regional trade with non-FTA partners to total trade (3) = (1)–(2)	Countries in the region that are not FTA partners
ASEAN+3	47.2%			
ASEAN	54.8%	54.8%	0.0%	None
China	26.3%	19.1%	7.2%	Japan
Japan	41.9%	15.2%	26.7%	China/Korea
Korea	43.7%	36.3%	7.4%	Japan
ASEAN+6	48.7%			
ASEAN	60.3%	60.3%	0.0%	None
Australia	64.4%	61.5%	2.9%	India
China	31.1%	21.8%	9.3%	Japan/India
India	27.7%	15.0%	12.7%	China/Australia/ New Zealand
Japan	47.0%	19.9%	27.1%	China/Korea/ New Zealand
Korea	48.5%	41.1%	7.40%	Japan
New Zealand	56.4%	30.4%	26.0%	India/Japan

Source: Authors' calculations based on data from the Asian Development Bank's Asia Regional Integration Center.

The table shows that a significant portion of intra-regional trade is not covered by trade agreements that protect against current and possible future protectionism. This is especially true for Japan, which has the highest ratios of intra-regional trade uncovered by any FTAs in both the ASEAN+3 and the ASEAN+6 groups, with ratios of 26.7 and 27.1 per cent, respectively. For the ASEAN+6 group, India has the second highest ratio of intra-regional trade uncovered by any FTAs at 12.7 per cent, as well as the lowest ratio of intra-regional trade at 27.7 per cent. As ASEAN has formed FTAs with all trading partners in ASEAN+3 and ASEAN+6, all of its intra-regional trade is covered by at least one FTA.

It should be noted that Table 7.1 overestimates the ratio of intra-regional trade protected by FTAs in many ways. Most importantly, most FTAs have exempted certain products from tariff reductions through lists of sensitive products that are subject to later liberalisation or possible trade remedies. Even products that are subject to tariff reductions can still face costly rules of origin (ROOs) and discriminatory non-tariff measures (NTMs). Nevertheless, Table 7.1 provides a useful snapshot of the current state of trade liberalisation in East Asia. It confirms that East Asia has a good deal of room for intra-regional trade expansion through tighter economic integration.

The objectives of this chapter are threefold. First, the chapter aims to assess the progress of regional integration in East Asia, with a focus on ASEAN. Second, it aims to analyse the prospects of deepening regional integration through ASEAN, RCEP and the TPP, and to propose some recommendations on further regional integration. Finally, the chapter draws some policy implications for Thailand, many of which should be useful to other ASEAN countries.

ASEAN economic integration: The state of play

ASEAN announced the official launch of the AEC in late 2015 and, in 2017, it celebrated its 50th anniversary. Although ASEAN has realised some political achievements during the past five decades, its economic integration project remains very much a work in progress, and it is expected to remain so for many years, or even decades, to come. The term 'Community' (the 'C' in AEC) is a misleading description of ASEAN's economic integration goals. The term connotes the idea of supranationality, which has never been on the negotiation agenda among ASEAN members, except in very limited dimensions (Kausikan, 2016).

The ASEAN Secretariat claims that the implementation of the AEC Blueprint 2015—the AEC's foundational strategic document—has been substantively achieved in many areas, including in eliminating tariffs, facilitating trade, advancing the services liberalisation agenda, liberalising and facilitating investment and facilitating skilled labour mobility (ASEAN Secretariat, 2015a). As a result, the AEC scorecard (ASEAN Secretariat, 2015b) claimed a high reported completion rate (see Figure 7. 3). However, these claims are far from convincing. Some argue that the uncompleted issues are by far the more important ones. In addition, the AEC scorecard measures the implementation of milestones and priority actions identified in the AEC Blueprint 2015. In other words, it measures the means, rather than the ends, of the AEC (Menon & Melendez, 2015).

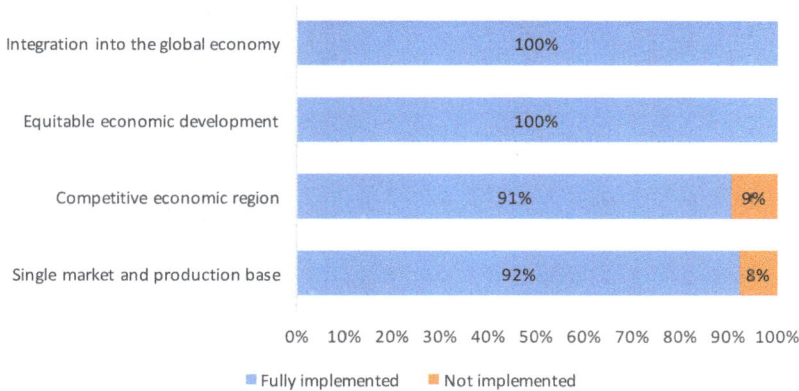

Figure 7.3: ASEAN Economic Community (AEC) scorecard measures, fully implemented ASEAN-wide and high-priority measures, by AEC Pillar, 2008–2015: Number of measures (as of 31 October 2015)
Source: ASEAN Secretariat (2015b).

In fact, levels of integration vary greatly by sector (see McKinsey 2014). The only clear success that ASEAN can claim is the reduction of tariffs among member countries. Since the implementation of the Common Effective Preferential Tariff (CEPT) agreement as part of the AFTA in the 1990s, tariff rates on about 99 per cent of AFTA countries' product items have been reduced to zero. The new ASEAN members—Cambodia, Laos, Myanmar and Vietnam (CLMV)—have reduced their tariffs to the range 0–5 per cent for 93 per cent of their product items. As a result, average CEPT tariff rates in ASEAN countries now stand at 0.04 per cent for the original ASEAN members (ASEAN–6, i.e. Indonesia, Malaysia, the Philippines, Singapore, Thailand and Brunei) and 1.33 per cent for CLMV (see Figure 7.4).

The ROOs under ASEAN are relatively simple and transparent, either requiring 40 per cent regional value added or the 'change of tariff heading' method. The latter involves examining the intermediate goods that make up a final product, and noting whether changes in tariff classification have occurred in the transformation. In many cases, businesses have options to use either rule to qualify for preferential treatment under AFTA. According to Cadot and Ing (2016), the simple average ad valorem equivalent of ASEAN's ROOs is estimated to be 3.4 per cent across all sectors and the trade-weighted average is estimated to be 2.1 per cent. Thus, the ASEAN ROOs do not appear to be overly restrictive. However, the restrictiveness differs from sector to sector. In particular, ASEAN ROOs are less restrictive in sectors such as electronics and capital equipment, but more restrictive in sectors such as leather products, textiles and apparel, footwear, and automobiles.

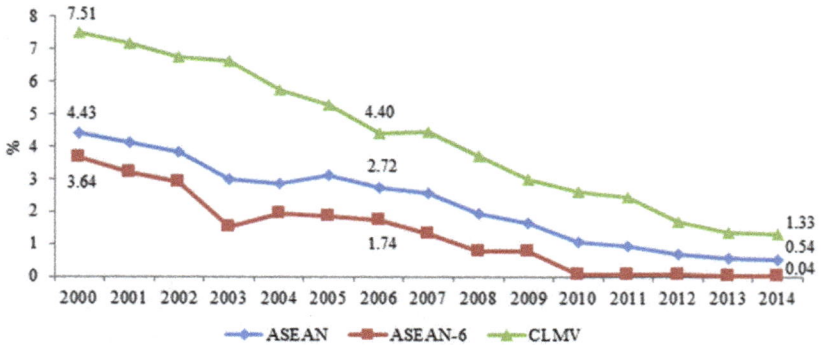

Figure 7.4: Average Common Effective Preferential Tariff rates in ASEAN countries, 2000–14
Source: Compiled using data from OECD (2016).

The free flow of goods among ASEAN member countries continues to be hindered by the prevalent use of NTMs. Although the average tariff rates of ASEAN countries decreased from 8.9 per cent in 2000 to 4.5 per cent in 2015, the number of NTMs increased from 1,634 to 5,975 over the same period (Ing, de Cordoba & Cadot, 2016). These NTMs may have adverse consequences for the sourcing decisions of firms, the structure of trade and the structure of related industries. In addition, the increase in NTMs may explain the slow rise of intra-ASEAN trade (Cadot & Ing, 2016). The extent and nature of NTM usage differs across sectors and ASEAN countries (Thailand Development Research Institute [TDRI], 2013; Cadot & Ing, 2016).

TDRI (2013) found large variations in the use of NTMs among ASEAN countries. For example, Singapore applies fewer NTMs than other ASEAN countries. The measures that it does apply are reasonably transparent and non-discriminatory, aiming primarily to protect Singapore's consumers and the environment. Conversely, countries such as Indonesia and Malaysia that have active industrial policies apply more NTMs. Some NTMs are marked 'red' by the Coordinating Committee on ASEAN Trade in Goods Agreement (CCA), indicating that they are 'core NTMs', also known as non-tariff barriers (NTBs). These include non-automatic licensing, quantitative restrictions, prohibitions, enterprise-specific restrictions, single channels for imports and foreign exchange market restrictions. For example, car assemblers in Thailand have long complained about Malaysia's import licensing system that allows only domestic car producers to import cars into the country, thus discriminating against foreign automakers. A study by the Economic Research Institute for ASEAN and East Asia (ERIA, 2012) confirmed that Indonesia and Malaysia have the highest incidence of NTBs, whereas Thailand and the Philippines have the least (see Figure 7.5).

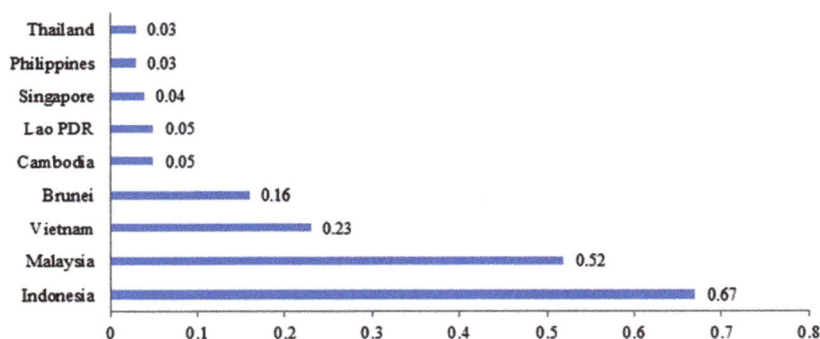

Figure 7.5: Core non-tariff measures restrictiveness index in ASEAN, 2009
Note: Higher numbers indicate greater restrictions.
Source: Compiled using data from ERIA (2012).

Although minimising NTBs is an action target in the AEC Blueprint, ASEAN has relied on a voluntary approach to reduce them, with very limited success. A study by TDRI (2013) examined its lack of success. First, information on existing NTMs is not fully available or easily accessible. This is because the use of NTMs is scattered among many agencies and often embedded in executive decrees, regulations or announcements that are available only in local languages. More importantly, under the voluntary approach, member countries may have incentives to under-report the NTBs that they are using. Second, there is no effective monitoring system to keep track of changes in NTMs among member countries. Third, ASEAN has no power to compel its members to revise NTMs that are found to be non-transparent or to eliminate the measures identified as NTBs.

High trade costs associated with moving goods and services across borders are another factor hindering intra-regional trade. Intal (2015a) reviewed the state of trade facilitation initiatives in ASEAN countries.

The review focuses on customs modernisation, the national 'single window' system (which allows trading parties to lodge all information required by regulators at a single national entry point) and national trade repositories (online references with comprehensive information on each country's tariffs and NTMs). He found that, although there has been significant progress in trade facilitation in the region in recent years, there remains a huge gap among member countries. The gap seems to be correlated with the overall development gap. The main challenges in trade facilitation in ASEAN include inadequacy of funds, availability of technical talent, the technical infrastructure of the system and coordination issues among related agencies.

Another study by the World Economic Forum (2013) found that most ASEAN members, with the exception of Singapore, perform poorly in terms of efficiency and transparency of border administration. Thus, the ASEAN Single Window (ASW) has been established to link national customs and trade regimes. However, only the original ASEAN members and Vietnam are ASW-ready.

Further, the level of investment liberalisation in ASEAN is different across countries and sectors. Intal (2015b) measured the level of foreign investment liberalisation under the ASEAN Comprehensive Investment Agreement. He used a weighted average of the foreign equity liberalisation rate and the liberalisation rate of other investment restrictions—namely, restrictions on national treatment and other market access restrictions. He found that the level of investment liberalisation was high in manufacturing, with the exceptions of Indonesia and Vietnam. In contrast, the level of liberalisation in the agriculture and mining sectors varied greatly across ASEAN, with some countries being very open and allowing foreign investment participation and others being more restrictive.

ASEAN has been negotiating service liberalisation since the creation of the ASEAN Framework Agreement on Services (AFAS) in 1996. The AEC Blueprint has established clear liberalisation targets to substantially remove all restrictions on trade in services for four priority service sectors: air transport, e-ASEAN (information and communication technologies), health care and tourism—the latter by 2010 and all other sectors by 2015. Milestones for progressive liberalisation are marked by a gradual increase in ASEAN equity participation in various service sectors.

Table 7.2: Foreign equity participation in services sectors (per cent)

Sector/Sub-sector	Target 2015	AFAS ninth package commitments									
		Thailand	Malaysia	Singapore	Philippines	Indonesia	Brunei	Cambodia	Laos	Myanmar	Vietnam
e-ASEAN											
Mobile phone services	≥70	49	70	73.99	40	49	100	100	100 (F)	100	<65 (NF) <49 (F)
Online data and database services	≥70	49	100	100	100	51	100	100	100 (F)	100	<65 (NF) <49 (F)
Consultancy services on computer hardware installation	≥70	49	100	100	100	49	100	100	100 (F)	100	100
Health care	≥70										
Hospital services	≥70	49	70	100	>50	70 (East) 51 (Medan/ Surabaya)	100	100	100	70	100
Medical services	≥70	49	100	100		70 51 (Makassar/ Manado)	100	100	100 (no clinics)	70	100
Dental services	≥70	49	70	100		70 51 (Makassar/ Manado)	100	100	100 (no clinics)	70	100
Tourism	≥70										
Hotel lodging services	≥70	49	70	100	100	100 (East) 70 (Others)	70	100	100	100	100
Catering services	≥70	49	70	100	100	70 (East)	70	100	100	100	100
Tour agent services	≥70	49	70	100	70	<49	70	51	70	100	<100
Construction	≥70	49	51	100	40	<55	55	100	100	100	100

Note: F = facility; NF = non-facility; AFAS = ASEAN Framework Agreement on Services.

Source: Authors.

However, some ASEAN countries, especially Thailand, the Philippines and Indonesia, were not able to meet these targets by the 2015 deadline (see Table 7.2). The World Bank (2011) found that service trade restrictions were higher in more developed countries, such as the Philippines, Indonesia and Thailand, and lower in less developed countries, such as Cambodia and Vietnam (see Figure 7.6). The lower restrictiveness in the latter group may be the result of an underdeveloped regulatory regime in these countries (World Bank, 2013) or a lack of domestic providers with vested interests. The resistance of more developed ASEAN countries to service liberalisation is clearly shown in Indonesia and Thailand's specific commitments under the latest (2015) ninth package of commitments (see Table 7.3). Table 7.3 clearly indicates that, although more service sub-sectors are nominated for liberalisation in the ninth package, many commitments are inconsequential or worthless.

Table 7.3: Some commitments of Indonesia and Thailand under the AFAS ninth package

Indonesia's commitments
CPC 832 Other rental services, limited to video tape rental services CPC 873 Investigation and security, limited to shoplifting investigation services CPC96321 Museum services limited to museums of jewellery CPC 71224 Passenger transportation by man or animal-drawn vehicles CPC 71236 Freight transportation by man or animal-drawn vehicles
Thailand's commitments
CPC 64340 Bicycle courier service for food delivery CPC 93321 Day care services for children with disabilities CPC 66300 Transport service via space, including space passenger transportation service (excluding launching and placing of satellites in space) Railway car cleaning service

Note: AFAS = ASEAN Framework Agreement on Services; CPC = Central Product Classification.

Source: Authors. Data from countries' specific commitments under AFAS ninth package.

Narjoko (2015) examined the progress of liberalisation in the AFAS by measuring changes in the rate of liberalisation of the AFAS commitments between the seventh package, concluded in 2009, and eighth package, concluded in 2010. He found a marginal improvement only in the depth of services liberalisation rate between the two packages, although there were significant increases in the number of sub-sectors covered in the eighth package. Analysing the changing liberalisation rates across the member states, he found that the offers became more liberal only in Brunei Darussalam, Cambodia, Malaysia and Singapore, whereas decreases were recorded for the other member states.

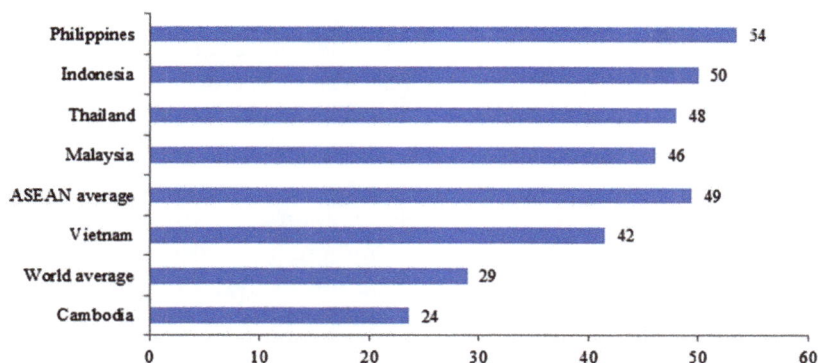

Figure 7.6: Overall services trade restrictiveness index in ASEAN, 2008–11
Note: A higher number indicates greater restrictions.
Source: Compiled using data from World Bank (2011).

Progress in trade liberalisation efforts has been extremely slow over the last 20 years. Although concrete quantitative liberalisation goals have been set, the AEC Blueprint allows for flexibility in attaining such goals, as follows (Nikomborirak, 2013):

- If a member country is not able to meet the parameters of commitments set in the previous round, it may catch up in the next round.
- If a member country is not able to make commitments on liberalising agreed sub-sectors, it is permitted to substitute sub-sectors outside the list of agreed sub-sectors.
- Liberalisation through the 'ASEAN minus X' formula is permitted; under this rule, if a member country cannot meet the liberalisation target, the remaining member countries may proceed to implement the liberalisation measure among themselves.

According to Nikomborirak (2013), these flexibility provisions are inconsistent with ASEAN's liberalisation goals. First, the AEC Blueprint stipulates that there shall be no 'backloading' of commitments; however, allowing countries to catch up on commitments in following rounds would undoubtedly lead to such a problem. Second, allowing a member country to substitute priority service sub-sectors scheduled for early liberalisation with other non-priority sub-sectors would render the specification of priority sectors meaningless. Finally, the option of liberalisation through the 'ASEAN minus X' formula dilutes what are meant to binding commitments to 'best effort' commitments.

Moreover, service liberalisation under ASEAN contains no commitment to address behind-the-border issues, such as interconnection for telecom services or access to ATMs for banking, which are crucial to the creation of effectively competitive markets. The difference in laws and regulations among member countries is also problematic. As a result, service liberalisation under ASEAN in its current form would not create a single service market. For example, data localisation regulation in Indonesia requires 'electronic system operators for public service', a broad and undefined group of companies, to establish data and disaster recovery centres in Indonesia for the purpose of law enforcement and data protection. Vietnam requires that all organisations establishing websites or social networks establish at least one server inside the country that contains the entire history of information posted and shared (Bauer, Makiyama, van der Marel & Verschelde, 2014). Nazir Razak, the chairman of Malaysia's CIMB Group Holdings and a co-chairman of the ASEAN Business Club, has commented that CIMB cannot establish a centralised back office operation because of the differences in national laws, despite having a significant presence in Malaysia, Indonesia, Thailand and Singapore (Tan, 2016).

ASEAN's aim is to achieve financial and capital market integration through financial services liberalisation, capital account liberalisation and capital market development. However, even banking integration, the area making the most progress, has advanced very slowly so far (Asian Development Bank, 2013; Almekinders, Fukuda, Mourmouras, Zhou & Zhou, 2015). This is partly because the level of financial development varies greatly among ASEAN countries. Financial integration in ASEAN will be a long-term project, given the flexibilities permitted, such as the 'ASEAN minus X' formula, and the ability for ASEAN members to set their own conditions and timelines for liberalisation. Nevertheless, ASEAN has been successful in setting up a macro-economic surveillance mechanism through the ASEAN+3 Macroeconomic Research Office and a regional financial safety net through the Chiang Mai Initiative Multilateralization (ERIA, 2012).

In promoting cross-border movement of labour, ASEAN has also achieved very little. From an economic development perspective, the opening up of unskilled labour markets through FTAs would be a beneficial policy option, given the relative abundance of unskilled labour in many ASEAN countries. However, the AEC Blueprint attempts to facilitate only the mobility of skilled professionals, currently comprising just eight professions—engineers, physicians, dentists, nurses, architects, surveyors, accountants and tourism professionals. This excludes, among others, senior staff at regional banks, telecom operators and other service providers. It shows that service liberalisation under the AEC Blueprint 2015 Mode 3 (services delivered through commercial presence) and Mode 4 (services delivered through the presence of a natural person) are not linked.

To facilitate the movement of the aforementioned professionals, ASEAN has adopted an approach involving mutual recognition arrangements (MRAs). However, the arrangement is considered to represent, at most, partial recognition, as noted by the Organisation for Economic Co-operation and Development (OECD, 2016). Under the MRA scheme, ASEAN professionals intending to work in other member countries are required to comply with the domestic regulations of host countries under the same pre-existing conditions. In the case of Thailand, for example, the requirements imposed on ASEAN professionals are the same as those imposed on professionals from the non-ASEAN countries. For instance, a requirement to pass an examination conducted in the Thai language is applied in medical professions to block the professional mobility of foreign practitioners. Many ASEAN countries impose similar requirements.

Moreover, for professional services, such as engineering and architectural services, policies applied in some countries are far more liberal than the MRA regime. As a result, even if there are signed MRA agreements, professionals have little incentive to use them because existing regulations are more liberal. In summary, the movement of professionals under the AEC continues to face as many hurdles as ever. Unsurprisingly, the uptake of the scheme has been low. In practice, many professionals choose to work in other ASEAN countries by registering themselves as consultants (Fukunaga, 2015).

Our review of the progress of trade and investment liberalisation in ASEAN in this section shows that, although there has been some limited tangible progress towards the goals of regional integration, to date, actual implementation continues to lag far behind the targets set in the AEC Blueprint 2015.

Despite this, ASEAN has declared that its regional integration project has been successful, claiming accomplishments in:

> Eliminating tariffs and facilitating trade; advancing the services trade liberalization agenda; liberalizing and facilitating investment; streamlining and harmonizing capital market regulatory frameworks and platforms; facilitating skilled labor mobility; promoting the development of regional frameworks in competition policy, consumer protection and intellectual property rights; promoting connectivity; narrowing the development gap; and strengthening ASEAN's relationship with its external parties. (ASEAN Secretariat, 2015a)

Despite these claims of success, which are made in the opening pages of the AEC Blueprint 2025, the proceeding item is a call for ASEAN countries to finish all remaining unimplemented works. Like the 2015 version, the aspirations of the AEC Blueprint 2025 are to create a deeply integrated and highly cohesive economy, engender inclusive growth, foster robust productivity growth, promote good governance, widen connectivity and reinforce ASEAN centrality in the emerging regional economic architecture. However, the AEC Blueprint 2025 does not clarify how future implementation efforts will improve on past efforts.

To critical observers, ASEAN integration has so far produced very few tangible results. For example, Elms (2016a) concluded that 'ASEAN officials shifted the rhetoric as the deadline loomed to argue instead that the AEC itself should be viewed as process and not a destination'. *The Economist* commented mockingly that 'when it comes to elevating form over substance, and confusing a proliferation of meetings and acronyms for a deepening of ties, ASEAN is the Zen master' (Banyan, 2016).

The lack of momentum in deepening regional integration within ASEAN largely stems from the protectionist stances of the majority of the member countries, with Singapore, perhaps, the only exception. Many ASEAN countries view other members as rivals in their pursuit of exporting to the global market or attracting FDI. Domestic political conflicts and the lack of strong and stable governments mean that the political leaders of many ASEAN countries look inward and lose their appetite for regional integration. Unless it squarely and urgently confronts the core problems of its integration project, ASEAN will not become a single market and a single production base, despite the vision of the AEC Blueprints.

The future of regional integration

Formal regional integration in East Asia began with the formation of the AFTA in 1993. Later, in the 2000s, a number of bilateral FTAs were formed between ASEAN countries and North-East Asian countries, including the China–Thailand FTA and the Japan–Malaysia FTA. Then, ASEAN as a whole began to produce bilateral FTAs with the 'plus one' countries, beginning with China in 2005, Korea in 2007, Japan in 2008, Australia and New Zealand in 2010 and India, also in 2010.

Bilateral FTAs proliferate over broader FTAs because they are usually easier to negotiate and, thus, they are preferred by politicians seeking short-run successes. However, bilateral FTAs rarely align with the way in which business is actually conducted by firms because few buy and sell goods or services in just one market—even if that one market is huge (Elms, 2016b). Moreover, a set of bilateral FTAs does not provide an efficient production platform for multinational corporations in the regional production networks. This is because the ROOs do not allow for pairwise accumulation of regional value added. Consequently, a more seamless regional architecture is needed.

The next section considers the future of regional integration in East Asia by analysing the prospects for three regional integration initiatives: deeper integration in ASEAN, the fate of the TPP after the US presidential election and the future of RCEP. We do not discuss the proposal to form a Free Trade Area of the Asia–Pacific (FTAAP), previously proposed by Canada and again, more recently, by China, because we consider that if it is formed, it will be.

Deeper integration in ASEAN

ASEAN prides itself on being the hub of bilateral FTAs in East Asia. The concept of ASEAN centrality emphasises its role in facilitating economic integration in the region. However, so far economic integration among ASEAN members has focused on offering a more attractive package to multinational corporations seeking to operate in the region, rather than on creating stronger bonds between member economies (Fields, 2016). The negotiation of the TPP shows how fragile the idea of ASEAN centrality is, as the proposed arrangement did not include most ASEAN countries.

For ASEAN to be central to East Asia's economic integration, two related conditions are required. First, integration among ASEAN economies must be significantly strengthened so that ASEAN becomes close to operating as a single market and production base. This requires ASEAN members to pool their sovereignty in certain areas; for example, the identification and reduction of NTBs in the case of trade in goods. Second, the institutions and organisations of ASEAN, specifically the ASEAN Secretariat, must be strengthened.

To strengthen its economic integration, ASEAN must aim to achieve critical targets and ignore trivial ones. In other words, ASEAN needs to be much more focused than it is now. The current ASEAN agenda is overly ambitious, considering its limited resources. The AEC Blueprint established 17 core elements and 176 priority actions, covering large subject areas, including the free flow of goods and capital, the movement of skilled labour, the development of small- and medium-sized enterprises and of infrastructure, capital market integration, equitable development and protection of intellectual property rights, to name just a few.

A sharper focus would help ASEAN to accelerate its liberalisation process, and deliver meaningful and tangible results, without depriving member countries, especially less developed ones, of their limited resources. This requires ASEAN to return to the core missions of an FTA: reducing barriers to trade and facilitating cross-border trade in goods and services and the movement of factors of production.

As tariff reduction is almost accomplished and ROOs are already relatively liberal, ASEAN should focus on reducing NTBs. In this regard, CCA needs to be empowered; although it has previously identified many NTMs used by ASEAN countries as non-transparent or discriminatory, it lacks the power to oblige these countries to abolish or improve them.

ASEAN should switch from its current positive-list approach to a negative-list approach in negotiating its service liberalisation, as suggested by Dee (2015). She also usefully suggested the inclusion of a ratchet mechanism, whereby any future domestic reforms would be automatically bound into AFAS schedules.

ASEAN should synchronise the commitments of Modes 3 and 4 in service liberalisation to implement the ideas of a single market and single production base as suggested by Fukunaga and Ishido (2015) and Dee (2015). Fukunaga and Ishido (2015) also recommended that the

Second, from an economic perspective, there are many welfare-decreasing provisions in the agreement. One of the most obvious examples is the notorious 'yarn forward' rule of origin imposed on garment products. The rule is likely to create trade and investment diversion away from lower cost non-member countries. Also highly controversial is the chapter on intellectual property rights. Many experts have pointed out that the TPP would jeopardise access to affordable medicine for the poor, and raise the prices of agricultural chemicals and seeds in the member countries because of its lengthy patent protection and data exclusivity provisions. In addition, the TPP grants extraordinarily long copyright protection—to a minimum specified as the term of the creator's life plus 70 years. Many leading economists have argued that such a long protection term provides marginally little benefit to creators but generates high costs to society.[4]

Despite the successful conclusion of the negotiation, the ratification of the TPP has been uncertain from the beginning, particularly in the US. According to the concluded text, the TPP will become effective if either 1) all the member countries complete their own domestic ratification procedures; or 2) at least six countries, which have at least 85 per cent of the total GDP of the original members, ratify it within two years.

Many member countries have opted to delay TPP ratification, waiting for the US Congress to do so first. This was rational, as ratification by the US is essential for the TPP to take effect—the US alone constitutes about 60 per cent of TPP members' aggregate GDP.

Lawmakers from both major political parties in the US criticised the deal. The complaints raised by members of Congress were concentrated around three major issues: the shorter period of data protection for biologic medicines than that provided under US law, the exclusion of financial services from the prohibition on data localisation measures under the electronic commerce chapter and the exclusion of tobacco products from the benefits of investor–state dispute settlement (Lincicome & Picone, 2016). There was also broader concern about how to ensure that other TPP members would fully implement the commitments.

---

4   In total, 17 prominent economists, including five Nobel Prize winners (George Akerlof, Kenneth Arrow, James Buchanan, Ronald Coase and Milton Friedman), submitted an amicus brief opposing the US bill from which the TPP borrows its text when it was challenged in court in 2002 (see cyber. harvard.edu/openlaw/eldredvashcroft/supct/amici/economists.pdf).

The prospect of TPP ratification became bleaker during both major parties' primary elections and the subsequent general US presidential electoral campaign. Donald Trump outrageously claimed that the TPP is a 'rape of [the US]', despite the fact that the entire text was largely drafted by the US team. In an atmosphere of heightened protectionism, Hillary Clinton changed her stance to oppose the deal. Senate Majority Leader Mitch McConnell and House Speaker Paul Ryan said that they would not schedule a vote for the ratification of the TPP in the lame duck session and insisted that several provisions of the agreement be renegotiated.

After the presidential election, Donald Trump made it clear that he would withdraw from the TPP and indicated his preference to enter into bilateral trade deals instead. This shift of position seriously undermines the US's negotiation credibility, as the TPP text has already accommodated US demands more than those of other countries. A study by Allee and Lugg (2016) found that, out of the 74 previous trade agreements that TPP members have signed since 1995, the text of the TPP most resembles that of existing US FTAs. This is particularly true in chapters that are of greatest concern to US political leaders, such as the investment chapter, where nearly half the 16,000-word text was lifted directly from past US FTAs.

The collapse of the TPP would certainly disappoint the governments of the negotiating partners, including Japan, Australia and Vietnam, as they have not only put in significant efforts to negotiate the draft agreement but also taken the political heat from interest groups in their countries. More importantly, it is a big setback for regional integration for two reasons. First, an attempt to create a mega-FTA that integrates countries in the Pacific rims has not borne fruit. Second, the momentum for concluding a high-standard RCEP may not be maintained without the ratification of the TPP.

The future of RCEP

The idea of a free trade area covering the ASEAN+6 countries was first proposed by Japan. With the TPP under negotiation, China, which initially pushed for the ASEAN+3 FTA, agreed to the ASEAN+6 deal, which later became RCEP. Proposed by Japan, and later endorsed by India, ASEAN was assigned to the 'driver's seat'. This reiterates the idea of ASEAN centrality in the emerging regional economic architecture.

Unlike the US-centric TPP, RCEP is Asian-centric. Even though RCEP is more populous, its aggregate GDP (US$22.6 trillion in 2015) is smaller than that of the TPP (US$27.5 trillion). However, the total economic size of RCEP is likely to overtake that of the TPP within the next 15 years, assuming the current growth rates of their respective member countries. While the TPP aimed at setting a 'gold standard' for international trade agreements, RCEP has never aimed to do so. It was designed from the beginning to be more accommodating and to focus on traditional trade policies.

At the launch of RCEP negotiations in November 2012, the leaders of ASEAN and its FTA partners endorsed the 'Guiding Principles and Objectives for Negotiating the Regional Comprehensive Economic Partnership'. According to the document, RCEP would encompass trade in goods and services, economic and technical issues, intellectual property and investments, and dispute settlement mechanisms. It also aims to improve on the existing ASEAN+1 FTAs in terms of breadth and depth, while recognising the individual and diverse circumstances of the participating countries. The guiding principles document explicitly includes a 'provision for special and differential treatment plus additional flexibility' for participating countries. RCEP reached its 15th round of negotiations in October 2016. Although the negotiation details are kept secret, progress has reportedly been very slow so far, and the 2016 end-of-year deadline for conclusion has already been missed.

Elms (2016c) suggested that there are four potential outcomes for RCEP. First, a complete failure of negotiations. This would be deeply problematic, but not entirely unexpected. Second, RCEP could conclude in relative short order, but only if leaders fudged issues and left details of the deal to be worked out by officials in the 'legal scrub' or 'translation'. This would be risky if the agreement is not sufficiently close to conclusion. Third, RCEP could conclude on schedule with a 'built-in agenda' to negotiate unsettled issues. However, ASEAN's experience of using built-in agendas indicates that the progress afterwards could be extremely slow. Fourth, RCEP could announce an 'early harvest' and keep negotiating. While this is not ideal for many dialogue partners, Elms considered that a small comprehensive package that does not dilute the interest of most members to maintain talks might be worthwhile.

We concur with Elms's (2016c) conclusion. Ultimately, for RCEP to be meaningful and relevant, it has to deliver significant additional benefits to all participants compared with the current ASEAN+1 FTAs. To add significant benefits, RCEP should strive for deeper regional integration and trade facilitation. It can emulate certain parts of the TPP and avoid provisions that are clearly welfare decreasing.

First, RCEP should mandate the elimination of all tariffs and other restrictions on trade in goods for virtually all goods, with few exceptions or carve outs. ROOs should aim at achieving an 'upward harmonisation' of those ROOs of existing ASEAN+1 FTAs; that is, RCEP should have the most liberal ROOs per product among ASEAN and all ASEAN+1 FTAs, as suggested by Medalla (2015). In addition, it should avoid using restrictive product-specific rules, such as the yarn forward rules adopted in the TPP. With less than upwardly harmonised ROOs, RCEP would just add another layer of rules and become irrelevant.

Second, RCEP should adopt a negative-list approach in negotiating service liberalisation and a ratchet mechanism and it should allow linkages between the commitments in Modes 3 and 4.

Third, it should refrain from including the clearly welfare-decreasing provisions embedded in the TPP text. These include the many provisions that grant overly stringent intellectual property rights protection, mentioned in the previous subsection. In addition, provisions on issues not directly related to trade should also be avoided. These include provisions related to currency manipulation (see Gupta, 2015) and cyber security (Baker, 2015).

The real obstacle to concluding a high-quality RCEP is the politics of protectionism. To give just one example, India is reportedly unwilling to reduce its tariff rates. At one point in the negotiation, it had proposed a three-tier schedule of tariff liberalisation, apparently to block imports of steel, aluminium and chemical products from China (Pailit, 2016). India's protectionism is also evidenced by the fact that it is one the most frequent users of anti-dumping and safeguard measures in the world.

In this context, RCEP's most important problem is that no one country is really in charge. To make RCEP meaningful and relevant, negotiating countries that have liberal trade policies, including Australia, New Zealand, Singapore and Japan, should take the leadership role. RCEP should aim at setting an ambitious target of deep economic integration, with a reasonable transition period for less developed countries. For example, a limited number of provisions may become binding to a less developed country only when its income per capita reaches a pre-specified threshold.

Learning from the TPP's ratification predicaments, RCEP may allow a lower threshold to become effective among the ratified members. This would prevent the failure of a few countries to ratify from sabotaging the whole agreement.

Implications for Thailand

This final section of the chapter will draw out some policy implications for Thailand, based on the developments in economic integration in East Asia discussed in the chapter. It is hoped that the implications analysed here will be useful to other developing countries in ASEAN.

The objectives of trade policy should not be limited to increasing a country's export opportunities. Rather, trade policy should aim at stimulating and facilitating domestic reform to improve the country's productivity and competitiveness in the long run. With the aim of increasing export opportunities through preferential treatment, Thailand was very active in negotiating FTAs with its trading partners during the 2000s. As a result, the ratio of Thailand's exports to FTA partner countries compared to its total exports rose rapidly from 19.3 per cent in 2001 to 53.5 per cent in 2010.

Thailand launched FTA negotiations with the US in 2004, the European Free Trade Association in 2005 and the EU in 2013, but none of these negotiations was successfully concluded. The negotiation with the US was officially terminated after eight rounds of negotiations, whereas those with the European Free Trade Association and the EU have been suspended.

Since 2010, Thailand has not secured any new FTAs with its major trading partners. The most recent effective FTA (implemented in 2012) was with Peru, which is a minor trading partner, with a trade share of just 0.16 per cent for Thailand. As a result, the share of exports to FTA partner countries has organically increased from the 2010 level of 53.5 per cent to 56 per cent by 2014. Thailand's FTAs with Turkey and Pakistan, if successfully concluded, would have a marginal effect in terms of increasing Thailand's market access opportunities.

Unlike Japan and Australia, both of which used trade agreements as a catalyst for structural reforms, Thailand has never aimed at facilitating domestic reform through its FTA efforts. According to the Thai Department of Trade Negotiations, the strategic goals of Thailand's FTA initiatives are to expand exports, seek inbound and outbound investment opportunities, seek external resources to cut production costs, and develop human resources and technologies. Regrettably, the goal of using trade policy for structural reform is missing in Thailand. Further, the Thai negotiation team aims to ensure that no legislative acts need to be amended as a result of the trade negotiations. This reflects the broader mindset of the Thai government, which appears to believe that Thailand can upgrade itself into a high-income country—through increasing goods and services exports, and attracting FDI and investment in infrastructure—without facing the difficulties of structurally reforming the economy. The government initiative closest to structural reform is its effort to facilitate the ease of doing business by improving the country's standing in the World Bank annual ranking. However, deregulation is just one part of the real structural reform required.

This mindset is reflected in the Twelfth Economic and Social Development Plan (2017–21) approved by the Thai cabinet. A key pillar of the plan is to promote economic growth through regional and international cooperation. In particular, the plan sets an average growth target of 5 per cent per year throughout the 10-year period. This would be achieved by increasing labour productivity and total factor productivity, each at 2.5 per cent per year, across the manufacturing, agricultural and service sectors.

With regard to trade strategy, the plan aims to expand trade and investment cooperation with 'like-minded' countries to:

- increase market access opportunities for Thai products and services
- develop physical connectivity within the region
- promote Thailand as an investment destination by developing border special economic zones
- promote outward investment of Thai businesses
- form trade and investment partnerships with other countries in the region.

The plan does not explicitly mention trade liberalisation as a policy instrument, nor any structural reforms of the agricultural and service sectors.

The service sector constitutes roughly half of Thailand's GDP and labour force. However, its productivity level is only half that of manufacturing. The agricultural sector, which constitutes 35 per cent of the country's labour force and 12 per cent of GDP, has an even lower productivity level. The low level of productivity in both sectors is partly the result of limited competition in the sectors, arising from Thailand's restrictive foreign investment regime. The regime is most restrictive in the agricultural sectors and, to a lesser extent, in the service sectors (Nikomborirak, 2013).

For Thailand to escape the 'middle-income trap', it needs to refocus its development priorities towards reforming its economy in general and increasing productivity levels in the service and the agricultural sectors, in particular. With only 16 per cent of its labour force working in factories, Thailand can no longer rely on its export-oriented manufacturing sector as its sole economic driver in a global economy characterised by lower growth. Thailand needs to shift towards promoting domestic demand, which requires policies that can help lift the income of the masses.

The first-best option to reform the Thai economy is to unilaterally liberalise its market by amending existing laws and regulations that prevent the country from having more competition and better resource allocation. However, such reforms are usually difficult to carry out because of opposition from interest groups that stand to lose from foreign competition. It is in this context that regional integration is critical for the future of the Thai economy.

With the collapse of the TPP, Thailand should actively contribute in the negotiation to make RCEP meaningful by pushing it to a high standard along the lines proposed in the previous section. Ultimately, Thailand should realise that it is no longer possible to propel itself to high-income status by pursuing a narrow trade policy agenda without major economic reforms.

References

Allee, T. & Lugg, A. (2016). Who wrote the rules for the Trans-Pacific Partnership?, *Research & Politics*, *3*(3), 1–9.

Almekinders, G., Fukuda, S., Mourmouras, A., Zhou, J. & Zhou, Y. (2015). ASEAN financial integration. *IMF Working Paper* WP/15/34. Retrieved 4 January 2017 from: www.imf.org/external/pubs/ft/wp/2015/wp1534.pdf

Asian Development Bank. (2013). *The road to ASEAN financial integration: A combined study on assessing the financial landscape and formulating milestones for monetary and financial integration in ASEAN*. Retrieved 4 January 2017 from: www.adb.org/sites/default/files/publication/30202/road-asean-financial-integration.pdf

Association of Southeast Asian Nations Secretariat (ASEAN). (2015a). *ASEAN economic community blueprint 2025*. Retrieved 16 October 2016 from: www.asean.org/storage/images/2015/November/aec-page/AEC-Blueprint-2025-FINAL.pdf

Association of Southeast Asian Nations Secretariat (ASEAN). (2015b). *A blueprint for growth—ASEAN economic community 2015: Progress and key achievements*. Retrieved 16 October 2016 from: www.asean.org/storage/images/2015/November/aec-page/AEC-2015-Progress-and-Key-Achievements.pdf

Baker, S. (2015, 6 November). Cybersecurity and the TPP. *The Washington Post*. Retrieved from: www.washingtonpost.com/news/volokh-conspiracy/wp/2015/11/06/cybersecurity-and-the-tpp/?utm_term=.62dbb01743ac.

Banyan. (2016, 3 September). Agreeing to agree. *The Economist*. Retrieved from: www.economist.com/news/asia/21706264-south-east-asian-summitry-apogee-form-over-substance-may-be-no-bad-thing-agreeing.

Basu Das, S., Sen, R. & Srivastava, S. (2015). AEC vision post-2015: Is an ASEAN customs union feasible? *ISEAS Economics Working Paper No. 2015-1*. Retrieved from: www.iseas.edu.sg/images/centres/asc/pdf/EWP20151.pdf

Bauer, M., Makiyama, H. L., van der Marel, E. & Verschelde, B. (2014). The costs of data localisation: a friendly fire on economic recovery. *ECIPE Occasional Paper No. 3/2014*. Retrieved 31 October 2016 from: www.ecipe.org/app/uploads/2014/12/OCC32014__1.pdf

Cadot, O. & Ing, L. Y. (2016). How restrictive are ASEAN's ROO? *Asian Economic Papers, 15*(3), 115–34. doi.org/10.1162/ASEP_a_00461

Dee, P. (2015). Monitoring the implementation of services trade reform towards an ASEAN economic community. *ERIA Discussion Paper Series 2015–44*. Jakarta: Economic Research Institute for ASEAN and East Asia.

Economic Research Institute for ASEAN and East Asia (ERIA). (2012). *Mid-term review of the implementation of AEC Blueprint*. Jakarta: Economic Research Institute for ASEAN and East Asia.

Elms, D. (2016a, 14 September). ASEAN: Still more process than destination. *Asian Trade Centre Talking Trade Blog*. Retrieved 10 October 2016 from: www.asiantradecentre.org/talkingtrade// asean-still-more-process-than-destination

Elms, D. (2016b, 7 September). TPP collapse? Plan B for everybody else. *Asian Trade Centre Talking Trade Blog*. Retrieved 10 October 2016 from: www.asiantradecentre.org/talkingtrade//tpp-plan-b-for-everybody-else

Elms, D. (2016c, 19 July). RCEP: Status update. *Asian Trade Centre Talking Trade Blog*. Retrieved 12 October 2016 from: www.asiantrade centre.org/talkingtrade//rcep-status-update

Fields, S. (2016). Trouble ahead for ASEAN. *Berkeley APEC Study Center Newsletter, 18* Winter 2015/16. Retrieved from: basc.berkeley.edu/wp-content/uploads/2016/04/BASC-Newsletter-Winter-15_16.pdf

Fukunaga, Y. (2015). Assessing the progress of ASEAN MRAs on professional services. *ERIA Discussion Paper Series*. Jakarta: Economic Research Institute for ASEAN and East Asia.

Fukunaga, Y. & Ishido, H. (2015, March). Values and limitations of the ASEAN agreement on the movement of natural persons. *ERIA Discussion Paper Series 2015-20*. Jakarta: Economic Research Institute for ASEAN and East Asia.

Gupta, S. (2015, 17 May). Keep currency clauses out of the global trading system. *East Asia Forum.* Retrieved 16 October 2016 from: www.eastasiaforum.org/2015/05/17/keep-currency-clauses-out-of-the-global-trading-system/

Ing, L. Y., de Cordoba, S. F. & Cadot, O. (2016). Non-tariff measures in ASEAN. *ERIA Discussion Paper Series.* Jakarta: ERIA and UNCTAD.

Intal, P. (2015a, May). AEC blueprint implementation performance and challenges: Trade facilitation. *ERIA Discussion Paper Series 2015-41.* Jakarta: Economic Research Institute for ASEAN and East Asia.

Intal, P. (2015b, April). AEC blueprint implementation performance and challenges: Investment liberalization. *ERIA Discussion Paper Series 2015-32.* Jakarta: Economic Research Institute for ASEAN and East Asia.

Kausikan, B. (2016, 1 September). Never mind territorial spats—ASEAN's priorities are economic. *Nikkei Asian Review.* Retrieved from: asia.nikkei.com/magazine/20160901-ASEAN-THE-GREAT-PUZZLE/On-the-Cover/Never-mind-territorial-spats-ASEAN-s-priorities-are-economic

Lincicome, S. & Picone, B. (2016, May). Evaluating the Trans-Pacific Partnership. *White & Case LLP.* Retrieved 30 October 2016 from: www.whitecase.com/publications/alert/evaluating-trans-pacific-partnership

McKinsey Global Institute. (2014). *Southeast Asia at the crossroads: Three paths to prosperity.* McKinsey & Company. Retrieved from: www.mckinsey.com/global-themes/asia-pacific/three-paths-to-sustained-economic-growth-in-southeast-asia

Medalla, E. M. (2015). Towards an enabling set of rules of origin for the Regional Comprehensive Economic Partnership. In Ing, L. Y. (Ed.), *East Asian integration* (pp. 93–121). Jakarta, Indonesia: Economic Research Institute for ASEAN and East Asia.

Menon, J. & Melendez, A. C. (2015, May). Realizing an ASEAN economic community: Progress and remaining challenges. *ADB Economics Working Paper Series No. 432.* Retrieved from: www.adb.org/publications/realizing-asean-economic-community-progress-and-remaining-challenges

Nair, D. (2016, February). A strong secretariat, a strong ASEAN? A re-evaluation. *ISEAS Perspective Issue 2016 No. 8,* Singapore: Institute of Southeast Asian Studies.

Nambiar, S. (2016, 13 February). Is the TPP really a leap forward for Malaysia? *East Asia Forum.* Retrieved from: www.eastasiaforum. org/2016/02/13/is-the-tpp-really-a-leap-forward-for-malaysia/

Narjoko, D. (2015, May). AEC blueprint implementation performance and challenges: Services liberalization. *ERIA Discussion Paper Series 2015-39.* Jakarta: Economic Research Institute for ASEAN and East Asia.

Nikomborirak, D. (2013, June). Service liberalization under the ASEAN economic community: Myths and reality, opportunities and challenges. *TDRI Quarterly Review, 28*(2) 3–9.

Organisation for Economic Co-operation and Development (OECD). (2016). *Economic outlook for Southeast Asia, China and India 2016: Enhancing regional ties.* OECD Publishing. doi.org/10.1787/saeo-2016-en

Pailit, A. (2016, 30 September). India inches towards liberalisation at RCEP. *East Asia Forum.* Retrieved 16 October 2016 from: www. eastasiaforum.org/2016/09/30/india-inches-towards-liberalisation-at-rcep/

Plummer, M. (2006, February). An ASEAN customs union? *Journal of Asian Economics, 17*(5). doi.org/10.1016/j.asieco.2006.08.013

Rodrik, D. (2002). *Feasible globalizations.* Unpublished research paper. Retrieved 31 October 2016 from: drodrik.scholar.harvard.edu/files/dani-rodrik/files/feasible-globalizations.pdf

Schott, J. J. & Jung, E. (2015). An assessment of the Korea–China free trade agreement. *Policy Brief Number PB15-24.* Peterson Institute for International Economics. Retrieved from: piie.com/publications/policy-briefs/assessment-korea-china-free-trade-agreement

Tan, C. K. (2016, 1 September). CIMB chief calls on the private sector to move integration forward. *Nikkei Asian Review*. Retrieved from: asia. nikkei.com/magazine/20160901-ASEAN-THE-GREAT-PUZZLE/ On-the-Cover/CIMB-chief-calls-on-the-private-sector-to-move-integration-forward

Thailand Development Research Institute (TDRI). (2013). *Increasing the competitiveness of Thai industries under Thailand's international economic policy.* Final report submitted to the Office of Industrial Economics, Ministry of Industry (in Thai).

White House. (2015). *Here's the deal: The Trans-Pacific Partnership.* Retrieved 1 October 2016 from: www.whitehouse.gov/blog/2015/ 11/06/heres-deal-trans-pacific-partnership

World Bank. (2011). *World Bank services trade restrictions* (database). Washington, DC: World Bank. Retrieved from: data.worldbank.org/ data-catalog/services-trade-restrictions.

World Bank. (2013). *ASEAN integration monitoring report.* Washington, DC: World Bank. Retrieved 15 October 2016 from: documents. worldbank.org/curated/en/915081468234873037/pdf/839140 WP0P14480Box0382116B00PUBLIC0.pdf

World Bank. (2016, January). Potential Macroeconomic implications of the Trans-Pacific Partnership. *Global Economic Prospects*. Washington, DC: World Bank.

World Economic Forum. (2013). *Enabling trade valuing growth opportunities.* Retrieved 16 October 2016 from: www3.weforum.org/ docs/WEF_SCT_EnablingTrade_Report_2013.pdf

8

India's Asian trade strategy

Dhiraj Nayyar[1]

The global context

The year 2016 was a bad one for global economic integration. Two events defined the move towards a new autarky: the vote by a majority of the citizens of the UK to leave the EU on 23 June and the election of Donald Trump to the Presidency of the US on 8 November on an explicit platform of protectionism. One of President Trump's first acts as leader of the US was to withdraw from the Trans-Pacific Partnership, the most ambitious agreement for free regional trade since the abject collapse of the Doha Round of negotiations at the multilateral World Trade Organization (WTO). Global trade is experiencing a period of unprecedented slowdown; indeed, given the contraction in recent quarters, shrinking may be the more appropriate description. India has been reluctant about opening up unabashedly to trade—a legacy of four decades of import substitution and statist policies. The events of 2016 may have led it to consider that the world, usually obsessed with trade creation and trade diversion, was finally coming around to share its preference for trade *aversion*.

1   The author is Officer on Special Duty and Head of Economics, Finance and Commerce at the National Institution for Transforming India (NITI Aayog), Government of India. The views expressed in this chapter are personal and do not reflect the views of NITI Aayog. NITI Aayog does not take responsibility for the data used in this chapter nor does it accept any consequences of its use. The author would like to thank Professor David Vines and Mr Andrew Elek for their comments on a presentation on the same subject during PAFTAD 38 in Canberra in November 2016.

The starkest indicator of India's trade aversion is the country's share of global merchandise exports. At just 1.6 per cent of a US$18 trillion market (Ministry of Commerce and Industry, Government of India, 2016), India trails the EU, China and the US (each of which has about a 13–14 per cent share) by a long distance. The second indicator of India's reluctant attitude towards trade comes from a statistic about intra-regional trade. South Asia is home to almost 1.6 billion people but just 5 per cent of its trade is intra-regional, compared with 55 per cent for the EU and 25 per cent for the Association of Southeast Asian Nations (ASEAN). For Asia as a whole, intra-regional trade is 50 per cent of total trade. Of course, responsibility does not lie with India alone—India's neighbours must share the blame. However, as the largest country and economy in the region, it must accept a greater amount of responsibility for that outcome.

There are two ways for India to interpret the new circumstances. The first is to feel comfortable about the emerging global order on trade and rejoice that there is unlikely to be any pressure from the major advanced economies to sign on to 'big ticket' free trade deals. This would be in line with the trade establishment's long-term defensive view on trade. The second option is to view this global scenario as an opportunity. With just 1.6 per cent of the share of global merchandise trade, India has huge scope to make an improvement in its share of trade, even if the total pie of global trade is stagnant.

There are several reasons why it is in India's interests to opt for the second response. A rapid growth in merchandise trade could not only power India's growth to double digits, but could also provide gainful employment for millions of Indians in labour-intensive industries, which have not been an area of strength for India. It is often argued[2] that India has a large internal market and it need not target international markets. However, the total size of India's economy is around US$2 trillion, whereas the total size of global trade is nine times that; the argument that India can simply rely on internal markets is not convincing.

Apart from necessity, there is also opportunity. China, the world's factory for the last three decades, may finally be ceding some space in manufacturing. There are two factors at work in this trend. First, the rise in real wages is rendering some types of manufacturing uncompetitive in China. Second, the economy needs rebalancing away from an overdependence on exports

---

2   Former Reserve Bank of India Governor Raghuram Rajan was a proponent of this view (see Rajan, 2014).

towards an orientation towards internal consumption (in many ways, the opposite of what India needs to do). Global manufacturing is looking for alternative destinations. India, with its still-low wage levels, is an obvious alternative but it must realise that it is not the only alternative. Relatively close to home, Vietnam, Bangladesh, Indonesia and the Philippines are competing for the same space. Crucially, this may be the last window of opportunity for India to become a global manufacturing hub. The onset of the 'fourth industrial revolution' posed by automation and artificial intelligence may mean that, two decades from now, manufacturing will have a whole new connotation and an entirely different set of jobs, demanding much higher skill levels. Further, by other measurements, India is not as isolated from world trade as one may think. The share of exports (including manufacturing and services) in India's gross domestic product (GDP) is close to 23 per cent, about the same as China's. Therefore, India has become quite an open economy, even if not entirely by design.   should embrace greater openness.

India's choices

Despite the overwhelming case in favour of greater and freer trade, there are reasons why India may choose not to seize this opportunity. There is genuine concern about the competitiveness of Indian manufacturing should it be opened up to trade. Several sectors of the economy already struggle to compete with imports, particularly those from China. In the one experience that India had with major trade liberalisation, during the economic reforms of 1991, there was little evidence to suggest that manufacturing had received a boost. Instead, there may have been some deindustrialisation in sectors that were totally uncompetitive (see Sharma, 2014). In addition, there is a concern that free trade negotiations inevitably centre around goods, in which India is not so competitive, rather than services, in which India is relatively more competitive. The services that interest India the most, such as information technology services, are heavily dependent on the movement of persons, a subject that is fraught in today's global scenario. Therefore, there are good reasons for the political economy of India being tilted against a more open trade strategy.

A significant question that arises is, if the major advanced economies are turning to protectionism, where will India find the markets for its exports? The answer is relatively simple. Although it is true that the US is becoming more anti-trade, there is no similar evidence that

Europe is. The anti-globalisation sentiment there appears to be centred on immigration. Therefore, opportunities may exist—the UK has already expressed openness towards a free trade agreement (FTA) with India (Press Trust of India, 2017). More significantly, the one engine of the global economy that is still revving, even if at a slower rate than earlier, is East Asia. Many of the global value chains (GVCs) that are critical to global trade are located in this region. India is geographically close to this region. Therefore, India's trade strategy must be an Asian strategy, centred on East Asia and South Asia, which have enormous potential for integration.

However, for an Asian strategy to take shape, India needs to do its homework—quite literally. The first step in an Asian strategy must be to address the bottlenecks in the domestic economy that render Indian industries uncompetitive in the first place. If a domestic strategy is combined with an external strategy, India could make its mark on global manufacturing trade and become a leader for the cause of integration in a world that is moving away from an important source of economic prosperity.

Homework is critical

In a highly globalised world, constructed around GVCs for products, investors, whether Indian or foreign, must choose which location is best to establish their businesses. The difficulty of doing business in India is best summed up by its ranking in the annual World Bank study on the ease of doing business. In the latest (2017) rankings, India comes in at 130 in a list of 190 countries. India has been languishing in the 130s since 2010. A number of competitor countries rank much higher: China, 78; Vietnam, 82; Indonesia, 91; the Philippines, 99; and Sri Lanka, 110. The countries are ranked on a number of parameters, including starting a business, construction permits, obtaining electricity, registering property, paying taxes, obtaining credit, trading across borders, enforcing contracts and resolving insolvency. India fares particularly poorly on some of these indicators; it ranks almost at the bottom (185) in construction permits and its ranking is not significantly better in enforcing contracts and paying taxes (172 for both). Its best performing indicator is obtaining electricity, for which it is ranked 26 (World Bank, 2017a).

However, there is a determined push from the government to improve India's standings in these rankings. Prime Minister Narendra Modi has publicly exhorted his officials to lift India into the top 50 in rapid time. Of course, given the quantum of improvement required in a range of areas, progress may take time. On some indicators, such as resolving insolvency, in which India is ranked at 132, there may be a dramatic upward surge following the legislation introducing a new bankruptcy law. Once the law is codified and put into practice, at least that parameter should experience a sharp improvement.

Factoring in imperfect factor markets

India's lack of competitiveness in manufacturing is not limited to red tape. There are several distortions in critical factor markets—in land, labour and capital—that need to be addressed. Land is a necessary resource for the setting up of industries. Until 2013, land acquisition via eminent domain in India was governed by archaic 1894 legislation, introduced during the period of colonial rule. It can reasonably be stated that the law did not provide adequate safeguards to those whose land was being acquired, whether for industrial use or for the construction of infrastructure so vital to attracting other investment. Unfortunately, the legislation enacted in 2016 that replaced this old law mired the entire process of land acquisition in bureaucracy, delays and unnecessary costs. Given the sensitivity of the political economy to land-related issues (in a relatively poor country, land is often the only major asset for a large number of people) any easing or roll back of the law is fraught and unlikely to be successful. The only way forward is for India's individual state governments to enact their own, more liberal land acquisition laws. Constitutionally, land is a subject that belongs to the state governments. Usually, central government legislation prevails over any state government law. However, in the interest of economic growth, in this particular case, the central government could permit the state legislation to prevail.

There is a similar problem (and solution) in the vexed domain of labour laws. India's labour laws, drafted in the early years of independence, provide a great deal of protection to incumbent labour, but have created perverse incentives for industry to use capital in a country where labour is abundant. The statutes of the labour laws (there are several) make it nearly impossible to 'hire and fire'. That is why labour-intensive industries have never really taken off in India. Worse, the size of the formal sector (in which workers obtain benefits including pension contributions and insurance) is small. Only an estimated 10 per cent of the entire workforce is in the formal sector. Informal workers account for 60 per cent of the workforce in the organised sector. That proportion has not registered much change even 25 years after economic liberalisation, which, given that labour laws have remained untouched, is hardly surprising. The vested interests of incumbent labour will not make reform easy in New Delhi; the mere mention of labour reform the 2000–01 budget speech caused enough of a storm that the topic has not been mentioned since. However, as in the case of land, India's federal structure gives state governments the right to make their own labour laws. Some states, most notably Gujarat, have recently amended their labour laws, increasing the specified threshold on the number of workers above which the labour laws apply. Such reform by some states may eventually induce a competitive response from other states and result in a race to the top.

India's capital markets are its most reformed factor markets. In particular, significant changes were made in the market for equities, which has resulted in the development of robust stock markets, an important source of corporate finance and an instrument of corporate governance. However, the banking system continues to dominate the financial sector. State-owned banks control 70 per cent of all lending. The private sector has more efficient banks, but their market shares trail well behind the public sector banks. India has been slow to liberalise the banking space—too few private banking licences have been given in the past two and a half decades. However, the digitisation of banking and the arrival of payments banks could alter the landscape.

The building blocks of infrastructure

India's infrastructure woes are well known and well documented. What matters for competitive industry and efficient trade is excellent connectivity. India's record on roads, railways and ports, the three most critical pillars of a connectivity network for trade, is poor, especially in comparison to its closest competitors, even in nearby Asia. A full detailing of India's infrastructure woes would require a separate paper. Here, we focus on a handful of key infrastructure quality indicators to illustrate how India compares with (and trails behind) many of its competitor nations. The World Economic Forum's (2016) Global Competitiveness Report for 2015–16 presents some stark numbers for India. Overall, on the aggregated infrastructure index, India's rank is 81, well below most of its competitor countries in East Asia and in the emerging economies: Malaysia, 24; Russia, 35; China, 39; Thailand, 44; Mexico, 59; Indonesia, 62; Sri Lanka, 64; South Africa, 68; Brazil, 74; and Vietnam, 76. On the quality of roads, India ranks 61, ahead of Indonesia, 80; Vietnam, 93; and Brazil, 121; but below Malaysia, 15; Sri Lanka, 27; South Africa, 34; China, 42; Thailand, 51; and Mexico, 54. On the quality of port infrastructure, India ranks 60, ahead of Russia, 75; Vietnam, 76; Indonesia, 82; and Brazil, 120; but lower than Malaysia, 16; South Africa, 36; China, 50; Thailand, 52; Mexico, 57; and Sri Lanka, 58. On the index of air transport infrastructure, India ranks 71, which is below South Africa, 14; Malaysia, 21; Thailand, 38; Sri Lanka, 45; China, 51; Mexico, 55; and Indonesia, 66; but above Vietnam, 75; Russia, 77; and Brazil, 77. India slips to near the bottom of the pile vis-à-vis its competitors in the quality of electricity supply, in which it ranks 98. Out of the major emerging economies, only South Africa, ranked 116, is lower than India.

In some domains, including electricity, perverse policy incentives are a great hindrance to competitiveness. India has long followed a policy of cross-subsidies in the pricing of power or electricity, with industry being charged higher tariffs to cross-subsidise the agriculture sector. In China, by comparison, industry receives concessional tariffs. The high cost of power for productive manufacturing renders it uncompetitive. In railways, India has a long history of cross-subsidising passenger tariffs by charging higher rates for freight. The outcome of this policy is that 65 per cent of India's freight moves on trucks via highways and roads, with only 35 per cent moving by rail (World Bank, 2017b). This is the precise opposite of the scenario in most major economies, as road is much slower than rail. Thus, the perverse rail cross-subsidisation reduces the competitiveness of those engaged in trade and has other negative externalities, including congestion and pollution.

The obvious solution to perverse pricing is for the government to stop administering prices. Currently, there is more reason to be optimistic about a change in the power sector than in railways. In the power sector, several state governments have privatised distribution companies, which are more likely to price according to market factors. However, the electricity regulators have not always played an independent and neutral role in the matter of tariff policy. Making them genuinely independent could finally rationalise pricing in electricity. In railways, in which there is no private participation at all, rationalisation of tariffs requires great political will because it would mean an increase in passenger tariffs and a reduction in freight tariffs. The current government of Prime Minister Narendra Modi has carried out the first increase in passengers' fares in over a decade, but more remains to be done to get prices right.

GST and the single market

India has not just been reluctant about free and open trade outside its borders. Within its own borders, India deliberately avoided creating an architecture for a single market until about a decade ago, when it began to consider the idea of a goods and services tax. India has long had a complex system of indirect taxes under which the union government and 29 state governments levy a variety of taxes, often cascading in their effect. These include excise duties, value-added tax and the notorious *octroy*, which is a tax levied as goods cross from one state to another. This bevy of indirect taxes, which are far from uniform in their application, have hobbled the free and efficient movement of goods. The gains to internal trade and to economic efficiency from the reform of such a complex system are huge.

A well-designed GST, which would yield significant gains to the economy, should contain the following features: a single rate, a reasonably low rate and no exemptions. The GST as implemented in India in July 2017 satisfies none of these criteria. India's GST has been launched with four rates from 5 per cent to 28 per cent with several exemptions. The problem with multiple rates for different goods and exemptions for certain goods is that they encourage unproductive rent seeking, as interest groups spend resources lobbying for a favourable tax slab for their good. The problem with a rate that is set too high is that it encourages evasion, a perennial problem in India, given its history of high tax rates.

Introducing legislation in favour of the GST involves a constitutional amendment, which requires approval not just in the two houses of parliament, but also in a majority of state legislatures. Several of India's states, particularly those that are production hubs, were concerned that a shift in the levying of tax from the factory gate (in the old system) to consumption (under the GST) may lead to revenue losses. States wanted some protection of revenues, which explains their insistence on leaving alcohol and tobacco out of the remit of the GST, so that they could levy their own taxes on these high revenue-yielding items. In the end, some compromise between the union government and the state governments was necessary and it is likely that India's GST will begin with four rates, ranging from single-digit up to 28 per cent, and several exemptions.

It is estimated that the current incidence of indirect taxes on goods totals about 27 per cent. By comparison, most goods will see a reduction in rates under the GST. Significantly, the interstate border levy, or *octroy*, will be abolished, eliminating bottlenecks at state borders, as goods-carrying vehicles will no longer have to make long stops to fill out tax papers. The savings in fuel costs and time are not trivial. Moving forward, there is a commitment to lowering rates, reducing the number of exemptions and reducing the number of slabs (tax thresholds), once the uncertainty about the GST and tax collection sorts itself out in a few years. In the meantime, even in its current form, the GST will be a major improvement on the existing system that will increase the competitiveness of India-based manufacturers and, eventually, boost overseas trade.[3]

Fix the parts before the whole

It would be evident to any observer of the Indian economy that the list of reforms to be undertaken domestically, whether on regulations, infrastructure or taxes, will take a long time to be implemented in the context of India's competitive democratic system. It would be unwise and unrealistic for India to wait until every domestic reform to improve its competitiveness is undertaken before it opens up to trade. If anything, a greater opening up to trade could help push through domestic reforms. That said, it may be more realistic and feasible to create two or three economic zones, in which a speedier implementation of reforms may be possible. However, in a democratic federal polity, it is likely to be difficult to follow a China-style special economic zone policy. In China, certain regions along the coast were developed as a priority, while interior regions waited their turn. India's union government would find it difficult to favour some regions over others—it does so only in exceptional cases, where geographical terrain is a hindrance to economic activity— particularly if the prioritised regions were the already more prosperous areas along the coast.

---

3   A study conducted by the think tank National Council of Applied Economic Research (NCAER, 2009) for India's Finance Commission analysed the benefits of a GST for growth and trade.

However, India's federal polity can be leveraged to speed up reforms in some areas of the country.[4] State governments have considerable autonomy under the constitution to draft their own laws. In the case of politically sensitive reforms, such as land acquisition laws and labour laws, it makes eminent sense for state governments to take the lead. There is some evidence of this already. At least five states, among them Gujarat, have made local labour laws more flexible.[5] Some states have chosen to liberalise land laws creatively, by opting for solutions like land leasing (see Panagariya, 2016b) and land pooling, rather than blanket land acquisition. As long as the union government does not 'run roughshod' over what states do legislatively, reform can take place outside the politically charged atmosphere of New Delhi. The government of Prime Minister Modi is committed to cooperative federalism, under which the union government works with state governments as equal partners. It is also committed to competitive federalism. If some states reform, thereby attracting investment and jobs, other states may be forced to follow a reformist path by their demanding electorates.

Apart from reforms in factor markets such as land and labour, state governments can also play an important role in the speedier implementation of infrastructure projects. Although the funds for infrastructure may need to come from New Delhi, implementation can be made more efficient locally through quicker clearances and easier regulations at the state level.

Therefore, in India, rather than pursuing a centrally created special economic zone in the manner of China, the way forward appears to be giving more autonomy to states to push reforms, which will be supported by the union government. States like Gujarat, Andhra Pradesh, Maharashtra and Tamil Nadu, which are already the main centres of industry, have shown evidence of pushing forward at the state level, irrespective of what happens in New Delhi. That way, at least some progressive states can take a lead and breakaway from the vicious cycle of perverse policies and poor implementation that afflict India's overall competitiveness. This would provide a perfect platform for a more aggressive Asian trade strategy.

---

4   For a full exposition on the potential of coastal employment zones in India, see Panagariya (2017).
5   See NITI Aayog Vice Chairman Arvind Panagariya's blog on the subject of labour laws and state governments (Panagariya, 2016a).

South Asia first

The logical beginning of an Asian trade strategy for India should be in its immediate neighbourhood. Regional trade agreements have long been used as an engine to power growth. The global multilateral system, typified by the General Agreement on Tariffs and Trade and the WTO, has always moved slowly and, sometimes, not at all. In contrast, regional initiatives aimed at opening up trade have flourished in almost every part of the world. The EU was an early starter and remains the model for a common market, if not for a currency union, but the North America Free Trade Agreement (NAFTA), ASEAN in East Asia and Mercosur in Latin America have also had reasonable degrees of success. In South Asia, the South Asia Free Trade Agreement (SAFTA) was signed in January 2004 between eight countries in the region: India, Pakistan, Bangladesh, Sri Lanka, Nepal, Bhutan, the Maldives and Afghanistan. The aim of SAFTA was to reduce customs duties in the region to zero by 2016. Needless to say, that goal has not been achieved. Political tensions between India and Pakistan, the two biggest countries, have derailed aspirations for an economic union in the region. India has made more positive moves than Pakistan, at least in bilateral relations. India granted most-favoured nation status to Pakistan in 1995, but Pakistan failed to reciprocate, effectively rendering SAFTA a non-starter.

Fortunately, India has pushed ahead with alternative sub-regional arrangements in South Asia, which may have more potential to succeed than SAFTA. One such initiative involves Bhutan, Bangladesh, India and Nepal (BBIN).[6] In June 2015, the member nations signed a motor vehicle agreement,[7] with restrictions on and delays for vehicles of a member country driving on the other member countries' roads. A similar agreement had been proposed earlier under the South Asian Association for Regional Cooperation (SAARC) framework, which included Pakistan, but it did not come to fruition. A motor vehicle agreement is a crucial prerequisite for efficient trade, especially overland trade, between neighbouring countries.

---

6   On the opportunities and challenges of BBIN, see Pal (2016).
7   For a news report on the implementation of the motor vehicle agreement, see Law (2015).

Along with BBIN, a second vehicle for India's South Asian strategy is the Bay of Bengal initiative for multisector technical and economic cooperation (BIMSTEC). BIMSTEC has seven member states, five of which (India, Nepal, Bangladesh, Sri Lanka and Bhutan) are in South Asia and two of which (Myanmar and Thailand) are in South-East Asia, although in the geographical vicinity of South Asia. BIMSTEC was founded in 2004 but it has gained a renewed momentum recently (see ENS Economic Bureau, 2016), particularly since India moved to its proactive 'Act East' policy.[8]

The China obstacle

If Pakistan has long been the hurdle for a proactive South Asian strategy, then China is the elephant in the room when it comes to India's (East) Asian trade strategy. It is well known that India has a fraught political relationship with its northern neighbour. The two most populous countries in the world fought a war in 1962. Since then, the two countries continue to have a prickly relationship involving temporary border incursions because of a disputed border. China has made a territorial claim over the North-East Indian state of Arunachal Pradesh, which has ancient links with Tibet, but India considers the state its territory. China's implicit and explicit diplomatic and military support for Pakistan, against what India perceives as its interests, is an added political irritant to the bilateral relationship. The bilateral relationship between China and Pakistan is only growing stronger. China's massive investment in an economic corridor through Pakistan that will link China's relatively underdeveloped western region to a port (Gwadar) on the Arabian Sea is a sign of ever deeper engagement.

However, politics is not the only reason for a tense relationship between India and China. There is an economic dimension that has gained prominence in the last 15 years, as India has developed a highly skewed bilateral trade relationship with China. This is arguably a bigger hurdle to reducing barriers to trade than the political tensions that exist between the two countries. Consider this statistic: in 2000–01, India's trade deficit with China was under US$1 billion, but in 2008–09, it was US$22 million.

---

8   For the details of the policy, see the official Government of India statement (Ministry of External Affairs, Government of India, 2015).

In 2015–16, India's trade deficit with China had risen sharply to a massive US$53 billion. China's accession to the WTO in the early 2000s and its massive export expansion thereafter saw it build surpluses with several major economies. India was no exception. In India's case, it is not just the size of the deficit that is noticeable, it also the quality. India's imports from China are overwhelmingly higher value-added manufactured goods, while India's exports to China are largely lower value-added raw materials, mostly minerals. This situation is perhaps a reflection of China's superior competitiveness in manufacturing.

However, what the trade relationship does not reflect is India's comparative advantage; China's non-tariff barriers restrict the export of goods and services in which India is competitive. China maintains non-tariff barriers on a number of agricultural products from India, including regulatory requirements that restrict the import of pharmaceuticals from India. In the realm of services, regulatory restrictions inhibit the export of entertainment products from India and visa regulations make it difficult for Indian information technology service providers to export their services to China. Thus, India has good reasons to be exasperated with China and to be reluctant about opening up to trade. India is open to the import of manufactured goods from China (largely because of its commitments to multilateral trade agreements), but China is not open to importing goods and services in which India is competitive, and restrictions are permitted on the movement of these goods (agriculture and pharmaceuticals) and services (entertainment and information technology), even under multilateral trade agreement regimes.[9]

From India's perspective, the situation is worsened by the very limited amount of foreign investment received by India that could aid in financing the trade deficit in a sustainable manner. Between 2000 and 2014, Chinese investment in India totalled just US$400 million, a tiny fraction of the trade deficit. Of course, some of the blame for this situation can be ascribed to India, which has, from time to time, raised barriers to Chinese investment in sectors such as telecommunications, citing security concerns. In other situations involving Chinese investment, such as in the case of power projects, India objected to the use of Chinese labour instead of local labour. Needless to say, all the factors that deter investment in manufacturing in India apply to all investors, whether Indian, Chinese or

---

9   In 2010, India issued a démarche, a strong diplomatic notice, to China on the barriers to trade for Indian goods. See Nayyar (2010) for more detail.

from elsewhere. Nevertheless, compared with the foreign investment that India has received from the advanced economies in the last 15 years, the quantum received from China is small.

The East Asia (minus China) strategy

Given its vexed relationship with China, is it worthwhile for India to attempt to develop a sub-East Asian strategy (minus China), just like the sub-South Asian strategy (minus Pakistan) it has been moving ahead with? The challenge is that, when it comes to open trade, India has similar problems with the ASEAN countries as it does with China. The India–ASEAN FTA, which became operational in 2010, has evoked serious concern from Indian manufacturers. The automobile industry, particularly the automotive components industry, has found it difficult to compete with manufacturers based in Thailand. A study by one industry group, the Associated Chambers of Commerce and Industry of India (ASSOCHAM, 2016), suggested that, since the signing of the FTA, India's exports to ASEAN have remained virtually stagnant, whereas imports have grown by 33 per cent. None of this is entirely surprising because India's problems at home are at the root of its uncompetitiveness. If those problems, described in earlier sections of this chapter, are addressed, then India's competitiveness on trade will improve vis-à-vis ASEAN and China. As the trade deficit with ASEAN is nowhere near the alarming level of that with China, it makes sense to maintain an already open trade arrangement with ASEAN and use that pressure to improve domestic policies and infrastructure. In addition, the India–ASEAN relationship does not come attached with the political baggage of the China–India relationship. On the contrary, India could leverage the real tensions that some ASEAN countries (e.g. Vietnam) have with China to gain greater economic concessions for the member countries in return for a political alliance that could counterbalance China.

The significance of continued engagement with ASEAN also lies in penetrating some of the GVCs that are centred in Asia. As much of the global trade occurs within these value chains—from which India is largely excluded—ASEAN can help India gain a foot in the door. As China slows down and rebalances its economy away from exports to domestic consumption, some of the businesses that are based in China may move out to ASEAN and South Asian nations. India needs to compete to attract that investment. At any rate, it cannot afford to be out of the value chain. A defensive insular strategy will lead to exclusion.

India must also explore opportunities and synergies with some of the less developed ASEAN countries, particularly the Cambodia, Laos, Myanmar and Vietnam (CLMV) grouping. Interestingly, these four countries are geographically contiguous to India's east (the order of closeness is Myanmar, Laos, Cambodia and Vietnam) and, in many ways, they are India's closest neighbours within ASEAN (along with Thailand). The government of India is actively pursuing investment and trade opportunities with these countries in areas in which complementarities may be greater than competition (and, therefore, more palatable politically). The government has proposed setting up special purpose vehicles to aid investment in the region.[10] The fact that the region has an important geographical link with India's most backward north-east and eastern regions makes engagement a win–win for both sides.

Conclusion

India has a long history of trade with nations near and far, but, in the last 70 years, when India has been a modern, independent country, this relationship with trade has ceased. As a result of the effects of colonialism and the adoption of a broadly statist economy in the 1940s and 1950s, India veered onto a path of import substitution and trade aversion. In fact, this was the case in most post-colonial economies in the developing world. However, unlike the East Asian 'tiger' economies of Singapore, South Korea and Taiwan, which changed course in the 1960s and early 1970s, and China, which changed course from the late 1970s, India has continued to resist trade. It has persisted with a failing import substitution strategy and missed out on an opportunity to catch up through export-oriented growth. The major economic reforms of 1991, which included significant trade liberalisation, hardly led to an embrace of free trade. An uncompetitive manufacturing sector, protected through decades of socialism, was not able to stand up to competition from open markets. While its manufacturing sector remains unable to compete with the best in the world, India will continue to be reluctant

---

10   For a detailed study of India's engagement with the CLMV countries, see Das (2015).

about freer trade. Therefore, it is imperative that the factors that render Indian manufacturing uncompetitive are urgently addressed. India must begin by doing its homework on the appropriate strategy and reforms. However, a strategy that focuses on setting the right basic conditions for manufacturing—whether through simplifying the rules for conducting business, factor markets reform, tax reform or a focus on infrastructure development—should not be confused with an import substitution strategy. Although India has a big domestic market, the global market will always be much larger. It must make 'Make in India' for the world.

Therefore, India must enhance its engagement with open trade, even during the process of resolving its domestic problems, which will not be solved overnight, but will yield gradual improvements. Indian manufacturing has to become a part of the GVCs that are core to the manufacturing processes and, indeed, to trade. Given the global environment, which has lurched towards protectionism at least in the advanced economies of the West, the logical way for India to pursue a trade strategy is through Asia, the one region of the world that is still growing reasonably fast. India could begin by opening up to the South Asian region, minus Pakistan, and maintaining an open engagement with the East Asian region, without being overly concerned about China. The politics of this strategy are important, as the economies and countries in the Asian region seek a counterweight to China's power. India should also begin to more seriously explore the potential in larger regional arrangements, such as the Regional Comprehensive Economic Partnership. It should insist that other countries take steps to liberalise their services sectors, particularly those sectors that require the movement of natural persons, a comparative advantage for India.

The nature of the global economy—including manufacturing and trade—may undergo a fundamental change as the fourth industrial revolution comes to fruition in a decade or two from now. This means that India has a narrow window to finally catch up on manufacturing as we understand it today. It also means that India needs to get its house in order (i.e. undertake domestic policy reforms) before the onset of that revolution. A proactive Asian trade strategy could help to achieve that goal, which, in the long run, may be more critical than simply raising exports.

References

Associated Chambers of Commerce and Industry of India (ASSOCHAM). (2016, 1 September). *Exports to ASEAN stagnate while imports up 33 %; question mark on FTA*. Retrieved from: www.assocham.org/ newsdetail.php?id=5895

Das, R. U. (2015). *India's strategy for economic integration with CLMV*. New Delhi, India: Department of Commerce, Government of India.

ENS Economic Bureau. (2016, 15 October). India pushing for consensus on BIMSTEC free trade pact: Nirmala. *The Indian Express*. Retrieved from: indianexpress.com/article/business/business-others/india-pushing-for-consensus-on-bimstec-free-trade-pact-nirmala-3083355/

Law, A. (2015, 1 November). BBIN motor vehicles agreement implemented. *The Hindu business line*. Retrieved from: www.thehindu businessline.com/economy/logistics/bbin-motor-vehicles-agreement-implemented/article7829675.ece

Ministry of Commerce and Industry, Government of India. (2016). *India's share in global trade*. Retrieved from: pib.nic.in/newsite/Print Release.aspx?relid=154454

Ministry of External Affairs, Government of India. (2015). *Act East policy*. Retrieved from: pib.nic.in/newsite/PrintRelease.aspx?relid=133837

National Council of Applied Economic Research (NCAER). (2009). *Moving to goods and services tax in India: Impact on India's growth and international trade*. Report prepared for the Thirteenth Finance Commission, Government of India. Retrieved from: fincomindia.nic.in/writereaddata/html_en_files/oldcommission_html/fincom13/discussion/report28.pdf

Nayyar, D. (2010, 21 January). Dissatisfied with China on Indian exports, govt issues strong demarche. *The Indian Express*. Retrieved from: archive.indianexpress.com/news/dissatisfied-with-china-on-indian-exports-govt-issues-strong-demarche/569873/

Pal, P. (2016). *Intra-BBIN trade: Opportunities and challenges.* Observer Research Foundation. Retrieved from: www.orfonline.org/wp-content/uploads/2016/03/ORF-Issue-Brief_135.pdf

Panagariya, A. (2016a). Job creation in industry and services and shared prosperity. *National Institution for Transforming India (NITI Aayog).* Retrieved from: niti.gov.in/content/job-creation-industry-and-services-and-shared-prosperity

Panagariya, A. (2016b). Land leasing: A big win–win reform for the states. *NITI Aayog.* Retrieved from: niti.gov.in/content/land-leasing-big-win-win-reform-states

Panagariya, A. (2017). Jobs, growth and coastal economic zones. *NITI Aayog.* Retrieved from: niti.gov.in/content/jobs-growth-and-coastal-economic-zones

Press Trust of India. (2017, 18 January). UK expresses keenness to have FTA with India. *The Indian Express.* Retrieved from: indianexpress.com/article/india/uk-expresses-keenness-to-have-fta-with-india-4480620/

Rajan, R. (2014, 12 December). *Make in India, largely for India.* Bharat Ram Memorial Lecture, Reserve Bank of India. Retrieved from: www.rbi.org.in/scripts/BS_SpeechesView.aspx?Id=930

Sharma, M. S. (2014). *Restart: Last chance for the Indian economy.* New Delhi, India: Penguin Random House.

World Bank. (2017a). *Doing business: Measuring business regulations.* Retrieved from: www.doingbusiness.org/rankings/

World Bank. (2017b, 7 February). *Green signal for faster development: India's new freight corridor.* Retrieved from: www.worldbank.org/en/news/feature/2017/02/07/green-signal-faster-development-indias-new-freight-corridor

World Economic Forum. (2016). *Global competitiveness report.* Retrieved from: reports.weforum.org/global-competitiveness-index/

9

East Asia's transformation and regional architecture

Ponciano Intal, Jr

Introduction

Regional architecture has been defined as 'a reasonably coherent network of regional organizations, institutions, bilateral and multilateral arrangements, dialogue forums, and other relevant mechanisms that work collectively for regional prosperity, peace and stability' (Hu, 2009, p. 4). One remarkable development in East Asia[1] during the past three decades has been the emergence of regional architecture that has revolved around small and middleweight countries, especially the Association of Southeast Asian Nations (ASEAN) member states, Australia and New Zealand; been supported by the big powers; and been characterised by open regionalism and a cooperative multilateral security perspective. This regional architecture has contributed to, and been facilitated by, the economic transformation of East Asia, which has largely been anchored in outward-oriented economic policies and open regionalism.

Region building is a dynamic process and East Asia's economic and security architecture, based on open and cooperative regionalism, has been supported and shaped by a network of institutions in the region. Among

---

1   East Asia is construed broadly here to include Australia, New Zealand and India; effectively, East Asia defined as the ASEAN+6 grouping.

the official institutions and organisations, the most prominent have been the Asia–Pacific Economic Cooperation forum (APEC) and ASEAN and ASEAN-related arrangements, including the ASEAN Regional Forum (ARF) and East Asia Summit (EAS). Non-official or semi-official institutions and organisations, such as the Pacific Economic Cooperation Council (PECC), Pacific Trade and Development (PAFTAD) conference, and ASEAN – Institutes of Strategic and International Studies (ASEAN–ISIS) have been central to the framing of regionalism in East Asia (and, more broadly, the Asia–Pacific). Note that PECC, PAFTAD, ASEAN–ISIS and even the more recent Economic Research Institute of ASEAN Research Institute Network (ERIA RIN) are themselves networks of individuals or institutions. Indeed, it is likely that the prominence of networks—and networks of networks—at the official and non-official levels in the process of region building in East Asia has arisen from the fact that region building has been substantially shaped and facilitated by the small and middleweight countries. This has invited a more collaborative approach, which allows for greater flexibility and responsiveness to the fast-changing developments in the region.

Alongside the development of its regional architecture, East Asia has undergone a dramatic economic transformation in the past three decades. As an indicator of this economic transformation, developing East Asia's share in the total ASEAN+6's gross domestic product (GDP) rose from 20 per cent in 1985 to about 53 per cent by 2014 (where developing East Asia is defined as ASEAN, excluding Singapore and Brunei Darussalam, but including China and India, and ASEAN+6 is comprised of the 10 ASEAN members plus Australia, China, India, Japan, New Zealand and South Korea). At the same time, the share of the ASEAN+6's GDP as a proportion of total global GDP increased from about 18 per cent to about 27 per cent. Perhaps the most telling indicator is the huge rise in China's share of global exports, which increased from about 3 per cent in the mid-1990s to about 15 per cent in the mid-2010s. China, Japan, ASEAN as a group and India are now among the largest economies in the world, and the East Asia region (ASEAN+6) now has the largest share of global output.

This chapter argues that open and cooperative regionalism has flourished in the region because small and middleweight countries have provided a platform for region building. In turn, this regionalism has created a greater sense of community in East Asia, which is exemplified by the strong foundations for intra-regional economic linkages with the rest of the world, the accelerated economic transformation of the region's economies and the deepening regional cooperation on a wide range of areas and issues. In addition, an East Asian regionalism centred on small and middleweight countries has provided a flexible platform that can accommodate and adapt well to the changing economic and political fortunes of East Asian countries, as illustrated throughout the period that witnessed the rise of China.

Moving forward, developing East Asia is in a phase of growth and transformation, which provides both opportunities and challenges to the region and the world. It is worth noting that this transformation is occurring, and will continue to occur, in a world where much of the growth in global demand is from developing East Asia itself. The greater reliance on East Asia as a growth driver has become even more important in the context of the apparent inward-oriented policy bias in the US and the uncertainty in the EU following the Brexit vote. This is in stark contrast to the situation in the 1990s, when the US and the EU were important drivers of the growth and economic transformations of China and ASEAN. The export-driven strategies of China and ASEAN were, at that time, ultimately linked to the EU and US markets. Given the new environment, East Asia's regional architecture has arguably become even more important for the region and the world moving forward.

The rest of the chapter proceeds as follows. The first section discusses the economic transformation of East Asia. The second section describes the evolution of regional architecture during the past three decades. The chapter then considers major developments from 2015 until recently, and the challenges and opportunities they present for the region and its current architecture. The chapter concludes by highlighting the importance of further investment in a more robust regional, economic and security architecture that facilitates significant domestic supply-side reforms, particularly in developing Asia, so that the region can become a driver of the world economy and polity into the future.

The remarkable economic transformation of East Asia

The three decades since the mid-1980s witnessed a dramatic economic transformation of East Asia. The shift towards more export-oriented economic policies, together with a surge in foreign direct investment (FDI), led to rapid growth of manufacturing exports and higher economic growth in a number of ASEAN countries and in China. India's exchange rate and trade reforms in the 1990s have moved the country towards greater openness and export orientation, albeit at a more measured pace than in ASEAN and China. Nonetheless, India's reforms have yielded higher economic growth, particularly in its service export sector.

Arguably, the decade from the mid-1980s to the mid-1990s, prior to the Asian financial crisis, could be described as ASEAN's first golden era of high growth, with surging investment and manufacturing exports, and significantly declining unemployment and poverty. An important catalyst for this golden era was the appreciation of the yen. This, together with outward-oriented policy reforms in Indonesia, Malaysia and Thailand, and the opening up of China, led to a surge in export-oriented FDI by Japan, Taiwan and Hong Kong (the latter two primarily directed foreign investment flows to China). This phenomenon is sometimes described as the 'flying geese' pattern of development. Japan was the first to pursue this pattern, and it was followed by other newly industrialised economies. By the early 1990s, these geese were joined by several emerging ASEAN countries and China. Overall, this pattern provides a spatial description of the dynamic shifts of comparative advantage in the region. Japanese firms were major players in this process. This was largely in response to the yen's appreciation, the sharp rise in Japan's labour costs and the Japanese government's encouragement for firms to shift their low-wage and low-skilled labour-intensive manufactures to ASEAN countries and China. In addition, the establishment of the special economic zones in coastal China—the country's major initial experimentation in opening its economy—led to a massive relocation of Hong Kong's manufacturing sector to China's Pearl River Delta. At the same time, Taiwanese firms expanded into Chinese coastal areas like Fujian. Thus, the late 1980s to early 1990s saw the emergence of export-oriented manufacturing sectors in these countries and the foundation for the regional production networks that now define East Asia's industrial production linkages, especially in the electronics and machinery industries.

The founding ASEAN countries experienced an economic crisis in 1997–99. In large part, this arose from the so-called 'impossible trinity' that these countries pursued during the latter 1980s and the early 1990s, or the long-term incompatibility of a fixed exchange rate, an open capital account and an independent monetary policy. There was an initial setback in terms of national output as a result of the crisis, but relatively robust growth during the 2000s, owing to large currency depreciations in the affected ASEAN countries and much more prudent macro-economic policies. Combined with surging import demand and a commodity boom arising from the fast-growing Chinese and Indian economies, these factors provided the foundations for the export and economic recovery. The 2000s also saw a deepening of the region's production networks, which were increasingly centred on China, to the degree that China became the primary export market of many ASEAN and other countries, including Japan, Korea and Australia. This was a significant redirection of trade away from the US and, for a number of ASEAN countries, Japan.

The late 1990s to the 2000s and beyond saw the emergence of Cambodia, Laos and Vietnam (CLV); this group experienced much higher economic growth rates compared to the rest of ASEAN during this period. These higher growth rates, with an attendant surge in (primarily export-oriented) FDI and exports, arose from CLV's aggressive shift towards outward- and export-oriented economic policies. It was facilitated by favourable market access conditions in ASEAN, the EU and the US. Myanmar commenced a similar process in the 2010s, with the reforms of a new civilian-oriented government. Vietnam has been the stellar success story for ASEAN in the past two decades in terms of reforms, international economic relations and socio-economic performance, arguably second only to China worldwide.

In short, during the past three decades, developing East Asia was a rapidly growing, transforming and dynamic region. The results of this process can be gleaned from the substantial rise in developing East Asia's share of global investment, exports, trade in goods and services, and output (see Figures 9.1 and 9.2).

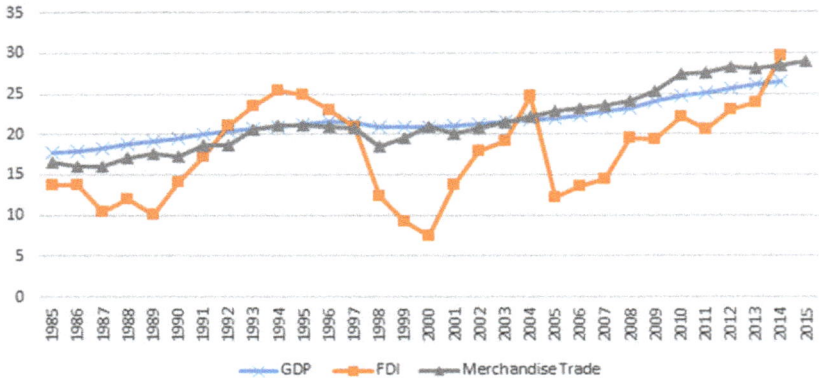

Figure 9.1: ASEAN+6's share of global GDP, foreign direct investment and total merchandise trade (per cent), 1985–2014
Source: UNCTAD (unctadstat.unctad.org/EN/).

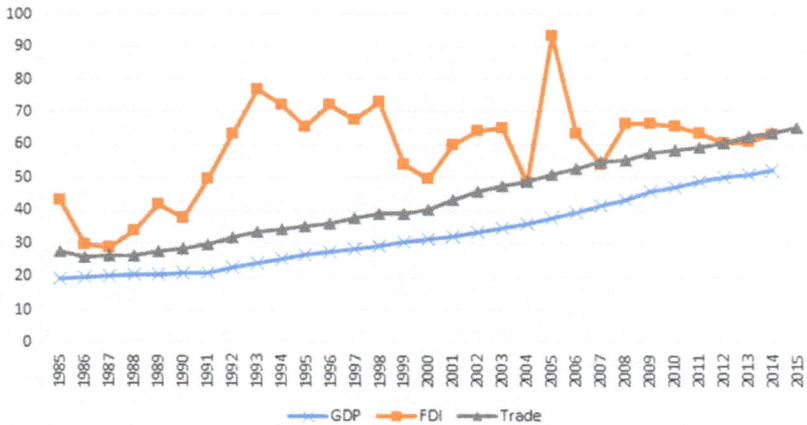

Figure 9.2: Developing Asia's share of ASEAN+6's GDP, foreign direct investment and total merchandise trade (per cent), 1985–2014
Source: UNCTAD (unctadstat.unctad.org/EN/).

Similarly, developed East Asian countries experienced significant change during the period. The flurry of reforms in Australia and New Zealand in the 1980s and 1990s effectively transformed these countries' relatively protectionist and rigid regulatory regimes into comparatively open economies, with regulatory regimes and systems that are now among the best in the world. Among the Organisation for Economic Co-operation and Development (OECD) countries, South Korea has been one of the most aggressive and consistent in improving its regulatory management system since the late 1990s. South Korea, Australia, New Zealand and Singapore have ranked among the best in the world in terms of regulatory quality, competitiveness and ease of doing business. Equally important, the four have been more resilient to global shocks compared with many other OECD countries. Perhaps not surprisingly, these four countries have been strongly engaged in regional integration efforts and developing East Asia's regional architecture.

The upshot of the region's widespread transformation was that, by 2014, the ASEAN+6 region had already taken over the EU's status as the region with the largest share of global output. The ASEAN+6 share in 2014 was 26.47 per cent, compared with the EU's 26.40 per cent and the US's 25.54 per cent. The shares for the EU and US reflect secular declines experienced by both, but especially the EU, which had a global output share of 36 per cent in 1985. East Asia has also eclipsed the EU and the US as the world's leading investment destination and is edging closer to the EU as the world's largest trading group. Intra-regional trade in East Asia has grown substantially. For example, ASEAN's trade with itself and with the '+6' group (the non-ASEAN countries that make up the ASEAN+6 region) increased from about 51 per cent in 1990 to about 64 per cent in 2015. The intra-ASEAN+3 (ASEAN plus China, Japan and South Korea) trade share rose from about 37 per cent in 1990 to about 47 per cent in 2015.[2]

An important factor in the significant rise of East Asia in global trade and investment has been the expansion of regional production networks in the region, much of it in parts and components, and primarily involving Japan, Korea, Taiwan, China and ASEAN members. It should be noted that the rise in the intra-regional trade share within the ASEAN+3 occurred in parallel with the intra-regional trade intensity, declining from 2.06 in 1990 to 1.66 in 2015. This reflects the fact that, as it deepened its intra-regional trade, East Asia also greatly expanded its trade with the rest of the world. Indeed, the past three decades has seen the development of the so-called 'Factory Asia', which refers to the production networks in the region that are geared to producing goods not only for the region, but also, importantly, for export to the rest of the world, especially the US and Europe.

---

2   Data taken from the Asian Development Bank (ADB) Asia Regional Integration Center.

These developments—the deepening economic linkages, the growth of production networks in East Asia and the rise of East Asia as the factory of the world—flourished in a fortunate context of convergent export-oriented trade policies and the growing economic openness of virtually all East Asian economies during much of the last three decades. This convergence was not solely the result of unilateral liberalisation obligations under the World Trade Organization (WTO). It was also the result of a surge in regionalism and the growth of regional architecture, as these facilitated deeper economic linkages intra-regionally without raising barriers against the rest of the world. Indeed, in many cases, the regional commitments were effectively multilateralised. Finally, the regional cooperative arrangement has brought peace and stability to East Asia during much of the period. This is the essence of the open and cooperative regionalism that has been the hallmark of East Asia's regionalism and regional architecture. A discussion on East Asia's regional architecture and regionalism follows below.

Evolution of East Asia's regional economic and political security architecture

Alongside the economic transformation of East Asia during the past three decades has been the remarkable development of the region's economic, political and security architecture. Of interest are the regional institutions and arrangements for regional economic integration and cooperation, as well as for regional peace, stability and security. After being largely undeveloped throughout the 1980s, East Asia's regional architecture underwent a flurry of region building from the 1990s and, especially, from the 2000s.

There were few regional arrangements, such as free trade agreements, for regional economic integration and cooperation before the end of the 1980s. Those that did exist were largely at initial tentative stages of implementation, or just proposals. Notable stillborn proposals include the Japanese-led Pacific Free Trade Area, consisting of Australia, Canada, Japan, New Zealand and the US, and the Organisation for Pacific Trade and Development, which was a proposal similar to the OECD (Asian Development Bank [ADB], 2010, pp. 57–58).

However, two classes of institutions established during that era, at the official and non-government levels, proved to be central to the development of regional economic architecture in the 1990s and beyond. At the official level was ASEAN (established in 1967) and, at the non-governmental level, were the PAFTAD conference series (established in 1968) and PECC, established in 1980. Essentially, this shows that there was a nascent regional architecture in East Asia until the late 1980s, with the networking primarily occurring among non-government institutions. The most significant intergovernmental effort at deeper regional economic linkages was the Closer Economic Relations (CER) free trade agreement between Australia and New Zealand, which was established in 1983.

From the 1990s, ASEAN became the centre of East Asia regional architecture. During its first three decades of existence (1967–97), the major benefit of ASEAN for the region was not economic but, rather, the engendering of peace, neighbourliness and cooperation among the founding ASEAN countries. This was important because, in the 1960s, South-East Asia was deemed unstable and characterised as the 'Balkans of the East'. ASEAN built confidence and dispelled mutual suspicion between ASEAN members through frequent meetings and other cooperative activities. It pushed for peace throughout the ASEAN region through the Zone of Peace, Freedom and Neutrality, and through efforts to end the Cambodian conflict, which culminated in the 1991 Paris Agreement. ASEAN's significant economic initiatives during the period—the Preferential Trade Arrangement, ASEAN Industrial Projects and the ASEAN Industrial Complementation Scheme—had, at best, modest results.

PAFTAD and PECC have been the most important groups shaping one of the key characteristics that defines East Asian regionalism: open regionalism. Together with the APEC Business Advisory Council (BAC), successor of the Pacific Business Economic Council, PECC has become a critical support institution for APEC since the latter's establishment in 1989. Perhaps the best characterisation of the important role of the non-governmental institutions, especially PECC, to East Asia's region building at that time was put forward by former Australian Prime Minister Robert Hawke, in a momentous speech in South Korea, on 31 January 1989, when he stated that: 'PECC's work has illuminated large areas of common interests within the region' (Hawke, 1989, p. 4). Indeed, as Hawke (1989) stated, to some extent, the conception of APEC as a 'more formal intergovernmental vehicle of regional cooperation … in the model, in a different context, by the OECD' was a follow up of PECC, which 'by its informality … has also made it difficult for it to address policy issues which are properly the responsibility of Governments' (pp. 4–5).

The decade from the late 1980s to the early 1990s was a momentous period in terms of global security and economic relations. In the political and security arena, it witnessed the fall of the Berlin Wall, the reunification of Germany and the eventual collapse of the Soviet Union. In the economic relations arena, the period was characterised by the establishment of the EU (and the accompanying fears of a 'Fortress Europe') and of the North American Free Trade Agreement (NAFTA). In addition, the Uruguay Round of trade negotiations started in 1988, which, despite their ups and downs, ended successfully in 1994.

All of these major international developments significantly accelerated East Asia's regionalism and the development of its regional economic architecture. Thus, the establishment of APEC was largely the result of the region's appreciation for its relatively open and non-discriminatory multilateral trading system. Other concerns in the region, such as the rising bilateral tensions caused by trade imbalances with the US, poor progress of the Uruguay Round and the formation of bilateral and regional trading arrangements that could undermine a truly multilateral trading system, were also contributing factors to APEC's establishment (Hawke, 1989). Hawke first presented the idea that eventually led to the formation of APEC in South Korea, a middleweight country. APEC's preferential bias for the multilateral trading system makes the concept of 'open regionalism' espoused by PECC a perfect fit for APEC. APEC's aims are trade and investment liberalisation and facilitation, deeper regional economic and technical cooperation and structural reform that is consistent with, and supportive of, the multilateral trading system. APEC has become a key fixture of East Asia's regional architecture since the 1990s. Given its voluntary nature, and the strong support from APEC, BAC and PECC, APEC has provided a platform for Asia–Pacific discussion and agreement on a wide range of border, behind-the-border and structural and regulatory reform issues. Despite the failure of initiatives such as voluntary early sectoral liberalisation, APEC has become an important complement to other regional integration and cooperative institutions and initiatives, including ASEAN, the next topic of discussion.

ASEAN and regional economic architecture

ASEAN has become more active in economic region building since the 1990s. Arguably, this is the area in which ASEAN centrality has been more pronounced and, at the same time, increasingly tested. In 1991, ASEAN established the ASEAN Free Trade Area (AFTA), in large part in response to the concerns generated by the establishment of the EU and NAFTA, which, it was feared, could curtail exports and even investments to an increasingly export-oriented ASEAN. AFTA was a significant leap forward from ASEAN's previous Preferential Trade Arrangement of the late 1970s–80s. The successful formation of AFTA was particularly impressive, given the domestic policy contestations between protectionism and greater economic openness that occurred in the region at that time. This occurred in Indonesia (see Drysdale, 2016b) and, later in the 1980s, in the Philippines. Thus, to a large extent, AFTA was not just a reaction to negative expectations in regard to ASEAN's external trading environment, but also a reflection of the growing confidence in ASEAN member states that export orientation and economic openness delivered better economic results than protectionism, as reflected in sharply rising exports of manufactures and FDI inflows.[3] AFTA was the second free trade agreement in East Asia after CER, but the first in which most of the members were developing economies—that said, they were also among the fastest growing economies in the world, until the Asian financial crisis.

It is worth noting that ASEAN's response to the Asian financial crisis was not to return to protectionism but to deepen and widen its open regionalism. A few months after the start of the financial crisis, ASEAN leaders signed the ASEAN Vision 2020, which became the foundation for the blueprint of the ASEAN Economic Community (AEC). ASEAN maintained its outward-oriented, open regionalism course despite the financial crisis because of a confluence of factors. These included the discussions and agreements within APEC (particularly, the Bogor goals and China's decision not to devalue the renminbi in view of the crisis), implementation of the Uruguay Round, the signing of the Information

---

3   The Philippines was the exception as it lagged in FDI and exports compared to other ASEAN member states. AFTA was an affirmation of the significant shift in its economic policy stance away from protectionism, which, at that time, was viewed by many as a major reason for the crisis that befell the Philippines in the early to mid-1980s.

Technology Agreement in 1996, the implementation of AFTA, the results of track two discussions (in PECC and ASEAN–ISIS) and the remarkable success of ASEAN in trade and FDI before the crisis.

East Asia responded to the crisis by deepening the regional financial cooperation that arose during the course of the crisis. This included establishing the Chiang Mai Initiative, the first regional currency swap arrangement launched by the ASEAN+3 countries in 2000; the Asian Bond Market Initiative; and enhanced regional macro-economic surveillance mechanisms. All of these financial cooperation initiatives were strongly supported by the '+3' countries and initially nurtured by the ADB. At the same time, the sharp drop of FDI in ASEAN in the aftermath of the crisis and the surge in Chinese investment and growth meant that the implementation of the AEC was brought forward from 2020 to 2015. This was done to revive ASEAN as an attractive investment destination and to assist it to regain its pre-crisis position as a premier direct investment destination in the developing world.

The 2000s saw an explosion of FTAs involving East Asian countries. The surge in bilateral FTAs in the region was the result of the difficulties experienced in the WTO Doha Round negotiations. Lack of progress within the WTO encouraged support for bilateral and regional FTAs and 'competitive liberalisation' as stepping stones to global reform. Another factor in this explosion was the use of such FTAs for trade expansion and investment attraction, in the face of the challenging international economic environment at the turn of the 2000s. Most FTAs were pursued by small and medium powers, such as Singapore, Malaysia and Thailand, as well as Mexico across the Pacific (see Aggarwal & Koo, 2006).

As highlighted by the East Asia Vision Group (EAVG, 2001), the 1997–98 Asian financial crisis provided 'a strong impetus to strengthen regional cooperation … [giving] rise to the recognition that East Asia needs to institutionalize its cooperation to solve similar problems and prevent new ones' (p. 7). China's proposal for an ASEAN–China FTA led to a similar proposal for an ASEAN–Japan Economic Partnership Agreement and, indeed, snowballed into the signing of ASEAN+1 FTAs with Australia–New Zealand, China, India, Japan and South Korea over the decade. The EAVG's proposal for an East Asia Free Trade Area, which involved the ASEAN+3 countries and was pushed by China, led to a counterproposal for a Comprehensive Economic Partnership for East Asia, involving the ASEAN+6 countries, which was primarily promoted by Japan. ASEAN's diplomatic response to these contesting proposals was to unveil the Regional Comprehensive Economic Partnership (RCEP) in 2012, with a variable membership, but initially comprising the ASEAN+6 countries. An important goal of RCEP was facilitating trade by eliminating the 'noodle bowl' effect from the varying rules of origin of the ASEAN+1 FTAs, and aiming for a high-quality and inclusive FTA. Meanwhile, the Trans-Pacific Partnership (TPP), initiated by small, open economies, including Singapore, Brunei Darussalam and Chile, gained prominence when the US joined in and substantially shaped negotiations. The TPP negotiations were completed in 2015, but US President Donald Trump withdrew the US from the grouping, leaving the remaining members to negotiate a way forward, and the RCEP negotiations are ongoing (2017).

It is remarkable that there was such an explosion of bilateral and regional FTAs in such a short period of time in East Asia. In part, this was consonant with deepening business linkages—especially production networks—in a world of increasing global competition. Deepening and geographically widening business networks require a reduction in service link costs to allow for more efficient slicing and dicing of production processes and stages across borders, which reduces overall costs and improves efficiencies. Another reason for the explosion of FTAs was that the region was the fastest growing market, with large potential for investment and trading in a variegated and growing range of businesses and networks. In short, the FTAs were effectively problem-solving and opportunity-enhancing initiatives, meant to further the dynamism and synergies of East Asian economies.

The operationalisation of the first two regional FTAs in East Asia—CER and AFTA, which is part of the broader AEC—effectively embody open regionalism. This is because ASEAN member states, as well as Australia and New Zealand, trade much more with the rest of the world than between themselves. At the same time, China is the centre of Factory Asia and, as such, its production networks must engage the rest of the world, both in terms of exports and imports. This is consistent with open regionalism. Similarly, Japan and South Korea's top export markets have included the US for quite some time. In short, an export-oriented region must necessarily follow open regionalism to remain the factory of the world, even as, increasingly, it becomes the market of the world.

ASEAN and regional political security architecture

Since the 1990s, ASEAN has become the centre of East Asia's regional architecture in the political and security arena. ASEAN received enhanced diplomatic recognition following both its success in ending the Cambodian conflict through the 1991 Paris Agreement and its confidence-building measure that provided the foundation for the ARF, established in 1994, as an offshoot of the ASEAN Post Ministerial Conference. The ARF is noteworthy for a number of reasons (Ba, 2016):

- It was the first official-level security dialogue involving regular multilateral regional discussions on regional security and cooperation in the Asia–Pacific after the Cold War.
- It signified ASEAN's break from its earlier emphasis on regional (ASEAN) autonomy, which implied resistance to collective institutionalised security cooperation with the big powers.
- It brought in a rising China (hitherto outside the Cold War–era US security alliances in East Asia) and Russia.
- It affirmed the importance and relevance of ASEAN's Treaty of Amity and Cooperation for the region.
- Most importantly—and in sharp contrast to the then prevailing realist, balance of power perspective—it employed a cooperative approach to security, considering that 'security is best gained not by working against others, but rather [by] working *with* them' (Ba, 2016, p. 5).

The cooperative security approach is an institutional innovation to regional security architecture. It is informed by ASEAN's emphasis on dialogue, diplomacy and consensus, and is, arguably, the most realistic means by which small and middleweight countries can assume diplomatic centrality in multilateral security arrangements that involve major regional powers. ARF emphasised non-traditional security issues (Ba, 2016; Leifer, 2009).

Two other ASEAN-related institutional innovations in East Asia's regional security architecture are worth noting. The first, an offshoot of ARF, is the ASEAN Defence Ministers Meeting (ADMM), established in 2006, and the ADMM Plus, established in 2010, which focuses on practical, functional security cooperation initiatives. Membership of both ADMM and ADMM Plus is limited to the membership of the EAS, a smaller grouping than the 27 or so members of ARF. The EAS, which includes ASEAN+6, as well as the US and Russia, is the other institutional innovation that is becoming an important leaders-level dialogue mechanism on regional security matters in East Asia; the ARF is only at the ministerial level (foreign ministers). Although there are other institutions and arrangements that have a bearing on East Asia's regional security architecture, such as the Shangri-La Dialogue, Six Party Talks and the Shanghai Cooperation Organisation, the EAS provides a platform at the leader's level for managing the challenges of East Asia's regional security environment—especially in the face of apparently growing China–US rivalry in the region.

East Asia's transformation and regional architecture moving forward

The years 2015–17 may prove to be a watershed period for the East Asian region. ASEAN (and East Asia) has furthered its commitment to regional economic integration and connectivity and, at the same time, the East and South China Sea issues have markedly raised regional security uncertainty in the region. More recently, the ascendancy of a more nationalist, less open and more populist 'America First' US administration has also drastically increased uncertainty on the economic and trading environment between the US and East Asia. These issues pose major challenges to further region building in East Asia and put tremendous pressures on the efficacy and credibility of current institutions and organisations in the region. The contentious US–China relationship has increased the importance of East Asia's regional economic and security architecture. The remarkable opportunities offered by a robustly growing, developing East Asia to the region and the world demand, as well as facilitate, the stronger regional economic and security architecture that currently exists in East Asia.

Opportunities in developing East Asia

Significant opportunities are offered by the robustly growing economies of China, India and ASEAN. Atsmon, Child, Dobbs and Narasimhan (2012, pp. 43–44) projected that the number of Chinese households with an annual income of US$16,000–US$34,000 would increase from about 14 million in 2010 to about 167 million in 2020, representing about 400 million individuals. The number of affluent households earning more than US$34,000 per year is predicted to increase from 4.3 million to around 21 million—about 60 million people—during the same period (Atsmon et al., 2012). This is clearly a huge market. By around 2030, as China moves towards becoming a high-income country—as per the World Bank definition—many more Chinese households and individuals will enter the consumer market; this has tremendous potential for expanded trade within the region (OECD Development Centre, 2016, p. 32). Similarly, McKinsey Global Institute (2007, p. 13) projected that India's middle class—households with annual incomes of US$4,380–US$21,890—will increase from 13 million households (50 million individuals) in 2005 to 128 million households (or 583 million individuals) by 2025. This would make India the world's fifth largest consumer market by 2025. Likewise, ASEAN (as a group) is already one of the largest economic zones in the world, and its 'consumer class'—households with incomes capable of making significant discretionary purchases—will increase from about 67 million at present to about 125 million households by 2025 (Vinayak, Thompson & Tonby, 2014, pp. 3–6). The sheer magnitude of the projected middle/consumer class in China, India and ASEAN makes developing East Asia the largest source of market growth in the future.

Engendering robust growth in developing East Asia will require, first, significant supply-side reforms to allow a successful rebalancing of China's economy towards greater consumption and a domestic economic focus, although it will remain deeply engaged with the international economy. Second, successful industrialisation and employment creation in India needs to occur. Third, ASEAN must be upgraded technologically to achieve greater competitiveness. Although much of this reform must be domestically driven, a concerted deepening of regional economic linkages will greatly contribute to the success of such domestic reform. Indeed, there is a significant internal dynamic and multiplier effect from cooperative reform and deeper integration within East Asia, as exemplified by the AEC and RCEP.

For East Asia as a whole, successful RCEP negotiations could facilitate the grasping of a 'historic opportunity', as Drysdale (2016a) put it. Cooperative reform and deeper integration calls for the complementarity of RCEP, AEC, APEC, the Asian Infrastructure Investment Bank (AIIB), the ADB and the Belt and Road Initiative (BRI), among others. Non-governmental institutions, such as PAFTAD, PECC and ERIA RIN, also have an important role to play in the successful transformation of the region, given their shared experiences, as well as their understanding of practices and analysis. In short, the regional economic architecture should be tasked with ensuring that open and cooperative regionalism in East Asia delivers for the region and its peoples.

ASEAN, the AEC and RCEP

Both AEC and RCEP are important forums through which ASEAN member states can maximise the benefits and opportunities from the growing East Asia region. AEC goes much further than enhancing regional integration, as it is about concerted and cooperative domestic reforms and regional connectivity. These are both critical elements for ASEAN to remain a major FDI destination and a significant production hub for the region and the world. RCEP, if successfully concluded, would expand market access, cooperative arrangements and reform impetus to the whole dynamic East Asia region.

For ASEAN, the end of 2015 saw the formalisation of the AEC. In the next decade, ASEAN countries will be required to address behind-the-border and at-the-border barriers to deeper integration, as well as the challenges of greater national and regional connectivity. The results of monitoring studies by ERIA on the implementation of the 2015 AEC blueprint showed that, despite significant progress, much remains to be done for ASEAN to become a relatively integrated production base and market, especially in the areas of services, mutual recognition arrangements, non-tariff measures, investment and trade and transport facilitation. AEC's unfinished business from 2015 tends to relate to areas for which implementation efforts are more sensitive and difficult, require more time and resources or involve in-country institutional and regulatory changes.

The new AEC 2025 Blueprint includes finishing the unfinished business of the 2015 Blueprint, as well as new initiatives, including the Good Regulatory Practice (GRP) initiative. A number of these issues are highlighted in the new Master Plan on ASEAN Connectivity (MPAC) for 2025. Behind-the-border regulatory, institutional and coordination changes are becoming increasingly important issues as ASEAN integration deepens. Equally important is cross-border regulatory, institutional and process coordination among ASEAN countries. To some extent, the implementation of the GRP under the 2025 AEC Blueprint could help address the domestic and cross-border issues raised above. For example, ASEAN's business sector has already raised issues regarding the different requirements and regulations among ASEAN countries without appropriate mutual recognition agreements, and the burdensome processes and inadequate transparency in several ASEAN countries. There remain huge differences among ASEAN members in terms of ease of doing business and trading across borders.

In addition, many ASEAN member states will need to invest more in improving their human capital as they lag behind China and India in this area. As human talent is a key basis for competitiveness, many ASEAN countries may need to further open their economies to foreign talent to leverage their local talents and develop competitive niches. Similarly, ASEAN countries will need to encourage greater technological diffusion and enhance their innovation and adaptation capabilities to raise productivity growth and move up the technology ladder. All of the above will assist ASEAN member states to avoid a middle-income trap.

Clearly, the implementation of the AEC 2025 Blueprint will be extremely challenging. However, a successful AEC is essential for ASEAN to maintain its role as a key facilitator in East Asia's regional architecture into the future, especially in light of a rising India and a superpower China. To this end, ASEAN could draw on learnings, synergies and complementarities between implementing the AEC and MPAC measures and those of the broader regional cooperation and integration initiatives in East Asia and the Pacific, such as RCEP, APEC, AIIB and China's BRI. Indeed, harnessing the complementarities of these institutions and initiatives, together with other regional institutions, such as the ADB, can further regional liberalisation, connectivity, facilitation and economic and technical cooperation.

Equally importantly, these synergies contribute to greater inclusiveness within countries as well as between developed and developing countries in the region. Indeed, the economic success of Cambodia, Laos, Malaysia and Vietnam in the past decade has stemmed, in large part, from the synergies of liberalised economic regimes, improved facilitation of trade and investment, greater connectivity through infrastructure and strengthened institutional capability. Thus, enhancing the synergies of liberalisation, facilitation, economic and technical cooperation, and connectivity will propel East Asia towards deeper regional integration and global competitiveness. In turn, this could underpin more robust and inclusive growth.

In this regard, RCEP and China's BRI are opportune for the region. RCEP combines liberalisation, facilitation reforms and economic and technical cooperation. In addition, the complementarity with the AIIB and BRI can be harnessed to facilitate connectivity and support institutional capacities to implement reforms in developing East Asia. The AIIB, which started operations in 2015, and the BRI are the flagship initiatives of

China's new 'neighbourhood diplomacy' (Chen, 2015). RCEP has come at a particularly opportune time because of the confluence of similarity in domestic reform imperatives in developing East Asia and the availability of enabling regional institutions and initiatives. As Drysdale emphasised, RCEP is a 'historic opportunity for East Asia to secure its future as the dynamic centre of higher than average global growth through deepening its integration and cooperative commitment to the reforms' (Drysdale, 2016a, p. 2). This is because much of developing East Asia is in need of supply-side reforms to rebalance economies (China), remain attractive to investors and move up the technology ladder (developing ASEAN states), join global value chains (India) and unlock further productivity potential.

As of 2017, RCEP negotiations were ongoing. There appeared to be a growing resolve among RCEP members to achieve substantial outcomes from the negotiations in 2017 (even if RCEP may be concluded in 2018), given that 2017 marks the 50th anniversary of ASEAN. To some extent, RCEP negotiations are daunting because RCEP is an indirect way of establishing FTAs among ASEAN RCEP partners. In addition, it appears that ASEAN member states have yet to reach common positions on a number of RCEP issues, such as services.

In principle, ASEAN countries should embrace RCEP because it can potentially deliver greater benefits than AEC (Itakura, 2012). RCEP aims to be a modern, comprehensive, high-quality and mutually beneficial economic partnership agreement among the ASEAN+6 countries. At the same time, RCEP emphasises inclusiveness and economic and technical cooperation. Indeed, in light of the non-negligible tariffs and varied levels of development and institutional capacities that exist, a successful conclusion of RCEP would likely have positive effects in terms of the liberalisation and facilitation of global trade.

The economic and technical cooperation exemplified by a robust RCEP could present an excellent example to the rest of the world. Given that trade barriers are higher among RCEP countries and that the RCEP region holds great potential for trade growth, if RCEP can instigate deeper integration initiatives among ASEAN's RCEP partners, it will advance global trade reform.

East Asia has effectively been promoted into a de facto global leadership role. This has occurred as a consequence of the US rejecting the TPP as part of its more inward-looking 'America First' stance, the internal challenges in the EU following Brexit and the apparent de-emphasis on North Atlantic Treaty Organization by the new US administration. This global leadership role for East Asia involves engendering and maintaining outward economies and open markets. A successful RCEP conclusion, the BRI and Japan's expanded quality infrastructure program are all important foundations for the global leadership of East Asia. However, a successful RCEP conclusion requires engaged and active leadership by ASEAN, with the support of Australia, China and Japan.

East Asia's regional political security architecture moving forward

Pan (2015) described the process of European regionalisation as progressing 'from the center to the periphery', whereas the logic of East Asian region building is 'from the periphery to the center' (p. 20), with the periphery being the middleweight economies. The gravitational pull of power in regional architecture appears to be towards the centre, especially in the light of a rising China. Nonetheless, peace, stability and prosperity in East Asia calls for the region's current and future big powers to remain wedded to, and supportive of, a coordinated and strengthened network of institutions, organisations and agreements mainly centred around the region's small and middleweight countries. A lack of unity among the four big powers—China, India, Japan and the US—in the political and security arena would lead to the fulcrum of East Asia's regional architecture resting on the shoulders of the region's small and middleweight countries.

Although the trajectory of the region's economy and architecture appears to be promising and its challenges manageable, significant uncertainty persists in relation to the region's political and security environment and architecture. During 2015–16, China flexed its muscles in the South China Sea in relation to its island-building agenda. Its behaviour raised uncertainty in a region characterised by a rising China and its prickly political and security relationship with the once-dominant US. Moreover, the new US administration has been antagonistic towards China regarding trade, Taiwan and the South China Sea. Japan's more assertive political and security diplomacy in recent years has also increased this uncertainty, especially in light of its territorial disputes and historical baggage with China.

However, there are other factors that temper the uncertainty of the security environment in the region. Despite being vigorously contested by China, the Hague Tribunal decision provided clarity on the nature of the South China Sea. Moreover, the Philippines decided to set aside the tribunal's decision, despite it being in the Philippines favour, to improve its bilateral relations with China. It is also worth noting that the strong economic linkages between the region's big powers—the US–China and the Japan–China trade relationships are among the largest in the world—provide a solid rationale for these countries to ensure a relatively stable security environment in the region.

The remarkable economic transformation of East Asia has been underpinned by a relatively stable regional security environment. ASEAN aims to create a binding code of conduct in the South China Sea as a means of defusing the region's lingering tension over the area. More broadly, managing the region's security challenges would involve investing much more into aspects of its regional security architecture that have propagated 'security multilateralism' and security cooperation (Bisley, 2013). The multilateral security mechanisms, embodied by ARF, ADMM Plus and EAS, 'provide the opportunity to improve information flows, reduce the prospects and consequence of miscommunication and generate regular lines of contact so as to build a basic sense of trust among the region's states' (Bisley, 2013, p. 36). From the Australian perspective, the region's regional security architecture complements the unilateral security investments and bilateral security arrangements that a country can employ to enhance its own national security. Investing in regional security architecture that espouses security multilateralism is particularly important for small and middleweight countries, such as the ASEAN countries and Australia, for which long-term security lies in a stable balance of power among the region's big powers.

Regional leadership contestations between China, Japan and the US mean that the current regional architecture, which espouses security multilateralism and the 'ASEAN way' of dialogue, consultations, consensus and non-interference, remains the most robust means of managing the changing security landscape in the region. Strengthening the current regional architecture primarily involves strengthening EAS, as it is the most important leaders-only forum in East Asia that covers all the region's big powers. As such, it can have significant effects on the region's security environment. Its remit is to act as a platform for the East Asia leaders' dialogue on broad strategic, political and economic issues of common interest and concern. Its relatively informal structure aims to encourage the candid exchange of views among the leaders as well as to 'establish and strengthen personal relationships between the leaders' (Singapore Institute of International Affairs [SIIA], 2014, p. 3).

SIIA (2014) proposed several ways to strengthen EAS, including making it the 'apex summit' in which contentious and strategic issues arising from other regional forums could be tackled, creating a 'Sherpa' system to shape the EAS agenda, and tabling hard issues to encourage informal discussions on sensitive topics. Track II institutions that foster non-government, informal and unofficial engagement, such as ASEAN–ISIS, can also contribute to the discourse on critical issues in the region. Indeed, as EAS deals with non-traditional security issues, it may need to bring the non-government sector into the discussion. Further, this group—along with the newly created EAS unit at the ASEAN Secretariat—can act as an important support structure to EAS, as made clear by the contribution of the EAS Permanent Representatives to ASEAN in crafting the EAS response to North Korea's nuclear and ballistic missile tests. Moving forward, a more unified voice can help ASEAN reinforce its normative power in the region and maintain its centrality in the EAS and regional architecture.

Conclusion

The above discussion suggests that, more than ever, East Asia will continue to be the locus of opportunity and, to some extent, of uncertainty for the region and the world. The question arises as to whether the current regional architecture is up to the task of managing the risks and capturing the opportunities. Addressing the challenges and opportunities in East Asia calls for further investment in making the regional architecture's network of institutions, organisations and agreements even more responsive. Such a flexible network approach allows for accommodation and enrichment among the institutions and agreements that remain centred on the small to middleweight countries, but also takes into account the varying concerns and interests of (as well as opportunities arsing from) the big powers. It is evident that the current and future network of institutions, both non-government and official, that define East Asia's regional economic architecture need to work together to better manage the challenges— and opportunities—of an ever more integrated, open and fast-changing East Asia.

References

Aggarwal, V. & Koo, M. G. (2006). The evolution and implications of bilateral trade agreements in the Asia Pacific. In V. Aggarwal & S. Urata (Eds.), *Bilateral Trade Agreements in the Asia-Pacific: Origins, Evolution, and Implications* (pp. 279–299), London: Routledge.

Asian Development Bank (ADB). (2010). *Institutions for regional integration: Towards an Asian economic community.* Manila, Philippines: Asian Development Bank.

Atsmon, Y., Child, P., Dobbs, R. & Narasimhan, L. (2012, August). Winning the $30 trillion decathlon: Going for gold in emerging markets. *McKinsey Quarterly.* New York, NY: McKinsey & Company.

Ba, A. (2016). *ASEAN's role in the regional security architecture: The institutional dimensions of regional order.* Paper prepared for the ASEAN at 50 project.

Bisley, N. (2013). *Asia's security and the prospects of multilateralism: Australian perspectives.* Paper presented at National Institute for Defense Studies, Japan. Retrieved 15 September 2016 from: www.nids.mod.go.jp/english/event/symposium/pdf/2013/E-02.pdf

Chen, D. (2015, 27 July). China aims to set the regional cooperation agenda. *East Asia Forum.* www.eastasiaforum.org/2015/07/28/china-aims-to-set-the-regional-cooperation-agenda/

Drysdale, P. (2016a, 1 May). *Asia's next growth frontier.* East Asia Forum. Retrieved from: www.eastasiaforum.org/2016/05/01/asias-next-growth-frontier/

Drysdale, P. (2016b). *ASEAN: The experiment in open regionalism that succeeded.* Paper prepared for the ASEAN at 50 project.

East Asia Vision Group (EAVG). (2001). *Towards an East Asian community: Region of peace, prosperity and progress.* East Asia Vision Group Report.

Hawke, R. (1989, 31 January). *Regional cooperation: Challenges for Korea and Australia.* Speech before the Korea Business Associations, Korea.

Hu, R. W. (2009, July). *Building Asia Pacific regional architecture: The challenge of hybrid regionalism*. CNAPS Visiting Fellow Working Paper. The Brookings Institution Center for Northeast Asian Policy Studies.

Itakura, K. (2012). *Impact of liberalization and improved connectivity and facilitation in ASEAN*. Paper prepared for the mid-term review of the implementation of the AEC Blueprint. Jakarta, Indonesia: Economic Research Institute for ASEAN and East Asia.

Leifer, M. (2009). ASEAN's search for regional order. In S. S. Tan (Ed.), *Regionalism in Asia: Critical issues in modern politics*. London, England: Routledge.

McKinsey Global Institute. (2007, May). *The 'bird of gold': The rise of India's consumer market*. New York, NY: McKinsey & Company.

Organisation for Economic Co-operation and Development (OECD) Development Centre. (2016). *Economic outlook for Southeast Asia, China and India 2016: Enhancing regional ties*. Paris: OECD.

Pan, Z. (2015). Dilemmas of regionalism in East Asia. *Korea Review of International Studies*. Retrieved 15 September 2016 from: gsis. korea.ac.kr/wp-content/uploads/2015/04/10-2-02-zhongqi-pan.pdf

Severino, R. (2014, 31 January). Let's be honest about what ASEAN can and cannot do. *East Asia Forum*.

Singapore Institute of International Affairs (SIIA). (2014, September). *Rethinking the East Asia summit: Purpose, processes and agenda*. Policy Brief.

Singapore Institute of International Affairs (SIIA). (2015, January). *ASEAN centrality in the regional architecture*. Policy Brief.

Sta Maria, R. (2016, 15 September). *RCEP: Challenging ASEAN centrality*. Presentation at ERIA. Retrieved from: www.eria.org/ERIA%20Senior%20Policy%20Fellow%20Dr%20Rebecca%20 Inaugural%20Seminar%20Presentation.pdf

Vinayak, H. V., Thompson, F. & Tonby, O. (2014, May). *Understanding ASEAN: Seven things you need to know*. New York, NY: McKinsey & Company.

10

Evaluation of regional economic integration in East Asia

Shen Minghui

East Asian regional economic integration

Free trade agreements (FTAs) in East Asia have proliferated rapidly for the past two decades. At the end of February 2016, according to the Asian Development Bank (ADB) database, there were 133 FTAs in East Asia, of which 79 were signed and in effect, six were signed but not yet in effect, 44 were under negotiation and five involved signed framework agreements. Before the 1990s, economic integration in East Asia was driven mainly by market forces; it has been strengthened by institutional initiatives since then. Unlike the EU, the institutional arrangements in East Asia have been driven by a competitive pattern. Aside from the bilateral FTAs, the FTAs between the Association of Southeast Asian Nations (ASEAN) and a number of individual nations, known as the ASEAN+1 FTAs, have formed the major integration frameworks, with the ASEAN–China FTA as the spearhead. In the context of negotiations for the US-led Trans-Pacific Partnership (TPP), ASEAN initiated negotiations for the Regional Comprehensive Economic Partnership (RCEP) in 2012, involving 16 other countries. RCEP has now become a major framework for regional economic integration.

Development of regional economic integration

The market has historically played a leading role in East Asian economic integration, backed by the market-friendly policies of regional governments (Zhang & Minghui, 2012). Most East Asian economies have adopted export-oriented strategies, received foreign direct investments (FDIs) and participated in both regional and international production networks. With increasing intra-regional trade (see Figure 10.1) has come demands for tariff reductions and other arrangements, which have assisted in reducing the cost of doing business in East Asia.

ASEAN became a pioneer in regional trade agreements in East Asia by establishing its internal FTA and the ASEAN+1 FTAs.[1] The Asian financial crisis in 1997 became a key factor in promoting East Asian regional cooperation because the spread of the crisis to other economies in the region required cooperative responses. The emergence of the ASEAN+3 cooperation framework was a direct response to the crisis. Two major institutions were initiated under this framework: the Chiang Mai Initiative, which has since made significant progress; and the East Asian FTA (EAFTA), which has become RCEP. RCEP is not simply a combination of the five existing ASEAN+1 FTAs; rather, it aims to create a high-level regional institution for economic integration and comprehensive cooperation.

---

1   The ASEAN FTA was signed in 1992, starting with the Common Effective Preferential Tariff (CEPT). Initially, it was signed by six members and four other new members subsequently joined. The ASEAN+1 FTAs started with the ASEAN–China FTA in 2002, which commenced with the signing of the ASEAN–China Comprehensive Economic Cooperation Framework Agreement and an Early Harvest Program. Other ASEAN+1 FTAs with Korea, Japan, Australia–New Zealand and India subsequently occurred.

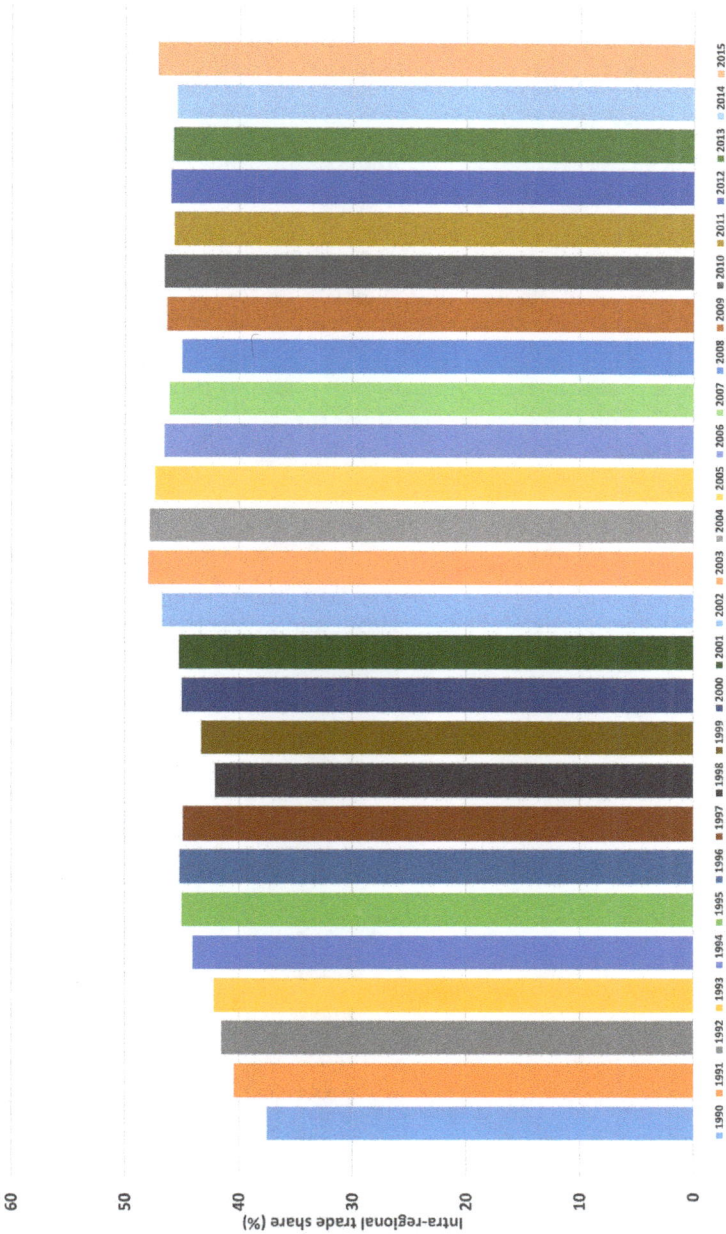

Figure 10.1: Intra-regional trade share of East Asia

Notes: The data cover ASEAN; China, including Hong Kong (China); Japan; and the Republic of Korea.

Source: Compiled using data from ADB (2016).

Characteristics of FTAs in East Asia

Active latecomers in integration

Over time, more and more ASEAN members have desired to extend their trading spaces and this has spurred the flourishing of regional arrangements such as FTAs. The emergence of mega-FTAs, such as the North American Free Trade Agreement (NAFTA) and the EU, placed pressure on economies that were outside of those agreements because of the exclusive nature of regional trade blocs.

East Asian economies were latecomers to regional integration. There were only two FTAs in the region in 1991, and no others were formed between 1993 and 1998. However, since the 2000s, FTAs in East Asia have proliferated. In 2002, China and the ASEAN leaders signed the Framework Agreement on China–ASEAN Comprehensive Economic Cooperation. This triggered the negotiation of FTAs with ASEAN by other countries, including Japan, the Republic of Korea (ROK), India, Australia and New Zealand. In addition, East Asian economies have been active in negotiating bilateral FTAs within and across the region.

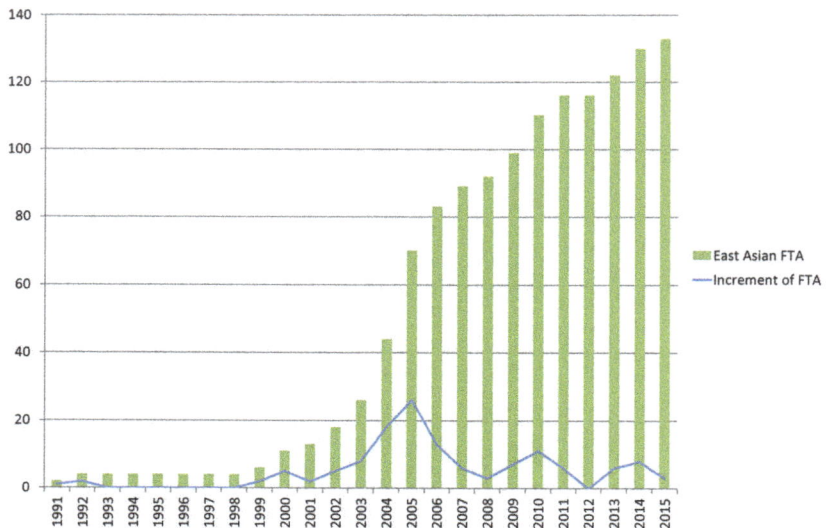

Figure 10.2: Free trade agreements in East Asia

Notes: The data cover ASEAN; China; Hong Kong (China); Taipei (China); Japan; and the Republic of Korea.

Source: Compiled using data from ADB FTA database (aric.adb.org/fta).

Partly as a response to East Asian regional integration, the US actively took part in FTA negotiations with Singapore, Australia, ASEAN (through the US's Enterprise for ASEAN Initiative) and the ROK, which culminated in the US making the decision to lead the TPP negotiations. Fierce competition between the different partners contributed to the proliferation of regional FTAs in East Asia (Figure 10.2); there were 92 FTAs by 2008 and 133 by 2015.

Proliferation of bilateral FTAs

Bilateral FTA negotiations are easier to conclude than multilateral or plurilateral negotiations because there are fewer players and narrower differences of interests. This factor, and the absence of a single powerful leader in East Asian regional integration, has contributed to the proliferation of bilateral FTAs. Most FTAs in East Asia are bilateral (see Figure 10.3).

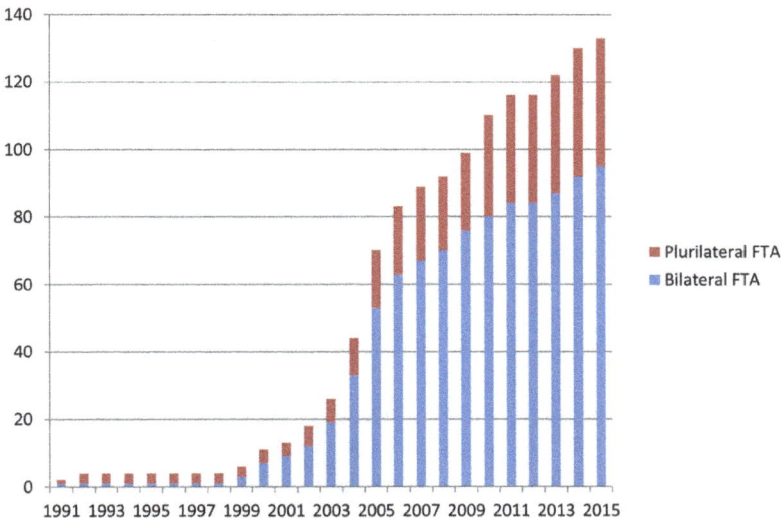

Figure 10.3: Bilateral free trade agreements and plurilateral FTAs in East Asia

Notes: The data cover ASEAN; China; Hong Kong (China); Taipei (China); Japan; and the Republic of Korea.

Source: Compiled using data from ADB FTA database (aric.adb.org/fta).

The pursuit of 'hub' status in regional integration has also promoted the proliferation of bilateral FTAs. According to the 'hub-and-spoke' theory, each hub economy obtains favourable access to spoke economies' markets, whereas spoke economies cannot achieve equal access to other spoke markets in the absence of FTAs. The advantage of being the one hub economy in Asia is clear; it provides incentives to the economies in the region to compete for the position. Under this terminology, an economy that has individually signed bilateral FTAs with many economies would serve as a hub. East Asia, Singapore and the ROK, in particular, have sought hub status for a long time and have made significant achievements in this direction. With a 77.2 per cent FTA coverage ratio, Singapore has been successful in maintaining a hub economy. It has concluded 13 FTAs with its important trade partners (ADB FTA database).[2] As of 2016, ROK has launched FTA negotiations with eight economies and concluded 14 bilateral FTAs with trade partners. Benefiting from its hub status, the FTA coverage ratio of ROK also ranks highly, at 41.1 per cent.

Practical approach to liberalisation

FTAs in East Asia have developed rapidly in terms of quantity, but most have involved low degrees of liberalisation. Traditional issues, including tariff reduction, rules of origin (ROOs), technological barriers, inspection and quarantine, trade remedy and dispute settlement, have been covered in the FTAs. However, more complex issues, such as post-establishment national treatment, performance requirements, intellectual property rights, competition policy, ecommerce and environmental policy, have seldom been incorporated. In addition, sensitive issues, including labour movement and state-owned enterprises (SOEs)—which the TPP agreement did incorporate—have not been popular inclusions in most FTAs in the region.

In Asia, most FTAs have adopted a positive list approach concerning market access to trade in goods. A negative list approach was explored in the ASEAN–ROK FTA, in which long lists of sensitive items are excluded from the FTA provisions to protect domestic markets. In addition, four of the ASEAN+1 FTAs (the exception is for Australia and New Zealand in the ASEAN–Australia and New Zealand FTA) have failed to accomplish zero tariffs for all trade in goods. For ASEAN economies, 94.5 per cent of customs tariff lines have zero per cent tariffs in the ASEAN–China FTA, 93.3 per cent in the ASEAN–ROK FTA, 89 per cent in the ASEAN–Japan FTA, 75.6 per cent in the ASEAN–India FTA and 93.8 per cent in the ASEAN–Australia–New Zealand FTA. Moreover, the FTAs in the region usually involve tariff reduction or elimination periods of 10 years or more, and tariff reduction periods are extended further for some developing economies.

---

2   aric.adb.org/fta

Table 10.1: ASEAN+1 free trade agreement coverage

		ASEAN–China	ASEAN–ROK	ASEAN–Japan	ASEAN–India	ASEAN–Australia–NZ
Trade in goods	Tariff reduction	√	√	√	√	√
	Rules of origin	√	√	√	√	√
	Technology barriers	√	√	√	√	√
	Customs border measures	*	*	√		√
	Inspection and quarantine	√	√	√	√	√
	Trade remedy	√	√	√	√	√
Trade in services		√	√	√		√
Investment	Post-establishment national treatment		√	√		√
	Post-establishment national treatment Most-favoured nation	√	√	√		√
	Performance requirement		√	√		√
Intellectual property rights		*	*	√		√
Government procurement				√		
Competitive policy				√		√
Ecommerce		*	*	√		√
Labour						
Environmental		*	*	√		
Economic technological cooperation		√	√	√		√
Dispute settlement		√	√	√	√	√

Notes: The symbol * refers to an 'cooperation' or 'facilitation' arrangement instead of a binding agreement. ROK = the Republic of Korea; NZ = New Zealand.

Source: ADB FTA database (aric.adb.org/fta).

Concerning trade in services and investment, few of the World Trade Organization–plus (WTO-plus) commitments have been adopted in the above FTAs. Access to the regional market is limited. There is no chapter on investment in the ASEAN–India FTA and no post-establishment national treatment clause. There is no performance requirement in the ASEAN–China FTA. Generally, East Asian countries have adopted a practical and gradual approach to liberalising their markets for trade in goods, services and investment.

RCEP and regional production network reconfiguration

In 2012, in response to the challenge presented by the TPP—particularly from four of ASEAN's own participating members (Brunei, Singapore, Malaysia and Vietnam)—ASEAN decided to initiate RCEP for the remaining ASEAN+6 countries (China, ROK, Japan, India, Australia and New Zealand). Based on the guiding principles proposed by ASEAN, RCEP negotiations commenced in 2013. The aim of RCEP is to create an open market with a higher level of liberalisation than exists between the five ASEAN+1 FTAs by integrating the complex EAFTA networks and untangling the negative 'spaghetti bowl effect' in the region. The intensive FTA arrangements complicate ROOs and often result in red tape and cross-border procedures that increase transaction and time costs, reduce enterprises' operational efficiency, distort regional FDI and ignite trade protectionism. This process has a negative effect on East Asian production networks (Xiangyun, 2010).

RCEP is intended to deepen regional economic integration through further liberalisation of trade, services and investment and through harmonisation of the policies, rules and standards governing trade and investment. Therefore, RCEP is regarded as part of a supporting policy framework for deepening regional production networks and supply chains (Zhang & Minghui, 2013).

Moving towards an integrated framework

Diversified efforts country by country

Owing to differences in industrial structure, sector development, trading status and economic development, the Asian regional economies proposed various FTA strategies to maximise their respective interests that had different, or even conflicting, aims. By insisting on the principle of ASEAN centrality, ASEAN is gradually upgrading its own institution from a free trade group to an economic community. At the same time, it has developed FTAs with other partners of the East Asian economies based on the ASEAN+1 formula. In 2012, as noted above, ASEAN initiated RCEP, which was aimed at building a comprehensive framework for liberalisation and economic cooperation, while retaining its own economic community as an independent identity.

Since its accession to the WTO, China has actively participated in and promoted FTAs, including initiating the China–ASEAN FTA, chairing the EAFTA feasibility study and pushing the China–Japan–Korea FTA to support RCEP. These efforts have been motivated by the Chinese economy's deep integration within East Asia production networks. Since the TPP does not include China, East Asian economic integration has become even more important for it.

Under its 'Look East' policy, India has placed great importance on participating in East Asian integration and cooperation. India prioritised negotiating the ASEAN–India FTA and RCEP; however, given the difficulties India has faced in liberalising its domestic markets, it has not negotiated bilateral FTAs with Japan, Korea or China.

Japan plays a central role in East Asian production networks; however, until 2000, it did not take an active role in negotiating FTAs. Japan began its first FTA negotiation with Singapore in 2001 and signed this agreement at the end of 2002. Later, it began FTA negotiations with each ASEAN member individually. In 2006, Japan proposed the Comprehensive Economic Partnership for East Asia (CEPEA) as an alternative to EAFTA. In fact, RCEP is based on the framework proposed by the CEPEA report. Japan, ROK and China concluded an investment agreement in March 2012, and all three commenced negotiating a trilateral FTA in March 2013. However, Japan's participation in the TPP altered its priorities regarding the regional FTA strategy to some extent, as it gave more emphasis to the potential benefits of the TPP.[3]

ROK is an active player in negotiating FTAs with East Asian countries. In addition to having FTAs with ASEAN, Australia–New Zealand and China, ROK is the only country in East Asia that has concluded FTA negotiations with both the US and the EU. In addition, ROK is active in the negotiations for RCEP and the Korea–China–Japan FTA. As an export-oriented economy, ROK appears to be more active than many other countries in forging FTAs.

---

3   When President Trump announced that America would leave the TPP, Japan, which had ratified the TPP before all other TPP members, was severely disappointed.

Australia and New Zealand have close economic relations with East Asia, which have encouraged them to participate in many types of regional economic integration, ranging from their ASEAN+1 FTA to RCEP. Australia and New Zealand are also involved in the TPP, which creates a much higher level of liberalisation than do the East Asia FTAs.

Although all the East Asian economies are interested in negotiating more FTAs with partners both inside and outside the region, they have common interests in forging an integrated FTA framework within East Asia.

The rationale of RCEP

Various simulation studies based on computerised general equilibrium modelling show that a region-wide FTA such as RCEP would reap more economic benefits than would bilateral or plurilateral FTAs (see Table 10.2). The economic gains for East Asia are significant if it moves from its current bilateral FTAs and ASEAN+1 FTAs towards RCEP (Kawai & Wignaraja, 2007). Even when compared with the TPP, the income effect of RCEP remains significant. Therefore, RCEP could play an important role in creating an intra-regional market and promoting international trade.

RCEP will seek to promote greater regional economic integration, progressively eliminate both tariff and non-tariff barriers, and ensure consistency with the WTO's rules. RCEP is expected to tackle issues including trade in goods, trade in services, investment, economic and technical cooperation, intellectual property, competition policy and dispute settlement. An open accession scheme has been adopted to allow future members to join, provided they comply with RCEP's rules and guidelines.

Although market-driven economic integration has contributed greatly towards East Asian production networks and supply chains, many impediments remain to be addressed, including cross-border measures, non-compatible domestic rules, discriminatory regulations and red tape, which increases business costs (Kawai & Wignaraja, 2009). Therefore, RCEP is regarded as part of the supporting policy framework for deepening regional production networks and supply chains.

Table 10.2: Effect of the Regional Comprehensive Economic Partnership on the GDP of economies (% GDP)

	Petri, Plummer & Zhai (2014)					Lee & Itakura (2014)			Wignaraja (2014)
	TPP12	TPP17	RCEP	FTAAP	RCEP	TPP(1)	TPP(2)	TPP(3)	RCEP
US	0.4	1.6	0.0	2.0	-0.1	0.1	0.1	0.1	
Australia	0.5	2.4	1.4	1.8	0.8	0.3	0.3	0.3	3.9
Canada	0.4	1.7	0.0	1.3	-0.1	0.6	0.6	0.6	
Chile	0.9	2.7	0.0	2.2	0.0	0.7	0.7	0.7	
Mexico	0.5	4.5	0.1	3.4	-0.1	0.8	0.8	0.8	
New Zealand	2.0	3.6	0.9	2.9	0.3	0.7	0.7	0.7	5.2
Peru	1.2	2.6	0.0	2.0	0.0	0.1	0.1	0.1	
China	-0.2	4.7	1.4	3.9	0.6	-0.2	-0.2	-0.2	1.3
Indonesia	-0.1	-0.6	1.7	-0.6	0.6	0.4	0.4	0.4	2.9
Philippines	-0.2	9.5	2.3	5.0	0.6	0.5	0.5	0.5	2.9
Thailand	-0.4	11.6	2.8	4.9	1.0	0.5	0.5	0.5	12.8
Brunei	0.9	8.4	5.8	5.5					
Japan	2.0	4.4	1.8	4.3	0.4	0.5	0.7	0.7	1.6
ROK	-0.1	6.4	3.9	6.1	1.5	1.2	1.2	1.2	6.4
Malaysia	5.6	10.5	3.3	8.9	0.3	0.8	0.8	0.8	6.3
Singapore	1.9	6.5	0.6	3.3	0.7	0.9	0.9	0.9	5.4
Vietnam	10.5	21.2	5.1	21.5	1.2	2.1	2.0	2.0	7.6
Cambodia									1.2
Other ASEAN	-0.4	-1.3	1.9	3.74	0.6	-0.1	-0.1	-0.1	0.3
India	-0.1	-0.6	1.7	-0.6	1.3	-0.1	-0.1	-0.1	2.4
Russia	0.0	-0.3	-0.2	9.3	-0.1	0.0	0.0	0.0	

Notes: TPP = Trans-Pacific Partnership; FTAAP = Free Trade Area of the Asia–Pacific; ROK = the Republic of Korea; GDP = gross domestic product.

Sources: Cheong (2013, p. 10), Lee and Itakura (2014), Petri et al. (2014) and Wignaraja (2014).

Considering the large development gap between East Asian economies, one FTA will not be capable of meeting the diversified needs in the region. Therefore, flexible and differential treatment may emerge to better serve less-developed countries. Although it is expected that comprehensive coverage will be insisted on, more importance may be attached to growth and development issues. Further, priority will be given to promoting balanced development in the region. In the meantime, issues such as connectivity can be treated in the RCEP. Further, from a dynamic perspective, the gains from trade and investment facilitation and economic cooperation and connectivity under the framework of FTAs will be much greater than the gains from lowering tariffs only. This new kind of regional economic cooperation in East Asia will improve the long-term environment to promote regional investment and to strengthen development cooperation.

The TPP and its effects

The nature of the TPP

Rule making by the US

The US has been challenged by the emerging economies in the East Asian region and by the proliferation of intra-regional FTAs there; both the ASEAN+3 FTA and the ASEAN+6 FTA—potential paradigms of East Asian cooperation—exclude the US. Therefore, the US has become concerned about the emergence of a trade bloc in East Asia that will curtail its long-term interests. More importantly, the larger one country's economy is, and the bigger the export market that it can provide, the greater influence on international rule making it may have. The US has to participate in and lead the TPP to avoid being excluded by regionalism in East Asia, especially after its failure to conclude the Enterprise for the ASEAN Initiative, an agreement designed to facilitate commerce between the US and ASEAN towards an FTA.

In November 2000, China proposed an initiative called the China–ASEAN FTA, triggering a series of FTAs in East Asia, most of which excluded the US. In 2004, the gross domestic product (GDP) of East Asia, calculated on the basis of the ASEAN+3, amounted to 69 per cent of US GDP. In 2006, based on the ASEAN+6, it reached 82 per cent of US GDP. Thus, by further strengthening their economic ties, it is possible for the East Asian economies to form a new economic bloc that could challenge the US leadership on international economic rules, with continuing consequences for US interests within the multilateral trading system. Former US president Barack Obama (2015), in his State of the Union address, asserted:

> China wants to write the rules for the world's fastest-growing region. That would put our workers and our businesses at a disadvantage. Why would we let that happen? We should write those rules.

Later, Obama (2016a, 2016b) commented that 'with TPP, China doesn't set the rules in that region, we do' and that 'the TPP would let America, not China, lead the way on global trade'. Thus, one of the main reasons that the US determinedly promoted the TPP was to sustain its leadership in international trade rule making.

Behind-the-border issues

As a twenty–first century agreement, the TPP was comprehensive and of a high standard. Traditional chapters regarding trade in goods only accounted for a small part of the TPP. Most of the chapters addressed behind-the-border issues or WTO-X policy areas, which included investment, cross-border trade in services, financial services, temporary entry for business persons, telecommunications, ecommerce, government procurement, competition policy, SOEs and designated monopolies, intellectual property, labour, environment, regulatory coherence, transparency and anti-corruption (Horn, Mavroidis & Sapir, 2010). Prior to the TPP, these WTO-X chapters had seldom been incorporated in existing FTAs in the region. Instead, developing economies had usually attached greater importance to traditional issues, such as trade in goods, customs and trade remedies.

Table 10.3: Comparison of negotiations areas between mega–free trade agreements and the WTO

	TPP	TTIP	RCEP	WTO
Trade in goods	√	√	√	√
Trade remedies	√	√	√	√
Trade facilitation	√	√	√	√
Technical barriers to trade	√	√	√	√
Sanitary and phytosanitary measures	√	√	√	√
Trade in services	√	√	√	√
Investment	√	√	√	**
Intellectual property	√	√	√	√

	TPP	TTIP	RCEP	WTO
Competition policy, state-owned enterprises	√	√	√	
Ecommerce	√	√	*	
Government procurement	√	√		***
Environment	√	√		
Labour	√	√		
Dispute settlement	√	√	√	√
Cross-cutting issues	√	√		
Standards and conformance, regulatory cooperation		√		

Notes: The symbol * indicates that the area is not explicitly stated as the category of negotiation but is included in other negotiating areas; ** indicates that the area is only under negotiation in trade-related investment measures (TRIM); *** indicates that the area is under negotiation in plurilateral agreements. TPP = Trans-Pacific Partnership; TTIP = Transatlantic Trade and Investment Partnership; RCEP = Regional Comprehensive Economic Partnership; WTO = World Trade Organization.
Source: Japan External Trade and Research Organization (2015, p. 44).

In terms of the agreement's text, the TPP focused on behind-the-border issues, such as intellectual property rights, labour and SOEs. These high-standard clauses represent the interests of sectors in which the US has a competitive edge. In short, the TPP was expected to create a potential platform for economic integration across the Asia–Pacific region, expanding US exports and advancing US economic interests with the fastest-growing economies in the world (Bergsten & Schott, 2010).

Model for the Asia–Pacific and WTO

European countries have historically challenged the US's dominance in writing international economic rules through the forum of the European Community, subsequently expanded to the EU—a unified economy possessing equal consumption market status to the US. For instance, in the early 1980s, after meeting strong resistance from the European Community, the US's attempt to open a new round of multilateral trade negotiations failed. Later, the US launched a US–Canada FTA, which forced European countries to agree to launch the Uruguay Round of trade negotiations. Subsequently, to break the persistent impasses of the Uruguay Round caused by the EU's refusal to compromise on issues concerning agricultural products, the US decided to negotiate with Canada and Mexico to establish NAFTA, which led to a prompt conclusion of the Uruguay Round. In this way, new issues, such as intellectual property rights, services and investment, eventually became incorporated into the General Agreement on Tariffs and Trade (GATT).

Table 10.4: The progression of issues in sequential trade agreements

Issues	US–Israel FTA, 1985	US–Canada FTA, 1988	NAFTA, 1992	Uruguay Round, 1994
Intellectual property rights	Article 14 provides for continued MFN and national treatment on intellectual property	Article 2004 provides for the parties' cooperation on this topic in the Uruguay Round	Part Six (Chapter 17) extends national treatment on intellectual property and establishes specific disciplines	Specific disciplines are set in an Agreement on Trade-Related Aspects of Intellectual Property Rights
Services	Accompanied by a non-binding Declaration on Trade in Services	Chapter 14 extends national treatment (with some exceptions) to covered services; special chapter on financial services	Chapter 12 extends national and MFN treatment (with some exceptions) to covered services; special chapters on financial and telecomm services	General Agreement on Trade in Services extends MFN treatment (with some exceptions) to covered services; special chapters negotiated or planned on financial, telecommunications and air transport services (with others to be negotiated later)
Trade-related investment measures	Clarifies that the investment provisions of an earlier bilateral treaty restrict the use of export-related performance requirements	Chapter 16 provides for national treatment (with some exceptions); prohibits performance requirements; sets rules on expropriation, dispute settlement, etc.	Chapter 11 provides for national and MFN treatment (with some exceptions); prohibits performance requirements; sets rules on expropriation, dispute settlement, etc.	TRIMs chapter provides only for a ban on certain performance requirements
Environment	(No provisions)	(No provisions)	Some provisions in the FTA, supplemented in 1993 by the North American Agreement on Environmental Cooperation	(No provisions; WTO working party established at the conclusion of the Uruguay Round)
Labour rights	(No provisions)	(No provisions)	Some provisions in the FTA, supplemented in 1993 by the North American Agreement on Labour Cooperation	(No provisions)
Competition policy	(No provisions)	(No provisions)	Chapter 15 establishes disciplines for monopolies and state enterprises, especially in the energy sector	(No provisions)

Notes: FTA = free trade agreement; NAFTA = North America Free Trade Agreement; MFN = most-favoured nation; TRIMS = trade-related investment measures.
Source: VanGrasstek (2000).

The US expected to negotiate the TPP with a group of like-minded trading partners and then to offer incentives for other economies to join over time. The TPP, like NAFTA, could have served as an incubator for new trade rules, providing a template for future negotiations in the Asia–Pacific region and in the multilateral system (Goodman, 2013, p. 4). Specifically, the US hoped to influence emerging economies in East Asia by using its leverage in the TPP, in the same way that it facilitated the Uruguay Round of negotiations by establishing the US–Canada FTA and NAFTA (see VanGrasstek, 2000). Emerging economies may have been forced to participate in the TPP for fear of being marginalised, and to accept its rules in multilateral negotiations. Thus, the regional rules embedded in the TPP would have become international rules in the long run.

Problems for the TPP

The TPP now faces many likely insurmountable challenges. Even before the rejection of the agreement by President Trump, it faced scepticism in the US. The TPP would only have involved a small increase in market access for the US. The official assessment report by US International Trade Commission (USITC) estimated that the US's real GDP in 2032 would be only 0.15 per cent higher as a result of the TPP (USITC, 2016, p. 22). Another report estimated that the TPP would only contribute to members' economies by about 1 per cent and their exports by 2–4 per cent (Petri, Plummer & Zhai, 2013, pp. 3–4). In fact, the limited new market access resulting from the TPP would hardly assist the TPP members to advance their economic ties with each other, thereby straining the resilience of the pact.

US President Trump confirmed that he would withdraw the US from the TPP on 21 November 2016. During his campaign, he called the TPP a 'potential disaster' from which he would withdraw when he took office (Dinan, 2016). To date, there is no indication that the Trump administration will consider revisiting the TPP negotiations. The Commerce Secretary Wilbur Ross regarded the TPP as a 'dumb deal' and favoured a bilateral FTA approach, considering that, in this way, the US could leverage market access to its huge market and acquire more concessions from its trading partners (Schott, 2016). This means that the Trump administration will not present the legislation necessary for US participation in the TPP to Congress.

Table 10.5: FTAs among TPP members

	Australia	Brunei	Canada	Chile	Malaysia	Mexico	New Zealand	Peru	Singapore	US	Vietnam	Japan
Australia		√		√	√		√		√	√	√	√
Brunei	√			√	√		√		√		√	√
Canada				√		√		√	*	√		*
Chile	√	√	√		√	√	√	√	√	√	√	√
Malaysia	√	√		√			√		√		√	√
Mexico			√	√				√	*	√		√
New Zealand	√	√		√	√				√		√	
Peru			√	√		√			√	√		√
Singapore	√	√	*	√	√	*	√	√		√	√	√
US	√		√	√		√		√	√			
Vietnam	√	√		√	√		√		√			√
Japan	√	√	*	√	√	√		√	√		√	

Notes: The symbol √ indicates that the FTA is signed; the symbol * indicates that the FTA is under negotiation. FTA = free trade agreement; TPP = Trans-Pacific Partnership.

Sources: ADB FTA database (aric.adb.org/fta); Bilaterals (www.bilaterals.org/).

Effects on East Asia

The TPP has had a significant influence on East Asia. First, as the US is the biggest market for East Asian exports, almost all East Asian economies were concerned about being excluded from the TPP and discriminated against. Consequently, seven countries from East Asia joined the TPP as initial members and others expressed their interest in participating in the next round of negotiations.[4]

China was initially concerned about its exclusion, but developed a pragmatic approach known as a quaternity, or set of four, strategy. Specifically, China:

- adopted a 'wait and see' attitude to TPP negotiations
- proposed the negotiation of an investment agreement with the US
- established four free trade zones domestically (Shanghai, Guangdong, Fujian and Tianjin) to experiment with high-level liberalisation, with the aim of facilitating market opening throughout the country
- took more active steps in the RCEP negotiation in terms of regional actions.[5]

In addition, China created the major 'One Belt and One Road' initiative, known as the Belt and Road Initiative (BRI), and the Asia Infrastructure Investment Bank (AIIB). Importantly, the BRI and the AIIB go beyond the traditional FTA approach for regional economic integration, and provide a different strategy for creating new growth engines by improving regional infrastructure (Gang, 2015).

The stance of ASEAN and the degree of consensus among its members will be crucial in responding to the challenges facing the TPP. By initiating RCEP, ASEAN ensured that it was a hub of the agreements and, thus, able to forcefully pursue its interests. In moving towards an integrated regional FTA, ASEAN may lose its centrality in regional integration. Considering the large economic disparities among its members, ASEAN needs to strengthen its capacity to engage other economies on an equal footing. Under its new charter, ASEAN established the goal to form

---

4   Australia and New Zealand are included in the East Asia group, as they participate in many economic integration and cooperation activities. The seven participating countries are Australia, New Zealand, Japan, Brunei, Singapore, Malaysia and Vietnam.

5   China favoured the ASEAN+3 framework (EAFTA) and led the EAFTA feasibility study during 2004–06.

a strengthened ASEAN community by 2015—the ASEAN Economic Community (AEC)—along with Security and Social Communities. Thus, it seems likely that RCEP will be concluded and accepted by ASEAN only after it succeeds in building the AEC. The best strategy for concluding RCEP may be to support ASEAN's efforts to build the AEC.

Initially, Japan was hesitant about joining the TPP; however, following lengthy discussions and much study, and despite challenges from the TPP regarding Japan's sensitive domestic sectors, including agriculture, it decided to join in 2013. To strengthen its power in FTA negotiations and ensure that it would be included in the drafting of future international trade rules, Japan indicated its political interest in joining the TPP. According to one study, the welfare effects for Japan from the TPP and RCEP are almost the same (Petri et al., 2013). Thus, economic factors alone do not explain why Japan prefers the TPP as its priority FTA. There is a widely held belief that the TPP has strategic importance in strengthening the US–Japan alliance (Bergsten, 2016).

As an export-led economy, ROK is quite active in forging FTAs with its trade partners. It has concluded several important bilateral FTAs with large economies including the US, China and the EU. ROK has been cautious in joining the TPP. However, after the China–ROK FTA came into effect, ROK expressed its interest in joining the TPP, stating that it would strive to join the mega-FTA in any form (Ji-young, 2015). At the same, it stressed that the ROK government would determine the timing of its entry after thoroughly analysing the effects on its national economy of joining the TPP (Ji-young, 2015). In fact, new market access from the TPP was not significant for ROK, as it could acquire the same market access by concluding the ROK–Japan FTA. The main reason that ROK may have preferred to join the TPP was fear of being excluded from rule making in the region.

When the TPP negotiations concluded in 2015, much progress had also been made in the RCEP negotiations, although these failed to be concluded by 2016. Considering the large development gaps in East Asia, as well as the diversified economic needs of those involved in the negotiations, it was difficult for the 16 economies to reach consensus. However, President Trump's executive order ending the US's participation in the TPP—signed on 23 January 2017 (Tharoor, 2017)—may divert the focus of the ASEAN economies to the RCEP negotiations and assist in building momentum for the deal to be concluded more rapidly.

East Asia and WTO

WTO in perspective

The global trading system is currently experiencing the largest round of reconstruction since the Uruguay Round. In the short term, owing to the comparatively low average most-favoured nation (MFN) tariffs of WTO members, costs will be high for developed countries to open up sensitive sectors and for developing countries to reform their behind-the-border measures. Therefore, the possibility of reaching a single undertaking of agreements in the Doha Round—the multilateral trade negotiation round at the WTO—is relatively low. The US joined and promoted TPP negotiations to create a comprehensive, modern template for future FTA negotiations. Its aims were to provide an alternative model for consolidating existing trade agreements (Petri et al., 2011, 2014) and to relaunch a new round of WTO negotiations. However, the rise of trade protectionism in the US and President Trump's attitude towards globalisation makes it unlikely that a new round of WTO negotiations will be launched. In addition, the High Level Trade Experts Group (2011) has argued that any efforts under a new round are unlikely to succeed.

In December 2013, 159 WTO members concluded negotiations on a Trade Facilitation Agreement at the Bali Ministerial Conference, as part of the wider Bali Package. The Trade Facilitation Agreement contained provisions for expediting the movement, release and clearance of goods, including goods in transit. It set out measures for effective cooperation between customs and other appropriate authorities on trade facilitation and customs compliance issues. Other provisions covered technical assistance and capacity building in this area. The Trade Facilitation Agreement in the Bali Package provided a timely lifeline for the multilateral trading system, the credibility of which was slowly being eroded (Kanyimbo, 2013). The benefits from the Trade Facilitation Agreement to the world economy are estimated to be between US$400 billion and US$1 trillion. These benefits arise from a 10–15 per cent reduction in trade costs and increases in trade flows and revenue collection, which create a stable business environment and attract foreign investment (WTO, 2013). To reap these benefits, priority needs to be given to this agreement; two thirds of members need to complete their domestic ratification process before the Trade Facilitation Agreement can enter into force.

With multilateral negotiations on hold, more alternatives for negotiations are being explored. One of these alternatives can be seen in the form of sectoral agreements reached in the WTO. For instance, the Information Technology Agreement (ITA) and the sectoral protocols to the General Agreement on Trade in Services were negotiated under the terms of existing agreements and the benefits are extended on an MFN basis (VanGrasstek, 2013, p. 553). Many participating economies urged a swift conclusion to ongoing negotiations around the expansion of the ITA product coverage—that is, ITA 2. This agreement is expected to contribute to growth in international trade. If ITA 2 is concluded successfully, more effort could be directed to utilising this sectoral agreement approach to explore a multilateral investment agreement under the WTO framework.

East Asia and multilateralism

East Asia has a vital stake in maintaining open markets and its continued success depends on an open, rules-based global system of trade and investment. As East Asia's economic success has relied heavily on integration with the global market (Chia, 2010), all economies in East Asia will continue to be interested in supporting multilateralism. As East Asian regional production networks are based on a highly open structure, East Asian regionalism is not in conflict with multilateralism (Zhang & Minghui, 2012).

By integrating into the global system, East Asian economies will benefit, not only from the liberalisation of manufactured exports, but also from the enhanced transparency and predictability of members' trade regimes. Although approximately 50 per cent of Asian exports go to markets outside the region, demand for final goods means consumption from outside economies accounted for more than 70 per cent of Asian exports in 2007 (ADB 2010). Thus, trade within the region is dominated by intermediate products. In fact, more than half of all intermediate goods are assembled in Asia (especially in mainland China) before they are consumed in external markets, including the EU and US. These two economies are the main destinations for Asia's final goods; in 2007, the US accounted for 23.9 per cent of Asia's total final goods and the EU accounted for 22.5 per cent. The Asian market only receives 28.9 per cent of its own final goods. It is notable that East Asian economies rely on exporting their products to outside markets—in particular, the US and the EU. Although proliferation of regional FTAs may assist East Asia to increase intra-regional trade, an open global market environment will continue to be important because the regional market is closely linked to the global market in many ways. Within production networks, it is multilateral arrangements rather than regional FTAs that benefit exporters in East Asia most.

Given the benefits that they receive from the multilateral trading system, East Asian economies have been reluctant to pursue regionalism. Since the late 1990s, East Asian economies have, understandably, felt compelled to negotiate their own agreements with critical markets in response to regionalism in other areas of the global economy, namely the EU and NAFTA. East Asian economies have feared that, unless they develop their own regional trade arrangements, they will be disadvantaged in global competition and multilateral negotiations. The push towards regionalism in East Asia strengthened considerably after the financial crisis in 1997. The silver lining of the crisis was that it created an East Asian economic identity because it highlighted the highly integrated nature of these economies (Kawai, 2005). As result, most of the FTAs in East Asia attach great importance to compliance with WTO principles. For instance, the Asia–Pacific Economic Cooperation forum (APEC, 2004) and the ADB (2008) have identified guiding principles for FTA best practice, which highlight consistency with GATT and WTO rules.

In practice, economies in East Asia are competing to negotiate FTAs with their trade partners to become hubs instead of spokes in the regional economy. Complex FTAs would potentially disrupt the processes of the cross-border production networks that have been central to the region's successful integration. Uncoordinated proliferation may lead to varying phase-in modalities and time frames for tariff concessions, as well as varying preferences across FTAs, especially on ROOs, which could hamper the process of production networking across economies in East Asia. RCEP is designed to deal with this noodle bowl of FTAs in the region. As Baldwin (2006, 2007) indicated, noodle bowls are building blocks on the path to global free trade, and a region-wide FTA that is GATT/WTO-consistent could eventually contribute to multilateralism.

East Asia's past economic success has relied heavily on an open and supportive global environment. Its rising integration within the global market has contributed significantly to the growth of international trade, and its commitments to the WTO and other international organisations could further deepen its integration and generate benefits for world economic development. Although East Asia needs to be cautious about its export-oriented growth model, and must consider how to rebalance its economy, its interest in the global market will not be reduced because its future economic dynamism will be closely associated with the global market environment. Nowadays, the world economy is threatened by sentiments against globalisation, apparent in phenomena such as Brexit and trade protectionism such as Trump's 'America First' rhetoric in the US. East Asia needs to fight against trade protectionism, which directly harms regional production networks. It must insist on unilateral liberalisation as well as regional integration to support free trade.

China's strategy and role

China's opening strategy

Since 1978, when reforms and opening began, opening to trade has played a key role in China's economic success. In 1986, China asked for a resumption of its member status in GATT. As GATT developed into the WTO in 1994, China, from 1995, had to negotiate its accession. The long negotiation and implementation process helped China to build a comprehensive foundation, based on an open market system. It also helped China to engage with the world market, using rules-based commercial behaviour. China strongly supports the multilateral system, as it benefits profoundly from its wide and deep engagement in the global market.

China has become active in forging FTAs with partners in East Asia and other regions in the world. To date, China has signed 14 FTA agreements, of which 12 have been implemented, covering 22 countries and regions from Asia, Latin America, Oceania and Europe. In addition, China has engaged in larger FTA negotiations, ranging from the China–Japan–Korea trilateral FTA to RCEP. Further, China plans to take a leading role in promoting the Free Trade Area of the Asia–Pacific (FTAAP) under the APEC framework.

Although China has been a leader in initiating its ASEAN+1 FTA, as a developing economy, it has had difficulty in negotiating FTAs with large developed economies. Thus, China adopted a 'learning by doing' approach, concluding FTAs with New Zealand, Switzerland, Singapore and ROK. It has also proposed investment agreements with the US and EU.

In 2012, China adopted a more aggressive strategy to forge FTA networks in a global context. The state council issued its first comprehensive and strategic document on FTA construction, which clarified the short-, medium- and long-term goals of China, as well as the specific requirements for each time frame for FTAs in neighbouring areas and regions. As well as prioritising negotiating FTAs with neighbouring countries, China has made efforts to negotiate FTAs with economies from other parts of the world, especially emerging economies, large developing countries, main regional economic groups and some large developed countries.

Belt and Road Initiative

In a speech on the Silk Road Economic Belt at Nazarbayev University (Kazakhstan) on 7 September 2013, Chinese President Xi Jinping praised the role of the ancient Silk Road in building close economic, social and cultural links, and in bringing peace between China and the outside world. The president called on China and Kazakhstan to build a modern belt together—that is, transportation and economic corridors that connect China to Europe and all other major Eurasian sub-regions. Speaking to the Indonesian parliament on 3 October 2013, Xi put forward a proposal to build a twenty–first century maritime Silk Road to broaden trade and other economic connections between China and other maritime countries of South-East Asia, South Asia, the Middle East, East Africa and the Mediterranean. The two initiatives are part of a package that covers vast regions of Asia, Europe and Africa, linking both land and maritime regions, with comprehensive agendas ranging from infrastructure and industrial parks to port networks and cultural exchanges. The National Development and Reform Commission, the Ministry of Foreign Affairs and the Ministry of Commerce, with State Council authorisation, issued a policy document in 2015, known as the Belt and Road Initiative (Vision and actions, 2015).

The BRI is not intended as a counterstrategy to the US 'pivot to Asia' strategy; rather, it is based on China's own needs.[6] The BRI will help to develop new market opportunities, which are of great significance for China's economic restructuring. After more than three decades of high growth, the Chinese economy is altering to a 'new normal' state— that is, it is shifting from a high-growth period to a moderate-growth period. To create a new dynamic growth engine, it is important to build up demand-led growth momentum and explore external market opportunities. The new growth frontier of the global economy lies in developing countries. However, the most significant bottleneck for developing economies is poor infrastructure for industrial supply chains. As most of China's neighbours are developing economies, it would be beneficial to China if their economic environment could be improved through participating in the BRI. By financing the infrastructure and industrial zones, it is expected that the BRI will create new growth potential in the relevant areas of Europe, Asia and Africa. China can play a key role under the BRI because it possesses special advantages in providing investment capital and supplying equipment and technology. It also has experience in developing infrastructure network and industrial zones, which will provide opportunities for Chinese companies in their 'going outside strategy' (Yonghua, 2014).

Direct investment will assist the Chinese economy to become more integrated with other economies. Many labour-intensive factories in China need to relocate to low-cost countries to maintain their competitiveness, and developing countries in Asia and Africa want to develop their own manufacturing capacity by using their endowments of cheap labour. In contrast with the past model of moving 'dirty' industries out, China will build new industries together with local countries, as all projects under the BRI framework are to be designed and built jointly by China and the host countries. This new kind of development cooperation differs from the traditional aid- and market-based reallocation of outdated production capacities.

---

6   As observed by Pitlo (2015), the celebrated revival of the Silk Road would seem to herald the return of China's charm offensive, winning over neighbours and other countries in the region through increased trade incentives and transport connectivity. If developing a sound soft power strategy is the mark of a rising world power, does this mean China is on its way?

The BRI is aimed at promoting orderly and free economic flows, an efficient allocation of resources and deep integration of markets, which would encourage the countries along BRI corridors to achieve economic policy coordination. It would further encourage them to achieve broader and more in-depth regional cooperation on higher standards and to jointly create an open, inclusive and balanced regional economic architecture. It is designed in the spirit of open regional cooperation and characterised by equality and mutual benefit, based on consultation, cooperation and sharing. The BRI seeks mutual benefit and will be 'open to all countries and international and regional organizations for engagement' (Ministry of Commerce, 2015).

Geographically, the Belt focuses on bringing together China, Central Asia, Russia and Europe (the Baltic nations), linking China with the Persian Gulf and the Mediterranean Sea through Central Asia and West Asia, and connecting China with South-East Asia, South Asia and the Indian Ocean. Its objective seems clear-cut and mission oriented. It will focus on jointly building a new Eurasian land bridge by developing economic corridors across China–Mongolia–Russia, China–Central Asia–West Asia, and the China–Indochina Peninsula. It will take advantage of international transport routes, rely on core cities along BRI corridors and use key economic industrial parks as cooperation platforms. The Road—which will focus on jointly building smooth, secure and efficient transport routes connecting major sea ports—is designed to go from China's coast to Europe through the South China Sea and the Indian Ocean, and from China's coast through the South China Sea to the South Pacific. The China–Pakistan and Bangladesh–China–India–Myanmar economic corridors will also be closely coordinated with BRI economies.

As the BRI is open and inclusive, its building process is open not just to countries along the routes, but also to all other countries in the world. As with the AIIB, the membership is open to all countries that have an interest in making a contribution.[7] Thus, connectivity is not only limited to these routes; instead, it should be read as encompassing diverse connectivity across the Eurasian continent (Summers, 2016). The geographical coverage of the BRI is flexible, as the aim is to encourage

7   AIIB was established on 25 December 2015 with 57 initial members; 37 from Asia and 20 from other regions.

a wide range of infrastructure development and socio-economic connectivity between China and those countries that are willing to participate.

Considering the economic diversity in the region, the BRI seeks to adopt a new model by closely connecting projects to the host country's development, as well as ensuring the efficient allocation of resources in China and in other countries. The economic development of most developing countries in the region has been hindered by inadequate infrastructure—the BRI is an important opportunity to break the bottleneck by designing and financing both in-country and cross-country highways and railway lines. A large number of projects are already being considered to connect various sub-regions, including high-speed railways, oil and gas pipelines and telecommunication and electricity links. Aside from direct financing from the Silk Road Fund and the AIIB, other financial institutions, including the ADB and the World Bank, will be actively involved because the BRI has established an inclusive framework, open to all who have an interest in participating. More importantly, it is the business community that is the major player; thus, both Chinese and foreign companies will be welcome to invest, based on established rules and a spirit of cooperation. The BRI, like many other initiatives, will face many challenges and difficulties, but China's aim is to do its best to succeed with the support of partners in the relevant areas.

China and the multilateral trading system

China's economic success has relied heavily on an open multilateral trading system. Following its entry into the WTO, China acquired significant economic benefits and its economy is now dependent on an open global system for trade, capital and resources. Although China has committed to change its export-oriented growth model and to create stronger internal demand, its interest in the global market will not be reduced because its future economic dynamism will be closely associated with the global market environment. China is likely to retain its 'number one' trade status even after domestic demand begins to play a major role in supporting economic growth.

China has contributed to the upkeep of the WTO and the maintenance of the principles of free trade, and also assists developing economies. It kept its promise to gradually eliminate tariffs and non-tariff barriers; this policy of openness has meant that China has maintained its trade growth rate at 20 per cent for many years. The development of China facilitated the growth of globalised production, leading to global welfare gains. Further, China actively participated in multilateral negotiations and helped developing countries by increasing flexibility around market access. In sum, China has strongly supported the current free trading system.

Although the Doha Round has been stalled for many years, and will likely never be completed as a multilateral round, China has not given up its confidence in the WTO processes. However, it is a complex developing economy simultaneously composed of low-performing and advanced sectors. Although China does not intend to abandon the WTO, it could act as an intermediary between developed members and developing ones. On 15 December 2015, President Xi Jinping stated that the multilateral trading system and regional trading arrangements were wheels that pushed economic globalisation. Regionalism will not impede multilateralism; rather, sooner or later, it will stimulate multilateral negotiation.

In retrospect, the new ITA negotiations, ITA 2, and the Environmental Goods Negotiations could not have been successfully concluded without China–US cooperation. In the future, a reconstruction of the global trading system is unlikely to succeed without consensus and cooperation between China and the US. The multilateral trading system remains the ideal trade policy paradigm. Properly managed, it can easily accommodate these two major economies. In this sense, the WTO is the most important component in maintaining the economic relations between China and the US. China and the US have a common stake in supporting a strong and resilient multilateral trading system. The challenge will continue to be uncertainty about the direction of US trade policy under President Trump.

References

Asian Development Bank (ADB). (2008, April). *How to design, negotiate, and implement a free trade agreement in Asia.* Mandaluyong City, Philippines: Asian Development Bank.

Asian Development Bank (ADB). (2010). *Institutions for regional integration: Toward an Asian economic community.* Mandaluyong City, Philippines: Asian Development Bank.

Asian Development Bank (ADB). (2016). *Integration indicators database.* Retrieved from: aric.adb.org/integrationindicators

Asia–Pacific Economic Cooperation (APEC). (2004). *Best practice of FTA/RTAs in APEC.* APEC Doc. No. 2004/CSOM/028rev.1, 2004. 16th APEC Ministerial Meeting, Santiago, Chile.

Baldwin, R. (2006). Multilateralising regionalism: Spaghetti bowls as building blocs on the path to global free trade. [Mimeographed]. Geneva, Switzerland: Graduate Institute for International Studies.

Baldwin, R. (2007). Managing the noodle bowl: The fragility of East Asian regionalism. *ADB Working Paper Series on Regional Economic Integration No. 7.* Retrieved from: www.adb.org/sites/default/files/publication/28464/wp07-baldwin.pdf

Bergsten, C.F. (2016, 27 November). The Trans-Pacific Partnership and Japan, *Nikkei Asian Review.*

Bergsten, C. F. & Schott, J. J. (2010, 25 January). *Submission to the USTR in support of a Trans-Pacific Partnership agreement.* Retrieved from: www.piie.com/publications/papers/paper.cfm?ResearchID=1482

Cheong, I. (2013, July). Negotiations for the Trans-Pacific Partnership agreement: Evaluation and implications for East Asian regionalism. *ADBI Working Paper Series Negotiations No. 428.* Tokyo, Japan: Asian Development Bank Institute.

Chia, S. Y. (2010, April). Trade and investment policies and regional economic integration in East Asia. *ADBI Working Paper Series No. 210.* Tokyo, Japan: Asian Development Bank Institute.

Dinan, S. (2016, 21 November). Donald Trump to withdraw US from Asian trade pact on his first day in office. *The Washington Times.* Retrieved from: www.washingtontimes.com/news/2016/nov/21/donald-trump-withdraw-us-trans-pacific-partnership/

Gang, A. (2015). East Asian cooperation under the perspective of 'one belt, one road'—An interview with Zhang Yunling, the Professor of Chinese Academy of Social Sciences. *World Affairs, 07,* 32–34.

Goodman, M. P. (2013, 14–15 November). *US economic strategy in the Asia–Pacific region: Promoting growth, rules, and presence.* Paper prepared for CNCPEC seminar. Beijing, China.

High Level Trade Experts Group. (2011, January). *The Doha Round: Setting a deadline, defining a final deal, Interim report*. Retrieved from: voxeu. org/sites/default/files/file/doha-round-setting-deadline-defining-final-deal-interim-report-jan-2011.pdf

Horn, H., Mavroidis, P. C. & Sapir, A. (2010). Beyond the WTO? An anatomy of EU and US preferential trade agreements. *The World Economy, 33*(11), 1565–88. doi.org/10.1111/j.1467-9701.2010. 01273.x

Japan External Trade and Research Organization. (2015). *JETRO global trade and investment report*. Tokyo, Japan: Government of Japan.

Ji-young, S. (2015, 6 October). Korea looking to join TPP. *The Korea Herald*. Retrieved from: www.koreaherald.com/view.php?ud=2015 1006001111

Kanyimbo, P. (2013, December). Trade facilitation in the Bali Package: What's in it for Africa? *ECDPM Briefing Note No. 61*. Retrieved from: ecdpm.org/wp-content/uploads/BN-61-Trade-Facilitation-Bali-What-is-in-it-for-Africa.pdf

Kawai, M. (2005). East Asian economic regionalism: Progress and challenges. *Journal of Asian Economics, 16*, 29–55. doi.org/10.1016/j. asieco.2005.01.001

Kawai, M. & Wignaraja, G. (2007). ASEAN+3 or ASEAN+6: Which way forward? *ADBI Discussion Paper No. 77*. Tokyo, Japan: Asian Development Bank Institute.

Kawai, M. & Wignaraja, G. (2009, August). Asian FTAs: Trends and challenges. *ADBI Working Paper Series No. 144*. Tokyo: Asian Development Bank Institute. Retrieved from: www.adb.org/sites/default/files/publication/155999/adbi-wp144.pdf

Lee, H. & Itakura, K. (2014, 5 June). TPP, RCEP and Japan's agricultural policy reforms. *Osaka School of International Public Policy Discussion Paper No. 14E003*. Osaka, Japan: Osaka University.

Ministry of Commerce. (2015). *Belt and road*. Retrieved from: english. mofcom.gov.cn/article/zt_beltandroad/

Obama, B. (2015, 20 January). *Remarks by the President in the State of the Union address* [Transcript]. Retrieved from: www.whitehouse.gov/the-press-office/2015/01/20/remarks-president-state-union-address-january-20-2015

Obama, B. (2016a). *State of the Union address as delivered* [Transcript]. Retrieved from: obamawhitehouse.archives.gov/the-press-office/2016/01/12/remarks-president-barack-obama-%E2%80%93-prepared-delivery-state-union-address

Obama, B. (2016b, 2 May). The TPP would let America, not China, lead the way on global trade. *Washington Post.* Retrieved from: www.washingtonpost.com/opinions/president-obama-the-tpp-would-let-america-not-China-lead-the-way-on-global-trade/2016/05/02/680540e4-0fd0-11e6-93ae-50921721165d_story.html

Petri, P. A., Plummer, M. G. & Zhai, F. (2011, 24 October). The Trans-Pacific Partnership and Asia-Pacific integration: A quantitative assessment. *East–West Center Working Papers, Economics Series No. 119.* Honolulu, HI: East–West.

Petri, P. A., Plummer, M. G. & Zhai, F. (2013, 7 March). Adding Japan and Korea to TPP—Asia–Pacific trade. Retrieved from: asiapacifictrade.org/wp-content/uploads/2013/05/Adding-Japan-and-Korea-to-TPP.pdf

Petri, P. A., Plummer, M. G. & Zhai, F. (2014). The TPP, China and the FTAAP: The case for convergence. In T. Guoqiang & P. A. Petri (Eds.), *New directions in Asia-Pacific economic integration* (pp. 84–85), Honolulu: East–West Center.

Pitlo, L. B. (2015, 17 February). China's 'One belt, one road' to where?' *The Diplomat.* Retrieved from: thediplomat.com/2015/02/chinas-one-belt-one-road-to-where

Schott, J. J. (2016, 5 December). *TPP can be fixed if you know what's wrong with it.* Retrieved from: piie.com/blogs/trade-investment-policy-watch/tpp-can-be-fixed-if-you-know-whats-wrong-it

Summers, T. (2016). China's 'new silk roads': Sub-national regions and networks of global political economy. *Third World Quarterly, 37*(9), 1628–43. doi.org/10.1080/01436597.2016.1153415

Tharoor, I. (2017, 24 January). Trump kills TPP, giving China its first big win. *The Washington Post*. Retrieved from: www.washingtonpost. com/news/worldviews/wp/2017/01/24/trump-kills-tpp-giving-china-its-first-big-win/

US International Trade Commission. (2016, May). *Trans-Pacific Partnership agreement: Likely impact on the US Economy and on specific industry sectors*. Retrieved from: www.usitc.gov/publications/ 332/pub4607.pdf

VanGrasstek, C. (2000). US plans for a new WTO round: Negotiating more agreements with less authority. *The World Economy*, *23*(5), 673–700. doi.org/10.1111/1467-9701.00296

VanGrasstek, C. (2013). *The history and future of the World Trade Organization*. Geneva: World Trade Organization Publications.

Vision and actions on jointly building belt and road. (2015, 28 March). Retrieved from: news.xinhuanet.com/english/china/2015-03/28/c_ 134105858_2.htm

Wignaraja, G. (2014). The Regional Comprehensive Economic Partnership: An initial assessment. In T. Guoqiang & P. A. Petri (Eds.), *New directions in Asia-Pacific economic integration* (pp. 84–85), Honolulu, HI: East–West Center.

World Trade Organization (WTO). (2013). *Days 3, 4 and 5: Round-the-clock consultations produce 'Bali package'*. Retrieved from: www.wto. org/english/news_e/news13_e/mc9sum_07dec13_e.htm

World Trade Organization (WTO). (2017). *Trade facilitation*. Retrieved from: www.wto.org/english/tratop_e/tradfa_e/tradfa_e.htm

Xiangyun, X. (2010). Role of origin in East Asian FTA system and East Asian production system. *Journal of Contemporary Asia-Pacific Studies*, *1*, 29–44.

Yonghua, S. (2014). *BRI leads China's companies to go abroad*. Retrieved from: world.people.com.cn/n/2014/1227/c1002-26285988.html

Zhang, Y. & Minghui, S. (2012). Emergence of ASEAN, China and India and the regional architecture. *China & World Economy*, *20*(4), 92–107. doi.org/10.1111/j.1749-124x.2012.01297

Zhang, Y. & Minghui, S. (2013, June). FTAs in the Asia-Pacific: A Chinese perspective. *Kokusai Mondai (International Affairs), 622.*

www.ingramcontent.com/pod-product-compliance
Lightning Source LLC
Chambersburg PA
CBHW040146270326
41929CB00025B/3403